"Bardhan and Gower synthesize theories and DEI literature from multiple disciplines to provide fresh perspectives and practical insights to address organizational climate, diversity, and inclusion issues in public relations practice. This is a 'must-read' book! Any leader in public relations and public relations faculty members and students will find this book's lessons useful – as the insights contained within are a needed contribution and signpost to guide future 'needle-moving' efforts and DEI pursuits in public relations education and practice."

Damion Waymer, Professor and Chair of Advertising & Public Relations, The University of Alabama, USA

"An artful balance of storytelling and data insights underpinned by academic rigor, the contextual buildup with each chapter of this book culminates with an unprecedented, pragmatic Leadership Model for Inclusive Diversity in Public Relations. It features recommended approaches for 1) accelerating DE&I progress and 2) eroding the field's glaring resistance to change, often masked by the cunning lip service of skilled communicators. The authors' findings are compelling for aspiring and current industry leaders."

Carmella Glover, President, Diversity Action Alliance, USA

"This book makes an enormous contribution toward addressing one of the most important issues facing U.S. public relations professionals in the coming years: the need for measurable, impactful, and faster progress on 'building inclusive diversity' in the PR profession. The authors make a compelling case that leaders embrace the idea that 'the horse of inclusion pulls the cart of diversity, and not the other way around,' and that leaders must be more responsible and accountable for actions that foster inclusive, equitable internal cultures. Every PR leader should read this and build on the model Bardhan and Gower propose for advancing the D&I imperative facing all of us."

Patrick Ford, Professional in Residence, College of Journalism and Communications, University of Florida, USA

The Role of Leadership in Building Inclusive Diversity in Public Relations

This book focuses on the relationship between leadership and diversity, inclusion and equity within the US public relations industry.

The authors argue that there is ample research evidence that diversity and inclusion efforts cannot succeed without leadership support that commits to and assumes responsibility and accountability for the structural and cultural changes required. Drawing on literature from three different areas – public relations, diversity and inclusion/equity in US societal and organizational contexts and leadership – the authors build a conceptual framework and model for inclusive leadership in public relations that addresses industry dynamics.

The book is timely as a resource for public relations scholars and as a supplementary text for advanced courses in public relations principles, theory, management, leadership and diversity. It also provides practitioners theoretical guidance on how to improve diversity, inclusion and equity in their organizations.

Nilanjana Bardhan is a Professor in the Department of Communication Studies at Southern Illinois University – Carbondale, USA.

Karla Gower is a Professor in the Department of Advertising and Public Relations at the University of Alabama – Tuscaloosa, USA.

The Role of Leadership in Building Inclusive Diversity in Public Relations

Nilanjana Bardhan and Karla Gower

Routledge
Taylor & Francis Group

NEW YORK AND LONDON

Cover image: © mangsaab / Getty Images

First published 2023
by Routledge
605 Third Avenue, New York, NY 10158

and by Routledge
4 Park Square, Milton Park, Abingdon, Oxon, OX14 4RN

Routledge is an imprint of the Taylor & Francis Group, an informa business

© 2023 Nilanjana Bardhan and Karla Gower

Library of Congress Cataloging-in-Publication Data
Names: Bardhan, Nilanjana, author. | Gower, Karla K., author.
Title: The role of leadership in building inclusive diversity in public relations / Nilanjana Bardhan and Karla Gower.
Description: New York, NY : Routledge, 2023. |
Includes bibliographical references and index. Identifiers:
LCCN 2022004886 (print) | LCCN 2022004887 (ebook)
Subjects: LCSH: Diversity in the workplace. |
Public relations--Management. | Leadership. Classification: LCC
HF5549.5.M5 B367 2023 (print) | LCC HF5549.5.M5 (ebook) |
DDC 658.3008--dc23/eng/20220421
LC record available at https://lccn.loc.gov/2022004886
LC ebook record available at https://lccn.loc.gov/2022004887

ISBN: 978-0-367-77154-6 (hbk)
ISBN: 978-0-367-76964-2 (pbk)
ISBN: 978-1-003-17002-0 (ebk)

DOI: 10.4324/9781003170020

Typeset in Bembo
by KnowledgeWorks Global Ltd.

Contents

Foreword   *ix*
Preface / Acknowledgments   *xiii*

1 Introduction   1

2 Public Relations, Diversity and Inclusion: A Story
   Unpacked with a Spotlight on Leadership   13

3 Diversity and Inclusion in the Context
   of the United States   44

4 Leadership and D&I: Where Is Public Relations?   75

5 Mind the Gap: The Story of Lackluster
   D&I Leadership in Public Relations   107

6 Digging Deeper: Practitioner/Educator/Student
   Leaders Elaborate on D&I   126

7 A Leadership Model for Inclusive Diversity
   in Public Relations   156

8 Conclusion: Looking Ahead   187

References   *198*
Index   *224*

Foreword

Diversity, equity and inclusion (DEI) are the topics of conversation in corporate, association and nonprofit boardrooms. As with most trending organizational topics, interest in these concepts waxes and wanes with the tides of industry and the focus of the moment. For example, at the start of the pandemic in 2020, communication officers placed internal communications as the main focus of their initiatives as societal institutions struggled to understand how to operate in this new reality of masks, airborne diseases and unknown realities. According to an Institute for Public Relations report, only 19 percent of communicators saw the need to communicate about diversity. Some even dismissed diversity, equity and inclusion as a concern or priority because they were not hiring (Institute for Public Relations, 2020). The centrifugal forces of COVID-19 messaging about safety and layoffs and beliefs that DEI does not matter during a crisis pushed diversity away from the center of conversations, although social inequities were amplified by the pandemic response, those who died in the early waves, and the lingering effects of systemic racism in healthcare (Jones, 2000; Kline & Quiroga, 2021).

Then, sparked by the recorded murder of George Floyd and the echoing plea of "I can't breathe" (a phrase that multiple men and women have said at the hands of the police and vigilantes), collective action swelled to a crescendo of marches, demonstrations and petitions as people acted to upend the status quo and address discrimination, injustice and a myriad of other traumas (Acosta, 2020; Becker, 2012; Krieger, 2020; Thomas et al., 2019). The international conversation switched to injustices within those same societal institutions and their responses to their stakeholders. For example, multiple agencies promoted or hired chief diversity officers, and many corporations, nonprofits and public universities released bland statements about diversity and equity following off-campus protests and campus demands for accountability and change. Brands have chosen to center their core audiences and reframe their values in light of the spate of well-publicized injustices (Edrington, 2021). Once again, the spotlight shifted, and what was once marginalized and considered nonviable and unimportant became essential.

The text of Bardhan and Gower comes at a key moment in time. Why this book? Bookshelves, both virtual and physical, are crammed with books about corporate diversity, equity and inclusion. This book stands out because Bardhan and Gower offer a crisp pivot to examine how public relations as an organizational function plays a role in inclusion. As communicators we know the power of words and visuals and we know that public relations resides in the liminality between the organization and its many publics. Boundary spanners provide key stakeholder insights and intelligence and serve as a communicative relay between and throughout the organization. If our role is important enough to handle communications internally and externally and our role accords a seat at the table of power, our industry and leadership should have an explicit DEI path to follow and use. This book provides that.

This work focuses on inclusion, which is the bedrock for diversity and equity. Often, in these discussions of diversity, equity, inclusion and accessibility, people start with the legal ramifications, affirmative action, and counting. Diversity is seen as an additive transaction: If we just add one of this group, we will have achieved diversity, and other things will change for the better. Few consider the organizational context: the structures, the culture, the institutional myths, the corrupted processes for hiring and retention, and the hidden curriculum of expectations and beliefs that one is assumed to know. A recent report from the Institute for Public Relations and the Wakeman Agency found a pervasive lack of knowledge about what diversity is, what the differences between equity and equality are, and what inclusion is (Institute for Public Relations, 2021a). According to that research, only 23% of practitioners perceived "inclusion" and "belonging" as separate terms. This snapshot of our field shows that we have a lot of work to do as communicators and as organizational cultural carriers. If DEI is the responsibility of all within the organization, we are a weak link.

Bardhan and Gower challenge industry leaders to make DEI a consistent, ongoing focal area. DEI cannot be supported only during heritage months, when the CEO makes unbearably racist and sexist remarks during a client meeting, or when it is convenient for the organization. Everyday struggles must be met with everyday commitments to progress and growth. For far too long, we have been told to wait and be patient. *We must do better* is a common refrain heard when doing DEI research and work. The phrase falls from the lips of students, practitioners, C-suite level executives, board members and professors. It is a clarion call often without direction and intention, a call to battle lacking strategy or the willingness to confront systems, policies, and the networks of complicity that allow bad actors and maddening actions to thrive. Diversity and equity are seen as a promise and a threat. Accessibility is treated as a non-issue, and inclusion is presumed to just happen. *We must do better* without substance is easy equity talking and diversity-signaling. Doing better as leaders and creating cultures and practices of inclusion are difficult terrains to navigate and traverse.

Finally, Bardhan and Gower rebut the dominant framework for DEI and public relations leadership, which is that these two things have nothing to do with each other and offer a compelling argument and model for real-world practice. Models are elegant yet flat versions of the true contours that organizations and people face in the real world. A two-dimensional graphical image on a page cannot account for every matter, attack or conundrum that gets thrown toward the organization. The authors have done an exceptional job providing a firm foundation upon which organizations can frame and build their own DEI programs within and across the organizations. For any effort to succeed, the effort must be seen as intentional and authentic. The superficial and shallow gestures and efforts made by those in a powerful in-group to benefit the identities of out-group members is what Leong (2021) considered identity capitalism. The efforts are not rooted in authenticity and genuine belief in diversity equity and inclusion. Rather, the efforts associated with identity capitalism are flush with power and self-absorption. It is the desire to receive pats on the back or congratulatory praise for one-dimensional attempts at diversity "without doing the hard work to make substantive. . . progress a reality" (p. 7).

This book comes now when it is most needed, providing tangible solutions to an ongoing wicked problem that the public relations industry has attempted to dodge, avoid and minimize. It is hard to write that this moment is a good time for anything. (I am muddling and puzzling through this foreword during the last weeks of December 2021.) Billionaires are engaging in a space race as the rest of us look on askance as natural disasters create havoc and climate refugees on every continent. Climate change activism is now a global conversation as governments twiddle their thumbs, corporations attempt to do something, and communities suffer. Labor strikes are gaining momentum as workers are pressed to their limits and as organizations forsake true inclusion, psychological safety, and physical safety in pursuit of profit and managerial surveillance. Juries convicted the neighborhood vigilantes and police officers who killed unarmed Black men.

We are living in a "failing trust ecosystem" (Edelman, 2021). Brands have addressed social injustices unevenly with some leaning into transparency and others cloaking themselves in rainbow washing, social justice washing and greenwashing. What we believed was the end of a pandemic is now the start of a global endemic. If this is not the time for rethinking the status quo and troubling the failing institutions and beliefs that brought us here, then when? If not these two authors who have published on global public relations, public relations education, public relations history, and public relations leadership and devoted significant chunks of time on The Plank Center's diversity, equity and inclusion initiatives, then who?

In the book, Bardhan and Gower offer the knowledge needed, the skills required, the attitudes congruent for leadership to do better in spirit, deeds, and action, not just words. Whether these new, spotlighted conversations prompted by this book, catalyzed by movements and activists for social good, or generated by scandal spur meaningful change are up to those in power in our agencies, those who are creating new curricula, and those who are sitting in our classrooms. This book provides hope and inspiration as well as a blueprint on how industry can make substantial shifts to accommodate and welcome all persons into what has been a lily-white, very female, and incredibly able-bodied field. It's time to stretch into this new reality or stagnate.

Natalie T. J. Tindall, PhD, APR
Isabella Cunningham Chair in Advertising, School of Advertising
and Public Relations, Moody College of Communication,
University of Texas at Austin

Preface/Acknowledgments

We began conceptualizing this book in 2015 when The Plank Center for Leadership in Public Relations board created its first Diversity and Inclusion (D&I) subcommittee under the leadership of Keith Burton, immediate-past chair of the board. Positioning the Center as a catalyst for diversity, equity and inclusion in the profession, keeping track of research on public relations leadership and D&I and conducting needed research on this topic were among the subcommittee's stated goals. The subcommittee gradually became a stand-alone committee as the D&I mission of the Center's work grew steadily through all its programming and events. In 2018, the Center held its first D&I Summit in Chicago. Since then, the summit has grown in success and visibility and has developed into a space that prioritizes dialogue for action and connects professionals, educators and students who are passionate about the topic of D&I and leadership in public relations.

Through all these efforts, we developed the concept and focus of this book. A clear lack of research was detected at the intersection of D&I and leadership in public relations. While everyone seemed to be talking about the importance of genuine leadership involvement and support for D&I success, no comprehensive research on the topic for our profession/discipline was available. This book addresses this glaring gap. We developed, researched and wrote it with the intention of producing a volume that would be useful to the three key audiences of The Plank Center – public relations professionals, students and educators.

We dedicate this book to Betsy Plank, a public relations leader and trailblazer, after whom The Plank Center is named. Three decades ago, she noted that D&I is "not only 'the right thing,' the proud thing – it is. . . the smart thing" to do (Plank, 1991). It is our strong hunch that Betsy would be excited about this book. We also dedicate this book to all public relations leaders who see diversity as a gift rather than a problem to be managed.

We thank The Plank Center and its board for supporting this project. We thank former board chairs Keith Burton and Ron Culp for their inspiring leadership and for channeling their D&I passion and commitment in ways needed to position the Center as a thought leader on D&I and leadership. We thank Pat Ford for his tremendous support after he joined the board and took on the role of cochair of the D&I subcommittee. We thank Bridget Coffing, our current board chair, for her ongoing support and enthusiasm for advancing D&I, and we thank Bruce Berger for his passion for research that inspires us in our own work. We thank our current D&I Committee cochair Diana Martinelli and all committee members and advisers for their valuable insights and genuine desire to make a difference. We thank Alexa Campbell and Derek Hooper, former graduate students at the University of Alabama, who assisted us with data collection, and we thank all the professionals, students and educators who generously shared their views through in-depth interviews. We are grateful for the valuable feedback on our manuscript proposal provided by reviewers, and we thank Felisa Salvago-Keyes, our Routledge publisher, for her advice, support and guidance throughout the publishing process.

Nilanjana would like to particularly thank Hugh Culbertson, professor emeritus at Ohio University, and Tee Ford-Ahmed, professor emeritus at West Virginia State University. Their mentorship, kindness and passion for public relations teaching and scholarship with an unwavering focus on D&I, both domestic and global, has shaped her own growth as a teacher and scholar for three decades. She also thanks her department chair Professor Sandy Pensoneau-Conway for her support, especially in the final months leading up to the completion of the manuscript. Karla would like to particularly thank Bruce Berger, professor emeritus at the University of Alabama, for his continued support, encouragement, mentorship and friendship. Both Karla and Nilanjana extend heartfelt thanks to Professor Natalie Tindall for taking time out of her busy schedule to write the foreword, and to all who read the manuscript and provided generous endorsements. The D&I journey is a collective one and we could not have produced this volume without all this support.

Nilanjana Bardhan, PhD
Professor, Public Relations and Intercultural Communication, School of
Communication Studies, Southern Illinois University – Carbondale, USA
Co-Chair, D&I Committee, The Plank Center for Leadership in Public Relations

Karla Gower, PhD
Behringer Distinguished Professor, Department of Advertising
and Public Relations, University of Alabama – Tuscaloosa, USA
Director, The Plank Center for Leadership in Public Relations

1

Introduction

A far, strange sound through the night,
A dauntless and resolute cry,
Clear in the tempest's despite,
Ringing so wild and so high!
Darkness and tumult and dread,
Rain and the battling of gales,
Yet cleaving the storm overhead,
The wedge of the wild geese sails:
...
Sure that the land of their hope
Waits beyond tempest and dread,
Sure that the dark where they grope,
Shall glow with the morning red!
                    Thaxter (1886, pp. 90–91)

We can learn much from geese when it comes to leadership qualities, especially responsibility, accountability and teamwork. The above stanzas from Celia Thaxter's poem "Wild Geese" may seem a little dark at first, but they convey an important message about leadership and hope for the future. Leadership is not an easy journey; it is not just about one heroic, visionary and charismatic individual leading the march with troops following behind. It is a journey of ongoing growth and learning that requires all of us, especially those at the helm of organizations, to flap our wings and face challenges and problems together by lifting each other up and soaring toward the morning light. Geese don't leave other geese behind.

DOI: 10.4324/9781003170020-1

We begin on this note because this book addresses a prominent problem and challenge related to leadership in public relations: the troubling lack of diversity and inclusion (D&I)/equity in the profession. This situation, if it persists, will have grave consequences for the reputation of the profession unless leaders take responsibility, band together like geese and provide the boost needed to make the profession more diverse, inclusive and equitable. About ten years ago, in their signature book on public relations leadership supported by The Plank Center for Leadership in Public Relations, Berger and Meng (2014a) wrote:

> The quality of public relations leaders and their day-to-day performance in organizations and in the profession has a great deal to do with the success, reputation, and future of those organizations and the profession itself, especially in a dynamic and fast-changing world in which the only certainty of the future is uncertainty.
>
> *(p. xxiii)*

Berger and Meng also pointed out that despite the important role of leadership in the success of the profession, surprisingly little research exists on the topic. Since the publication of their book, The Plank Center has continued to sponsor and fund research to build the body of knowledge on public relations leadership (see Chapter 4); however, the attention paid to D&I and leadership has been low and tangential, and our volume is an attempt to address this gap. With our focus at the intersection of D&I and public relations leadership, we hope the model for leadership for inclusive diversity in public relations that we have developed (see Chapter 7) will be useful for addressing the current dismal state of D&I leadership in the profession. Before we move on, however, we would like to mention that the focus of this book is on public relations leadership and D&I in the context of the United States. While some of what it offers may very well apply to other cultures and countries (especially in the western world), we caution readers away from the inclination to apply our model universally (Bardhan, 2003; Gower, 2006).

The writing of this book has been an instructive journey. We started the project, gathered our survey data and conducted all except two of our in-depth interviews before the combined racial/social justice and COVID-19 pandemic upheaval occurred in 2020. Our writing went through some significant turns and revisions as the D&I narrative in our environment surged and changed dramatically after the killing of George Floyd. Our first reaction was that our data would be dated given the turn of events; however, upon further reflection, we realized we were in a good position. Comparing what our data tell us with where the D&I narrative is at almost two years later is eye-opening and more realistic regarding where we are headed and how much of an impact 2020 really has had when it comes to concrete and meaningful

D&I advancement in the public relations profession. Recent reports have not been particularly encouraging (see Chapter 5).

In addition to wanting to produce a volume that will be equally useful to scholars/educators, professionals and students, the four main goals we set for ourselves in writing this book are as follows:

- Weave together large bodies of interdisciplinary literature on leadership and D&I and apply this to the state of D&I leadership in public relations. This work, to our knowledge, has not been done before (for a comprehensive and interdisciplinary literature on public relations and D&I, see Mundy, 2016).
- Emphasize inclusion. In other words, we wanted to put the spotlight on inclusion since diversity cannot thrive without inclusion. For too long we have put the cart (diversity) before the horse (inclusion) and it is time to turn our thinking around.
- Develop a model for D&I leadership in public relations which has applied value and potential for further theoretical development.
- Utilize a critical lens that aims to aid practice through critique. The common complaint from practitioners regarding critical public relations scholarship is that such scholarship is not practical enough. Critical scholars argue that their charge and imperative are to critique what is normalized in practice, especially from the perspective of power inequities and hegemonic systemic practices, since industry does not engage in such efforts. We made it our goal to take both arguments and attempt a fine balance. Without abandoning the critical lens, we aimed to develop a model and provide suggestions for practice (or praxis) which leaders in the profession can use on an everyday basis (see Chapter 7).

We now describe the main problem and challenge that this book addresses in more detail.

The D&I and leadership problem/challenge in public relations

After a 2019 review of its own numbers showed that about 88% of its executive leadership and 85% of its senior vice presidents and 75% of its overall professionals are White, Weber Shandwick CEO Gail Heimann stated:

> While diversity, equity and inclusion are core values we uphold at Weber Shandwick, the headline – on every level – is that people of color are grossly underrepresented in our agency. This data shows that our values simply aren't reflected in the make-up of our workforce …. We have to do better. And we have to move as quickly as possible. It will be a

> formidable journey and it will require an action plan devised with more
> rigor and more resources than we've designated previously ....
> *(Marszalek, 2020, paras. 4, 5)*

Weber Shandwick's numbers closely reflect the overall state of D&I in the industry. While no comprehensive industry-compiled D&I data currently exists, the US Bureau of Labor Statistics figures for race/ethnicity report that approximately 83–91% (depending on title/position) of the industry is White, 11–4% Black or African American, 3–2% Asian and 13–7% Hispanic (Bureau of Labor Statistics, 2020). Racial/ethnic diversity decreases further up the leadership ladder. According to a more recent benchmark report from the industry's recently formed Diversity Action Alliance (2021), 78% of the industry is White, 7% Black/African American, 6% Hispanic, 6% Asian and 3% of two or more races/ethnicities; top leadership is 93% White, 4% Black/ African American and 1% Hispanic. Information on other dimensions of diversity is difficult to find. In terms of gender, women constitute about two-thirds of the profession, but men dominate in leadership roles (Place & Vardeman-Winter, 2018). Data on other dimensions of diversity are hard to come by.

Heimann urges other leaders, especially in the agency domain, to be more transparent about D&I statistics and work with intentionality to move the needle faster. Other upfront leaders in the past have also sounded similar alarm bells and called upon colleagues to engage in action, but the situation on the ground remains largely unchanged (see Cohen, 2014; Cripps, 2015; P. Ford, 2017). In the face of a fast-changing cultural and demographic landscape in the United States, a country that will soon be a majority-minority society, public relations remains a "lily white field of women," with men mostly in leadership positions (Vardeman-Winter & Place, 2017, p. 326) (see also Chitkara, 2018; Logan, 2011; Mundy, 2015, 2016). Unfortunately, leaders like Heimann are few and far apart.

For the sake of context, we should mention the situation is not much rosier when it comes to related fields such as advertising and marketing, and in corporate America in general. During the racial reckoning and pandemic upheavals of 2020, Fuller (2020) wrote:

> With a national dialogue swirling around equity and inclusion, the data show that corporate America is still struggling with the basics of diversity and representation. ...
>
> So, what seems to be the hold up? For all the talk around the importance of diversity as well as its potential upside, why so little progress?
>
> One reason is that companies aren't approaching diversity the right way. The concept of diversity is generally greeted by most companies with an eye roll and a few perfunctory efforts. Talking to executives about

diversity has basically been the equivalent of telling kids to eat their vegetables: They will begrudgingly do it, but without any real enthusiasm, and mainly just to stay out of trouble.

(paras. 1, 5, 6)

Against the backdrop of this not very heartening macro context, our focus in this book is on the profession of public relations.

Just like any other profession, public relations has its own occupational culture with rules, rituals, hierarchies, practices and codes regarding how work is done, what is appropriate, what is not, what the norms are, what lies outside the norm and so on (Pieczka, 2002). Occupational culture, in turn, impacts D&I. Further, societal differences shape occupational cultures in specific ways (Sriramesh & J. White, 1992). For example, it would be inaccurate to assume that the gender dynamics of public relations practice are the same in all countries and cultures. Edwards (2011, 2015) helps us understand how to position public relations within larger sociohistorical contexts. Using sociologist Pierre Bourdieu's work, she explains societies have overarching fields of power within which reside other fields: "Each field is defined by a particular type of practice: occupations like public relations can be defined as a field…" (Edwards, 2011, p. 62). Describing Bourdieu's theory of habitus, she further explains the public relations profession's culture and power dynamics within a particular society are the product of a particular habitus. A habitus is a:

> … set of durable dispositions, developed and inculcated over time through family and education, that determine the way we comprehend our social environment and our role within it. … It is manifest in our values, beliefs and attitudes, evident in the language we use, and embodied in our behaviors, often unconsciously….
>
> *(p. 67)*

Habitus and social structures cannot be separated.

Edwards elaborates that the historically constructed racially homogenous nature of the profession in societies like the United Kingdom and the United States results in the public relations habitus being marked by racial privilege within the larger social structure: "If the field of PR attracts people from a similar type of habitus, drawn from a similar position from the social hierarchy, with a similar view of the world, then this will be reflected in PR practice, because habitus shapes practice" (Edwards, 2011, p. 70). Those entering from outside the habitus will not fit easily or will feel pressure to assimilate and code switch, i.e., they will not be able to be their authentic selves at work. Therefore, for D&I to thrive, the habitus must change. Such change is slow since people tend to seek out people like themselves for "fit" and avoid differences. "Fit" is the habitus-driven perception of how one will be able "to mesh and play well" within an organization's "cultural sandbox" (Tindall, 2016, para. 5).

Leaders play a prominent and impactful role in bringing about change in professional cultures. As the following chapters demonstrate in depth, the correlation between D&I success and visible leadership support and genuine commitment is loud and clear; additionally, there is now plenty of evidence that D&I success correlates positively with enhanced creativity, innovation and improvement in organizations' financial performance and competitive edge (e.g., Bassett-Jones, 2005; Dixon-Fyle, Dolan, Hunt, & Prince, 2020; Eswaran, 2019; Lorenzo, Voigt, Tsusaka, Krentz, & Abouzahr, 2018; Marketinsite, 2020). Therefore, leadership commitment to D&I is not just about legal compliance; it is a combined matter of ethics and social and financial responsibility. If the makeup of the profession does not reflect the cultural and demographic landscapes of the larger society it is embedded in, this means many are being excluded and viewpoints within the profession are culturally limited. As just described, the US public relations profession far from reflects the larger society in which it is embedded.

L. A. Grunig and Toth (2006) state that "Diverse standpoints ... reflect values about what is important to uphold" (p. 43). They point out that while all the international professional communication associations (e.g., International Association of Business Communicators, International Public Relations Association, Global Alliance for PR) include attention to and respect for cultural differences and diversity in their codes of ethics, the Public Relations Society of America's (PRSA's) code of ethics does not include a section pertaining to D&I. In fact, the words "diversity," "inclusion" and "equity" are not a part of any of the current codes. This fact about the missing D&I-related code of ethics conveys a lot regarding the habitus and story of US public relations' professional culture and ethical priorities. What is not said is as important as what is said. The language we use (or do not use) and the codes we develop (or do not develop) to define professional conduct say much about everyday practice, values and dispositions (i.e., habitus). There also seems to be an assumption that culture, difference and inequities apply only in international contexts. Public relations practice and scholarship in the United States has spent more time conceptualizing culture and difference as something that matters across national borders and largely ignored domestic diversity. According to Sha (2006), we should not "forget that publics within a national society are not culturally homogeneous, as we know to be true given the demographic shifts in the United States and other countries" (p. 48). Sriramesh (2009) cautions we should not ghettoize the study of culture and difference in public relations and assume that culture matters only in global/international contexts. Leaders need to look inwards and make some significant changes.

Leading with inclusion/equity: Putting the horse before the cart

Over the past few years, visibility of the term "inclusion," along with "equity," has increased in public relations trade discourse (in this book, we treat equity as an outcome of inclusion; see Chapter 3 for a detailed explanation). For several decades, the focus had been on "diversity" and terms such as "diversity management" were common in the discourse. But this recent shift in language indicates something important. There is a growing realization that increase in diversity does not automatically lead to inclusive and equitable organizational climates (Mundy, 2016; Roberson, 2006), i.e., we have been putting the cart before the horse and then wondering about the lack of movement and change. Gaither (2018) explains:

> At its core, cultural diversity is about *difference* in its many forms: races, ethnicities, genders, belief systems, orientations, and identities. Difference alone does not equal diversity; equally as important is the *context* – the climate or environment surrounding difference. Participatory environments – where difference is appreciated and welcomed can provide a transformative context to turn diversity from a buzzword into an organizational strength ....
>
> *(p. 472, emphasis in original)*

The "participatory environment" that Gaither refers to is the inclusion/equity piece. The reality on the ground is that the less attention we pay to inclusion/equity, the more retention becomes a problem. No one enjoys working in an organization where they feel excluded and discriminated against. According to talent and D&I consultants Bililies and Ndoma-Ogar (2021), "success with DEI hinges on making sure that your efforts aren't just a numbers game where you simply bring in talent embodying diversity. That's inauthentic, and it will only backfire" (para. 21). Therefore, one of the first mantras public relations leaders need to internalize is that the horse of inclusion pulls the cart of diversity, and not the other way around. Inclusion is the thread that stitches together diversity in ways that create welcoming and participatory climates in organizations.

Several recent studies from industry have highlighted the central role of inclusion in making diversity work (e.g., Bourke, 2018; Dixon-Fyle et al., 2020). In the same breath, several studies also point out there is little clarity regarding how to build inclusive climates. According to Tiffany Pham (2021), CEO of Mogul, a company that recruits diverse talent, when it comes to inclusion, most companies "are unsure where to start in a meaningful way that does more than just 'check off the boxes'" (para. 5). The situation in public relations is no different. In her study of senior public relations leaders,

Chitkara (2018) found that inclusion is what they seem to be struggling with. We found similar evidence in our data. Tying the inclusion piece to leadership, D&I scholar-practitioner/consultant Bernardo Ferdman (2021) emphasizes that to lead successfully in an increasingly complex and diverse work world, leaders must possess the skills needed to build inclusive organizational cultures. He explains:

> Inclusive leadership requires mindsets and skills for noticing, engaging with, and creating spaces for multiple dimensions of diversity, as well as the varying ways in which people deal with this diversity. It requires being able to explain how diversity matters, and to help people close the gap between the tendency to avoid, reject, or minimize differences in identities or cultures and the need to move toward approaches that highlight the value of diversity....
>
> *(p. 7)*

Therefore, our emphasis in this book and the model we have developed is on inclusion and leadership and how these two forces combined can make diversity work. Our goal is to assist public relations leaders to step up and start changing the D&I narrative so the profession can catch up with the times and embrace the future.

Story as metaphor and method: Understanding D&I through a narrative lens

"It's not a positive story, but it's an important one," states Weber Shandwick CEO Gail Heimann regarding the D&I problem in public relations (Marszalek, 2020)

Story is reality. We know that only too well in public relations. As Banks (1995) states, like any other profession, public relations communication includes "powerful messages about what is natural and what is right [or wrong]" and from a narrative perspective, this communication takes storied forms (p. 29; see also Elmer, 2011). Within communication theory and from a social constructionist perspective, the narrative paradigm offers a useful lens for understanding how the story form is deeply connected to how people make sense of their personal, social and professional worlds (Berger & Luckmann, 1966; Czarniawska, 1997; Littlejohn, Foss, & Oetzel, 2016). According to Walter Fisher, the main architect of the narrative paradigm:

> Many different root metaphors have been put forth to represent the essential nature of human beings ... I propose that *Homo narrans* be added to that list. ...The idea of human beings as storytellers posits the generic form of all symbolic communication. It holds that symbols are created and communicated ultimately as stories meant to give order to human

experience and to induce others to dwell in them in order to establish ways of living in common ....

(Fisher, 1987, pp. 62, 63, emphasis in original)

In other words, through symbolic interaction and activity, humans use the story form to construct reality and produce meaning; further, the meanings we make of things are connected to what we do, or do not do, about them. Storytelling is a powerful method for intersubjectively constructing realities within organizations, industries and the public sphere, and the narrative paradigm has been popular in management and organizational studies (Bardhan & Engstrom, 2021):

> [T]he notion of narrative knowledge uses the metaphor of the world-as-text – alerting us to the constitutive nature in which stories rule our lives and social institutions. ... our organizations, institutions, and professions are communicatively constituted through storytelling.

(p. 6)

When applied to D&I and public relations leadership, the narrative approach allows us to understand the problem primarily from a communication perspective. This is an appropriate approach for a communication profession.

The story approach permeates our entire book. At an overarching level, the story we tell (or construct) is the story of D&I leadership, practice and scholarship in public relations in the United States. At this level, story works as a metaphor or sense-making mechanism. In terms of methodology, we utilized the narrative paradigm (see Chapters 5 and 6) to design our online survey and in-depth interviews and analyze our data (i.e., the accounts we gathered from public relations professionals, scholars/educators and students). From a methods perspective, a story lens allowed us to evaluate the tone, texture, key moments, actors and direction of the D&I and public relations leadership story as surmised through analysis of communication (survey data and in-depth interviews). We then connected our findings with the larger literature to develop themes that construct the overall public relations leadership and D&I story. The story is an open-ended one since D&I is an ongoing journey.

Just to be clear, we do not wish to suggest that our narrative focus somehow disregards the material realities involved in the public relations D&I leadership problem/challenge (e.g., what concrete resources are committed to D&I efforts, how much diversity is actually present in an organization, and so on); what we are emphasizing is that over time, how we make sense of and what we do with material aspects are outcomes of the particular meanings we assign them through storied communication. What we do with the material is inseparable from how we narrate them.

Organization of the book

This book unfolds in four parts. The first part (the beginning; Chapters 1 and 2) sets the stage and delves into the D&I problem/challenge and what research tells us about it. The second part (Chapters 3 and 4) is mainly theoretical and conceptual. It delves into the interdisciplinary research on D&I and leadership and connects this literature with public relations leadership scholarship. The third part comprises data analysis and reporting (Chapters 5 and 6). The fourth part (not the ending, but continuation toward the future; Chapters 7 and 8) offers our model for public relations leadership for inclusive diversity, a definition of the same and suggestions for praxis and future scholarship.

In Chapter 2, we provide an in-depth history of D&I in the public relations industry in the United States and connect this narrative with leadership responsibility. We then review academic scholarship on public relations and D&I since the 1980s, further emphasize the key connections between leadership support and D&I success and conclude with key takeaways. In Chapter 3, we provide an interdisciplinary and in-depth overview of the literature that exists on D&I with a specific focus on disciplines such as organization studies, management, communication and social psychology. Next, we assess the state of D&I in the US public relations industry and scholarship in relation to this interdisciplinary literature and then conclude with key takeaways. Chapter 4 takes a broad look at how the concept of leadership has been studied for almost a century with a particular focus on the fields of management, communication, organizational studies and human relations. We describe how our study and understanding of leadership keeps evolving and shifting with the times and note overall trends in research. Next, we provide an overview of how public relations scholarship has theorized leadership and its relationship to D&I and connect the same with the larger literature. We conclude with implications and takeaways.

Chapters 5 and 6 present the data we gathered specifically for this project. In Chapter 5, using narrative analysis, we report the results of an online survey of public relations professionals practicing in the United States. This survey was a mix of closed- and open-ended questions designed to elicit responses which would provide storied insights into the relationship between D&I and public relations leadership. We conclude with key takeaways. The survey results formed the springboard for 30 in-depth interviews with public relations leaders (professionals, educators/scholars and students), and the analysis of these interviews is presented in Chapter 6. Through the interviews, we were able to dig deeper into the D&I and leadership relationship. We were also able to make comparisons between the results of the online survey and the in-depth interviews. We conclude with key takeaways.

We tie all the threads together in Chapter 7. That is, we weave together the larger literature with our data and develop 11 themes that constitute the overall public relations D&I and leadership narrative. Using these themes as our context, we present our public relations leadership model for inclusive diversity, describe the five core characteristics of the model and explain its various components. In Chapter 8, we highlight the primary and unique contributions of our book and offer practical advice and suggestions to leaders on how to apply our D&I leadership model. We conclude with suggestions for future scholarship on the subject and remind readers that the road ahead is full of exciting potential for leadership and D&I engagement in public relations. The ball is in leadership's court and what leaders do with it remains to be seen.

Conclusion

There are stories, both good and bad, inspiring and not-so-inspiring, regarding D&I and leadership. For example, leadership at IBM has demonstrated genuine commitment and the ability to develop strategic and measurable D&I plans and initiatives for its internal and external audience for several decades now ("Leading diversity," 2021). Another example is that of Hewlett Packard (HP) and how after its breakup, CEO Enrique Lores made board diversity a top priority since "[o]nce the board is sufficiently diverse, the commitment to diversity can come from the top and a corporate culture of diversity and inclusion can take shape" (Scott, 2020, para. 6). However, despite the good stories, the recent surge in D&I discourse from a moral perspective and the fact there is now plenty of research evidence that D&I is good for business, "many leaders still do not believe deeply that diversity is good" (Johnson & Lambert, 2021, p. 67). We need more stories like IBM and HP to change the narrative and bring about attitudinal and systemic level D&I change in public relations.

This challenge is steep since public relations remains a profession, or field, that is embedded within a larger historically specific and overarching field of power which does not yet tilt well in favor of D&I (Edwards, 2011, 2015). Diversity within Fortune 500 companies, particularly at the leadership level, is still quite dismal. According to a recent study by Deloitte and the Alliance for Board Diversity, while some gains have been made with more representation of women leading Fortune 500 companies, "it will take more than 50 years for minorities to comprise 40% of Fortune 500 board seats" (Colvin, 2021, para. 4). According to recent research by United Minds, a Weber Shandwick consultancy:

> A new study on diversity, equity and inclusion in the workplace shows a divide between corporate efforts to advance DE&I and the lived experiences of many employees. ... many employees are either

doubtful or uncertain about the effectiveness of their employer's DE&I efforts, and that even amid heightened attention on the importance of advancing DE&I, bad behavior and lack of commitment persists within organizations.

("United Minds Study Reveals," 2021, para. 1)

In this mixed environment, the public relations industry has ramped up efforts to move the D&I needle faster through initiatives such as the Diversity Action Alliance (DAA), which is a consortium of professional organizations dedicated to achieving, among other things, more transparency on D&I statistics in the profession (see Chapter 3 for more details on the DAA). Another major development which occurred recently as we were wrapping up our writing is that the Securities and Exchanges Commission (SEC) approved Nasdaq's proposal for mandating more diversity on the boards of publicly traded companies ("SEC approves," 2021). This change came about due to pressure from shareholders and governments around the world to diversify overwhelmingly White and male boards (Chapman & Choe, 2020). According to US Edelman CEO Lisa Ross (2021), the D&I momentum is not likely to reverse, and we are now in "an environment that's become more charged, more divided, more impatient and more ready to vote with their wallets and talents. This environment will only intensify" (para. 10).

Public relations leaders must allow the good stories to inspire and the not-so-good ones to teach us what not to do. The D&I story is an ongoing one, and research that keeps us on track with D&I progress (or lack of it), for example, books such as this one, are still very much needed for this important journey. The D&I promises made in 2020 were inspiring, but we must remain vigilant. We must ensure that diversity, inclusion and equity do not become empty buzzwords in public relations. Instead, we must create a momentum through which leaders and all employees can learn how to respect difference, work toward equity, creatively harness the advantages of diversity and build cultures of inclusion. We now further unpack the D&I story in public relations with a spotlight on leadership.

2

Public Relations, Diversity and Inclusion

A Story Unpacked with a Spotlight on Leadership

This chapter provides an in-depth look at the history and story of diversity and inclusion (D&I) in the public relations industry in the United States. Next, it reviews public relations scholarship on D&I since the 1980s. The extant research on the leadership and D&I link has emphasized this point for a while now, but the more recent upheavals against racial injustice have made it clear that we have a long way to go on the D&I front in our society and the organizations that populate it. We finally describe the importance of leadership engagement in D&I in public relations. As Marsha Pitts-Phillips, an African American professional and first D&I officer for the Minnesota chapter of the Public Relations Society of America (PRSA), emphasized after the killing of George Floyd in May 2020, leadership engagement is crucial for D&I success and for real change to take place: "Change starts at the top and with a company or organization's mission and values" (Pitts-Phillips in Jacques, 2020, para. 6). We conclude with key takeaways.

The industry story on diversity and inclusion

There is a context to every story, and this is true for the D&I story of public relations in the United States as well. For this context, we must go back at least 60 years. The Civil Rights movement and the women's liberation and gay pride movements of the 1960s and 1970s set the stage for the diversity imperative in the country, specifically in education and the workplace. With more women entering the workforce, the increase in diversity in society due to the opening up of immigration from non-European countries, affirmative action, equal opportunity and the overall growth of the discourse of multiculturalism, companies/organizations and institutions started to feel

DOI: 10.4324/9781003170020-2

the pressure to pay attention to these new realities and cultural shifts. However, and according to Pusch (2004):

> …most clung to the 'melting pot' approach and expected new populations to adapt to the corporate culture, which was built on the European American male culture. … Most of the employees from nondominant cultures who managed to 'fit in' at corporations did not like the price this extracted: giving up their own cultural identity, at least during work hours.
>
> *(p. 28)*

This expectation of assimilation resulted in high turnover of employees from underrepresented and historically marginalized groups. Furthermore, there was a tendency among companies to take a compliance approach to diversity to avoid legal hot water, thereby hampering the growth of genuinely inclusive and equitable work cultures.

Culture shifts challenge power structures, and those in positions of systemic/structural power usually do not simply step aside to make space for the historically marginalized. Structural and cultural changes require significant changes in attitude, especially among dominant cultural groups and demographics used to certain privileges and not used to probing their unconscious biases. This takes time. The diversity movement in the United States has been a struggle for voice, power-sharing and equity, and despite some gains it still remains so. The recent racial and social justice upheavals have led to a clear surge in support for D&I in our society and organizations in general and while we can and should be optimistic about this development, how much actual change will follow remains to be seen. This trajectory serves as the backdrop for the D&I story of the US public relations industry.

The discourse of equity in the profession began in the 1970s with gender. In its early decades, the work world of public relations comprised mostly men. Eventually, and fueled by the women's liberation movement, more women started joining the profession in the 1960s and, according to Gower (2001), it was in the early 1970s that "public relations women were awakening to their feminist consciousness" (p. 18). In a profession populated increasingly with women with mostly men in leadership positions of power, issues such as pay equity, glass ceiling constraints and sexual harassment rose to the top (L. A. Grunig, Toth, & Hon, 2001). The PRSA set up task forces in the 1970s and 1980s to advance these inquiries, and the topic of gender has remained high on the equity agenda ever since.

Attention to race and ethnicity as dimensions of diversity followed gender. In 1978, PRSA established the first task force on minority affairs. The Black Public Relations Society was formed in 1982, and the Hispanic Public Relations Association was formed in 1984 (Kern-Foxworth, 1991). Since then, some efforts have been made to chronicle the history of African

Americans in public relations, but the histories of Hispanics, Asian Americans and Native Americans remain virtually invisible to date. In the late 1980s, African American scholar, practitioner and educator Marilyn Kern-Foxworth emerged as a prominent actor and voice in the D&I discourse (L. A. Grunig, Toth, & Hon, 2001). Almost 30 years ago she urged the industry to recognize fast-changing societal demographics and diversify its ranks and wrote: "As our cities, towns and communities become more diverse and the size of non-White publics increase in size and economic clout, multi-ethnic markets will play key roles in American corporations and organizations" (Kern-Foxworth, 1991, p. 27). While recruitment efforts are better today, and more practitioners of color are in mid-level leadership positions, they remain starkly underrepresented at the senior levels; additionally, subtle discrimination and microaggressions are reported to still be quite common on a daily basis in the public relations workplace (Appelbaum & Walton, 2015; Tindall, 2009).

The business case for D&I has been prominent in industry arguments that have urged for greater change. The moral and social responsibility case has been less evident (Hon & Brunner, 2000; Mundy, 2016). For example, back in the early 1990s when the D&I discourse started gaining some momentum, practitioner James Strenski (1993) began an article on the importance of employee diversity in public relations in the *Public Relations Journal* with the words: "Companies that do not incorporate diversity as a key part of their business plan will be at a competitive disadvantage" (p. 33). Kern-Foxworth's quote above also follows an economic logic. In another often-cited article on the topic from the 1990s, Raymond Kotcher, then president of the public relations firm Ketchum, reported the outcomes of a survey of practitioners his firm had just conducted:

> … the public relations industry – a profession charged with identifying, monitoring and shaping trends in society – is still operating largely according to the traditional model of the American workplace. Needless to say, should the public relations industry continue to operate in this fashion, we could miss one of the most significant business opportunities we have seen in years.
>
> *(Kotcher, 1995, p. 6)*

The business case narrative also received a major boost from two published reports that caused a stir — *Workforce 2000* (Johnston & Packer, 1987) and *Workforce 2020* (Judy & D'Amico, 1997). The latter especially, along with year 2000 census data forecasting rapid diversification of US society and its workforce, added some urgency to the D&I discourse. Predictions grew about how demographically homogenous industries would fall behind as they would not be able to successfully connect with their more diverse clients, customers and stakeholders. Generally, there was increased emphasis after the turn of the century on research that attempted to show that companies with diverse teams and employees are likely to be more creative and, therefore, more competitive and lucrative (e.g., Bassett-Jones, 2005; Herring, 2009; Pandey, Shanahan, & Hansen, 2005; Phillips, Liljenquist, & Neale, 2010). Leading professional organizations (e.g., PRSA in the public relations profession) began funding more diversity-related research and setting up task forces to step up the pace of change. Overall, there was a general uptick in the D&I discourse.

The business case remains the prominent logic and narrative for D&I in the public relations industry today. Uysal (2013) analyzed the D&I content of the websites of 171 S&P 500 manufacturing companies and found that diversity was mainly positioned as a "competitive advantage," and it was only occasionally "linked to corporate social responsibility" (p. 8). Austin's study of the trade publications the *PR Strategist* and *PR Tactics* articles in the first decade of the millennium found that D&I matters were mostly boxed in special sections and columns, creating the sense that D&I is a separate matter from mainstream discourse, an add-on so to speak (see also Wills, 2020). Most articles opened with a tone of justification for D&I. Diversity was mainly framed as a journey and process and also as resource intensive. The importance of inclusion and the need to change organizational culture were highlighted, along with the sentiment that D&I is good for the profession. There was a clear bottom line focus, and attention was devoted mostly to groups depicted as significant because of their "growth" and "buying power" (mainly Hispanics and African Americans).

The traditional/historical diversity categories of gender and race/ethnicity dominated the industry's D&I discourse in the 1990s, and they generally continue to lead the charge (Austin, 2010; Bardhan, Engstrom, & Gower, 2018). There has also been growing interest in LGBTQ+ identities, mainly as markets and to a certain extent as practitioners (see Ciszek, 2020; Mundy, 2015; Tindall & Waters, 2012). Overall, more efforts have been made after the turn of the century to generally broaden the definition of diversity for the profession. One recent study of websites of the top 50 global public relations firms found that those firms that now address diversity on their websites tend to define diversity in very broad terms and tend not to focus too much on categories of historical inequities (i.e., race/ethnicity and gender/sexual orientation) (Wills, 2020). While the broadening of the definition of diversity has benefits and may be seen as more inclusive, downplaying or ignoring historically prominent inequities is problematic and an obstacle in the path of genuine inclusion/equity (this matter is addressed in more depth later in the chapter and in Chapter 3).

Recent attention has also emphatically focused on the entry of a new category – that of the millennials, who are now increasingly entering leadership positions. This generation is the most diverse one in the United States (although Gen Z, which is just beginning to join the work force, is now hailed as the most diverse generation of all times; see Lo Wang, 2018). The research on millennials in general, and what exists in public relations, shows that millennials are high champions of D&I. They look for D&I indicators while job searching, expect diversity in the workplace, are less engaged in non-inclusive environments, tune in quickly to discrimination at work, believe in bringing the whole self to work, are averse to covering (hiding aspects of identity), are more prone to being and accepting allies, have more of an intersectional approach to identity than any previous generation, and are overall more comfortable compared to other generations with discussing D&I (Brown, 2016; Essner, 2017; Gallicano, 2013; Kelly & Smith, 2014; Kochhar, 2016; Meng & Berger, 2018; Smith, Turner, & Levit, 2018). The millennial and Gen Z attitude toward D&I may be read as a hopeful sign for the future. They currently constitute about 40% of the workforce, they "want to work for organizations that excel at DEI," and they "want to follow leaders who clearly care about employees' well-being and who demonstrate ethical behavior" (Bililies & Ndoma-Ogar, 2021, para. 6). Furthermore, there is the related issue of digital communication and social media, which the millennial and Gen Z generations are most comfortable with and not hesitant to use to highlight discrimination and unethical behaviors of leaders and organizations. Companies must understand how the amplification power of social media and the increased ability of marginalized persons and groups to speak back can impact organizational reputations (Bililies & Ndoma-Ogar, 2021; Mundy, 2019). According to organizational behavior researcher Janine Yancey:

> The younger generation of our workforce have been raised to speak truth to power and to speak out when they see a wrong that needs addressing. … That generational characteristic, in combination with the power of social media, which allows people to organise online and share messages at scale, is a new framework of accountability that didn't exist even a few years ago. But it exists now, and it'll get even stronger as boomers and Gen Xers retire.
>
> *(Bishop, 2021, para. 18)*

On the other hand, the power of these communication technologies can also be harnessed to communicate and enhance D&I efforts. A future-oriented vision of D&I in public relations needs to stay in tune with these generational changes and indicators.

Defining D&I

How something is defined and described impacts how something is understood and acted upon. While no universal definition of D&I is possible or advisable since context powerfully shapes meanings of D&I, profession-specific definitions are possible. Ferdman (2014) broadly defines diversity in the context of the workplace as "the representation of multiple identity groups and their cultures in a particular organization or workgroup" (p. 3). No single industry-level D&I definition seems to stand out for public relations in the United States; however, a few definitions have emerged, especially from the Public Relations Society of America (PRSA), its leading professional body. Currently, the PRSA website states:

> The PRSA Diversity & Inclusion (D&I) Committee is committed to building consciousness by increasing visibility of D&I standards, resources and best practices for racial, ethnic, religious, sexual orientation and gender differences, as well as diverse skill sets, mindsets and cultures at all levels of the organization.
>
> *(PRSA, n.d., para. 2)*

Sha and R. Ford (2007) state that an inclusive and holistic definition of diversity in public relations should include differences that cannot be altered (e.g., race, age) as well as those that can be changed (e.g., religion, nationality). The PRSA definition focuses on a mix of non-alterable and alterable differences. The inclusion of "sexual orientation" and "religion" within the definition indicates an expansion from the traditional focus on "race/ethnicity" and "gender" up until about a decade ago; however, the logic for adding only these categories is not quite clear. For example, and for the sake of argument, why not add the category of "age" as well? And most importantly, the term "inclusion" itself is not mentioned at all. There is room for improvement in this definition.

A slightly older definition in the PRSA (2016) D&I toolkit designed for PRSA chapters provided a more expansive description. This document noted that PRSA changed the name of its "Diversity Committee" to "Diversity and Inclusion Committee" in 2015 and defined the role of the committee as follows:

> To champion diversity of thought, cultures, disciplines, ideals, gender, disabilities, sexual orientation and age in order to develop an inclusive Society. By reaching and involving members who represent a broad spectrum of differences, we will encourage and educate members about the benefits of a diverse profession by providing professional development, knowledge and support to help them succeed in public relations.
>
> *(p. 4)*

This definition combines non-alterable and alterable categories of difference and in its own words, aims for a "broad spectrum" approach to diversity. It also mentions "inclusion" and is more action-oriented in that it emphasizes the things that need to be done for D&I success (e.g., educate members about the benefits of D&I for the public relations profession). However, it does not mention a primary marker of difference and inequity in US society – race/ethnicity. This is a glaring omission. Beyond the definition, the toolkit emphasizes the importance of recruiting, retaining and mentoring underrepresented members and diversifying the senior leadership of PRSA. It recommends training for current leaders, adheres to the business case for diversity and emphasizes the creative problem-solving benefits that can accrue from diversity done right, stating: "Diversity and inclusion management provides a pragmatic, strategic advantage" (p. 6). And most importantly from the perspective of our main argument in this book, it emphasizes that leadership commitment is a must for D&I to succeed.

There are some points to be noted in the language of the toolkit. On the one hand, it upholds the view that D&I contributes to the bottom line, while on the other it emphasizes that D&I must be an organic part of every organization, i.e., a general lens through which all work is done, and that it is important that everyone understands why D&I is important and their own role in it. These two views form an awkward juxtaposition. The bottom-line approach tends to commodify those considered "diverse" (Mundy, 2016), and this can actually obstruct an organic approach to diversity and especially inclusion. Perhaps the toolkit was striving to attempt a balance between the two arguments since public relations is a profession after all and cannot ignore the bottom line (we address this matter in more depth in Chapter 3). The toolkit also states that both non-alterable and alterable diversity categories are equally important in that they can both be a source of conflict in the workplace. It explains that a broader definition is needed to include White males since "a narrow definition seems to engender resistance from white males and does not accomplish long-term cultural change that really focuses on utilizing the best talents of everyone, a primary objective for most diversity initiatives" (p. 4). There are a couple of problems with this argument. First, it assumes that all White males are threatened by the categories of race/ethnicity, gender/sex and sexual orientation; while many may be, not all are (see Brown, 2016; Miller & Katz, 2002). Second, while we wholeheartedly agree that everyone, including the dominant group (i.e., heterosexual White males), must be part of the D&I effort for real change, we do not support the view that downplaying historical inequities and power differentials is the way to do this (see Chapters 3 and 7 for alternative suggestions for including White males in D&I efforts).

The PR Council (PRC), founded about two decades ago, is a prominent trade association dedicated to promoting excellence and best practices among US public relations and communication firms. Compared to PRSA, this association has more language about diversity, and especially inclusion and equity, woven throughout its mission, code of ethics and principles, advocacy documents and D&I pledges for firms. One example of such language is:

> We aim to create cultures of inclusivity where professionals of all backgrounds – race, color, national origin, ancestry, religion, disability, medical condition, marital status, veteran status, sexual orientation, gender identity and/or expression, or age – are supported and encouraged.
>
> *(PR Council, n.d.)*

The focus on inclusion is clear in this statement, and numerous alterable and non-alterable characteristics of diversity are included. The long list of diversity categories suggests an intention of inclusion of many types of differences, mainly those that are related to historical inequities. The PRC, along with the trade journal *PR Week*, recognizes organizations and individuals annually for outstanding D&I work with internal and external stakeholders. Curiously though, while the association representing firms endorses inclusion and equity values and language, a recent study mentioned earlier of the top 50 global PR firms' definitions of diversity on their websites shows the opposite tendency – to shy away from historical inequities and lean toward more general differences or use vague language to define diversity; also, of the 50 firms studied, only 28 included any language on D&I on their websites and only nine of those 28 outlined clear programs and activities related to D&I (Wills, 2020). The author points out that not including historical inequalities in D&I language could lead to important disparities not being addressed, which in turn would result in poor inclusion and lack of equity. Another recent study of top 100 global public relations agency leaders (Chitkara, 2018) reported a lack of consensus on the definition of D&I among the leaders. There seems to be a discrepancy between language/values espoused and actual practice.

More recently, a comprehensive and more equity-oriented definition of D&I was offered by the Commission for Public Relations Education (CPRE). Founded in 1973, and currently comprising 18 national and international public relations professional and academic communication associations and accreditation bodies, the CPRE emphasizes the pressing need to make D&I an integral part of undergraduate public relations education so that the college-to-profession diversity pipeline is strengthened. It defines D&I as follows:

> Essentially, diversity is defined as all differences that exist between and among people. Typically, diversity is divided into primary and secondary dimensions, primary being characteristics that are innate and can't be changed (such as gender, age, nationality, sexual/affectional orientation, ethnicity and race) and secondary being characteristics that can be altered (such as religion, geographics, marital status and military service). Understanding the role these dimensions play in how people

communicate is as essential as ensuring that organizations demonstrate inclusiveness toward the diversity of their employees, volunteers and other key publics.

(CPRE, n.d., para. 6)

The CPRE further describes diversity as taking two forms, internal and external. The former is described as "diversity management" and the latter as "intercultural/multicultural communication." It elaborates: "The diversity management aspect of public relations involves human resource, staffing, team, vendor and personnel functions. Managing diversity well will improve the retention of diverse teams, which is considered beneficial to developing innovative solutions and campaigns" (para. 11). For successful D&I, the CPRE also emphasizes that practitioners should "keep pace with the changing demographics of the organization's external environment," "understand how immigration can enrich a culture," "demonstrate how public relations is making full use of the diverse backgrounds, skills and perspectives of all people, thus making working relationships stronger and more effective" and "recognize power imbalances that may exist between the organization and its publics and develop measures to ensure the organization is listening to and proactively engaging disenfranchised and other possibly marginalized groups" (CPRE, n.d., para. 13). Further, it emphasizes that "practitioners, educators and students must develop an introspective awareness of their own individual cultures, socialization and privileges" (para. 14).

The CPRE definition recognizes that successful communication across differences requires understanding the self as much as it requires understanding the other. While it does adhere to the language of "managing" diversity, which has been critiqued as too instrumental and commodified an approach to D&I (this matter is further addressed later in this chapter and in Chapter 3), overall the CPRE's definition is equity-oriented. It highlights inclusion and non-alterable and alterable differences, as well as the need to understand how various dimensions of difference impact communication with internal and external stakeholders. This focus on communication and relationship building is helpful for connecting the definition to the practice of public relations. The definition also focuses on how diversity can enhance creativity, the importance of context and the need to pay careful attention to inequities, privileges and power differentials which may apply to internal and external stakeholders. The focus on power differentials makes this definition stand out from the others.

The above definitions and descriptions suggest an ongoing struggle to define D&I in a profession that has been mostly White with mostly White, heterosexual, able-bodied male leaders for a very long time. While the overall language is supportive of D&I, there has been a tendency to keep the business case in the forefront and shy away from historical inequities (until the racial upheaval of 2020 forced the subject). The few available industry statistics and extant studies on D&I in practice suggest a disjunct between language and practice, or between talk and walk. The D&I needle is moving too slowly in public relations.

The leadership question

There is plenty of research that establishes the strong connection between successful D&I and genuine leadership support and engagement (see Chapters 3 and 4). According to Mundy (2019), "effective D&I [in public relations] must begin with – and be driven by – leadership. Leaders must champion D&I programs and visibly demonstrate that they are committed to success" (p. 36). Within the overall D&I narrative, the spotlight needs to shine harder on leaders in the industry. Despite research, numerous calls and initiatives for three decades, the D&I needle in the industry has barely moved. Therefore, it is necessary to ask what role leadership is playing (or not playing) in addressing this problem, and how dedicated they are to bringing about real change. Additionally, will the urgency and promises prompted by the recent racial unrest change how leaders prioritize D&I?

Over the last decade the public relations trade press has regularly and increasingly offered advice regarding the crucial role of leaders to advocates of D&I. According to senior practitioner Hugo Balta (2015): "In order for diversity to fulfill its true possibility, top leaders need to create a workplace environment where employees understand that their voices are valued and accepted" (para. 5). According to Van Camp (2012): "Engage top leadership on the issue and help them understand, if they don't already, that although often hard to quantify, diversity initiatives have a significant ROI" (para. 15). Dire predictions and outright admonishment of senior leadership have also emerged (see Cohen, 2014; Cripps, 2015). In 2014, an article in *PR Week* by senior practitioner and D&I advocate Joe Cohen made waves. In it, he threw out a challenge to all leaders in the industry to "walk the talk," writing "while I was aware of the lack of diversity in PR, I failed to take action. … I didn't do more than give lip service when it came to addressing the diversity issue" (para. 2). Cohen's call was unique because it was a challenge to fellow (White male) leaders in positions of power in the industry to participate in genuine action and be on the right side of the D&I conversation. More recently, senior leader Brad MacAfee (2017) wrote: "Organizations that are more diverse perform better on every metric. … diversity is a moral imperative. We must do all that we can to create diverse and inclusive environments because it is the right thing to do" (para. 9). While more leaders have become more vocal about the importance of D&I, a lot more leadership engagement with commitment for actual and measurable change is needed (Chitkara, 2018). The racial upheavals of 2020 have added to the urgency.

Overall, the crucial link between D&I success and leadership in the public relations industry requires careful scrutiny. Why is the needle not moving at a faster pace? Is D&I a genuine priority for leaders? What kinds of leaders does the industry need for real D&I successes? What must they believe, what must they do and how must they communicate about D&I to make real change happen? These are the central questions we address in this book because, "driving real results [in D&I] is nearly impossible" without senior leadership backing, funding and direct involvement, and that this is not an area in which organizations "can afford to fail" (Ternynck, 2021).

The story of public relations D&I scholarship

Scholarship on D&I in public relations spans about three decades, but it is sporadic in nature and low in volume compared to other more prominent research foci. Unlike the more muted tone of the industry discourse on D&I (until the recent racial unrest that is), the extant scholarship is less hesitant (especially more recent scholarship) to directly address the power-related historical inequities and other issues that continue to mark the composition, practices, and culture of the profession in the United States. Here we track some major studies and trends to map the story that extant research tells us.

The Excellence in Public Relations and Communication Management project, sponsored by the International Association of Business Communicators (IABC), started in the late 1980s and was first published in the early 1990s. At the time, it was the largest public relations research project ever undertaken (J. E. Grunig, 1992). Its primary goals were to delineate the characteristics of an excellent communication department, delve into how public relations can make an organization more effective (and, in turn, contribute to economic success) and build theory. This project, given its status and magnitude, had a significant influence on subsequent public relations scholarship. While D&I is, surprisingly, a slim focus in the study (there is more focus on societal culture and how that impacts practice in different countries), it made a point about diversity that gained traction and marked future D&I discourse and scholarship. For an organization to be effective and for communication to be excellent, the study argued, it must possess requisite variety. Borrowing this concept from organizational theorist Karl Weick, L. A. Grunig, J. E. Grunig and Ehling (1992) wrote:

> The principle of requisite variety, which Weick took from general systems theory, states that there must be at least as much variety – or diversity – inside the organization as outside the organization to build effective relationships with all critical or strategic parts of the environment. If, for example, an organization affects or could be affected by minority publics, it probably will not recognize those stakeholders as part of the environment if all the public relations practitioners are White.
>
> *(p. 85)*

Requisite variety is often interpreted literally as proportionate representation. Subsequent publications of the Excellence project clarified that requisite variety "does not mean there must be a representative of every group in the organization's public relations department. Rather it means that some diversity will force everyone in the department to interact and to think more diversely" (L. A. Grunig, J. E. Grunig, & Dozier, 2002, p. 489). In the 1990s, it became common to use the requisite variety logic, combined with the *Workforce 2000* report and the 1990 Census numbers (i.e., statistics predicting rapid changes in racial/ethnic demographics in the US workforce), to highlight the dismal state of D&I in the public relations profession and the glaring lack of awareness and support for D&I efforts in the industry. However, some research on D&I in public relations had already begun before the Excellence study popularized the logic of requisite variety.

Gender and race/ethnicity

As mentioned earlier, the public relations industry in the United States has emphasized gender as a priority since the 1970s. In 1989, a task force established by PRSA resulted in the Statement of Equality of Opportunity for Women. Academic research aligned with this priority and began examining gender in the 1980s, especially in the latter part of the decade, with a primary focus on pay disparity, discrimination and the lack of women in leadership roles (e.g., Cline et al., 1986; Toth, 1988, 1989). In the 1990s, PRSA continued to support efforts to challenge the glass ceiling and highlight various forms of gender discrimination (e.g., sexual harassment, pay inequity). Academic research moved beyond just the descriptive and focused more on applying feminist theory and conducting more theoretically oriented studies which accounted for gender (e.g., Aldoory, 1998; Creedon, 1993; Hon, 1995).

Toward the end of the 1990s and into the new millennium, gender research started focusing more on structure-related questions regarding systemic gender disparities in the industry, incorporating more feminist and critical theory, connecting power in more complex ways with gender and emphasizing theory-building along gender lines (e.g., Aldoory, 2005; Aldoory, Reber, Berger, & Toth, 2008; Aldoory & Toth, 2002; Choi & Hon, 2002; Daymon & Demetrious, 2016; Fitch, James, & Motion, 2016; L. A. Grunig, 2006; Place, 2012). However, some intersectional oversights remain. As Golombisky (2015) notes:

> Feminist scholarship in public relations … tends to focus on practitioners, relies mostly on liberal and radical feminisms, adopts sociological and sometimes psychological models of gender, and remains too White and too first world.

(p. 389)

According to Vardeman-Winter and Place (2017):

> The state of women's research in public relations is strong. However, different women's stories – as well as men's stories who are not part of the standard White, heterosexual, American experience – are severely underrepresented in public relations practice and research.
>
> *(p. 335)*

There remains a lack of complex conceptualizations of identities and the nature of gender itself. Gender is not a homogenous category, and its study needs to be diversified along race, ethnicity, transgender identities, sexual orientation, age, disability and other vectors of difference. As more diverse women have entered the industry and academia, especially since the 1990s, this reality has become more prominent. Some scholarship on these complexities has now begun to emerge (see later section on intersectionality).

Research on race/ethnicity and D&I picked up toward the end of the 1980s and showed that practitioners of color felt they were pigeonholed and hired to simply fill quotas. They experienced stereotyping, had little input in organizational policy and decision-making, and experienced slower advancement (i.e., the sticky floor syndrome) compared to their White colleagues. Research also noted that the role and contributions of people of color in the industry were not included in textbooks being used for education and that all of these reasons combined deterred people of color from being attracted to the profession (Kern-Foxworth, 1989a, 1989b; Zerbinos & Clanton, 1993). Studies also showed that pay discrepancy and tokenism continued to be challenges for practitioners of color and that they felt they were held to higher standards compared to their White counterparts to prove themselves. They also felt excluded from social activities where many business decisions are often made. In fact, such exclusion was the primary reason why more and more people of color started joining firms with predominantly minority employees (Bovet, 1994; L. A. Grunig, Toth, & Hon, 2001; Len-Ríos, 1998).

Around the latter part of the 1990s, research started showing that practitioners of color did not mind serving as liaisons and facilitators between clients and their racial/ethnic groups and did not see this as pigeonholing as long as they were not restricted to just that function (Len-Ríos, 1998; Tindall, 2009). Len-Ríos (1998) conducted a qualitative study of how African American, Asian American and Hispanic practitioners perceive and experience the D&I issue. Through an analysis of data from 13 in-depth interviews with practitioners in leadership positions in companies, she found that while these leaders felt there had been some improvement, minority practitioners still experienced some stereotyping and subtle to sometimes overt racial discrimination. This, along with a lack of mentorship opportunities for minority practitioners, impacted the latter's impression of public relations as a career choice. Two important findings, which Len-Ríos suggested should be topics for future research, were (1) men of color tended to experience more discrimination than women of color and (2) there seemed to be an indication that people of color were not included more in senior leadership positions because those already in senior leadership positions tended to not perceive them as part of their "comfort zone." These are troubling findings. First, they indicate a preference for homophily, which is antithetical to diversity. Second, they indicate some of the intercultural and historical power issues that have prevented the diversity needle from moving at a faster pace at the senior leadership level. What is even more troubling is that this reality has not changed much since 1998 when this study was published. According to Ellis and Gould (2018) in a recent article in *O'Dwyer's*, "In order to truly build a more diverse industry, PR firm owners and C-level executives must get out of their comfort zone, which tends to hover near Caucasians with degrees in PR, marketing or communications" (para. 8).

While the volume of research on race/ethnicity was not as much as that on gender in the 1980s and the 1990s, this aspect of D&I scholarship has become amplified since the late 1990s. As more people of color began joining the industry and academia (as public relations educators/researchers), their personal experiences, bolstered by reports such as *Workforce 2020*, led them to increasingly bring race and ethnicity to the table.

Scholarship at the turn of the century

Prompted by the scholarship in the 1990s, research in the new millennium began asking more pressing questions and urging the industry to realize the depth of the D&I problem. A qualitative study published at the turn of the century found that the diversity needle had moved slightly from the 1990s, but not much. Hon and Brunner (2000) conducted 33 in-depth interviews with public relations practitioners, mostly senior leaders, in a range of organizations and firms and found that while most of their interviewees acknowledged the benefits of D&I, only one third said some kind of D&I policy existed within their organization, and only four said D&I was an organic part of their organization's culture. Only a handful of interviewees said that D&I is irrelevant, a non-issue, a legal requirement only, and that they did not feel any pressure from clients regarding the matter. The authors did, however, note that in keeping with the business case lens on diversity, "[n]one of the interviewees addressed whether public relations has a responsibility to diversity beyond benefits for the organization" (p. 336). They concluded that D&I as social responsibility should be the ultimate organizational goal. These findings suggest that while there was a growing recognition of the D&I problem at the turn of the century, there was still no sense of urgency and moral recognition of the problem.

In 2005, a summit and subsequent report of the PR Coalition presented noteworthy insights that affirmed the findings of Hon and Brunner (2000).

The coalition, comprising 23 professional public relations organizations, reported results from a 2004 survey of coalition members which showed that 68% of organizations represented in the survey did not have a formal D&I process, nine in ten respondents felt that the industry needed to do a much better job with D&I, and only 15% reported that D&I is a top management priority. The report mentioned that unfortunately, while there is a lot of talk about doing the right thing, not much had actually changed. It emphasized that "[k]nowing where to look and knowing how to recruit and retain a diverse workforce are among the most critical steps in improving diversity" (PR Coalition, 2005, p. 3). The report recommended a three-pronged approach to the D&I effort − stepping up recruitment, mentoring diverse hires to enhance inclusion and the need for professionals in agency, corporate and educational settings to advocate for D&I in sustained and committed ways. It emphasized that significant engagement from senior leadership is needed for real change to occur, and it was decided that a D&I benchmark survey would be conducted every year. While survey results for 2006 are available, the effort lost momentum thereafter.

Since building and maintaining mutually beneficial relationships between organizations and publics is a primary goal of the profession, Brunner (2008) conducted interviews with agency, corporate and non-profit-based practitioners to examine whether diversity is considered necessary for building good relationships. She reported:

> The good news about diversity is that it is a part of everyday language, and it is an issue that is being addressed. The bad news is that discrimination complaints are not uncommon. The perplexing news is that some managers still ask why it is necessary to spend money, time, and energy on it.
>
> *(p. 156)*

Unfortunately, most research participants were unable to make the connection between relationship building and diversity, and it was perceived as being anywhere between a non-issue and a necessity. Brunner concluded that the focus needs to shift from just recruitment to retention (i.e., inclusion) and that this requires a true appreciation for what D&I can accomplish. She emphasized that leaders need to "step from understanding to engaging and responding" (p. 157).

An in-depth approach to D&I requires us to get closer to the complexities on the ground and look carefully at the relationships between identity, culture, power and difference. Public relations scholars are now asking sharper and less comfortable questions; they are questioning the culture of Whiteness that still pervades the industry, applying intersectional approaches and critical race theory to highlight historical and societal power inequities that are reflected in the industry, and highlighting structural and cultural changes that need to occur (Edwards, 2009, 2015; Logan, 2011; Munshi & Edwards, 2011; Pompper, 2005a; Pompper & Jung, 2013; Vardeman-Winter & Place, 2017; Waymer, 2012).

Complicating D&I, asking critical questions

The critical turn in public relations scholarship is more recent. This line of scholarship critiques the culture and practices of the profession from more systemic perspectives with a strong focus on power and inequities (see L'Etang, McKie, Snow, & Xifra, 2016). According to Edwards (2009), "Critical approaches to public relations examine the manner in which the profession sustains or generates social inequity and include theoretical critiques of scholarly work" (p. 251). The critical approach to diversity, therefore, is not organization-centric in nature; rather it is supra-organizational and metatheoretical in that it critiques the more instrumental approaches to diversity scholarship that do not take into account issues such as power relations, difference, inequities and hegemony that form the context for organizational life and industry practices.

In this social constructionist and critical vein, Aldoory (2005) in her work on gender and diversity writes that "public relations constructs meaning for publics" and that it is itself "constructed through power relations, gender, and difference (i.e., diversity and inclusiveness)" (p. 674). Regarding gender specifically, she writes that it should be studied in less essentialist ways and not conceptualized as just female (or the binary and biological opposite of male). She positions gender as a cultural and social construction and emphasizes the need for more feminist approaches to theorizing power in organizational contexts, noting that the feminist paradigm in public relations scholarship should contribute to theory-building and augment existing gender-neutral theorizing (e.g., how gender impacts organization-public relationships, leadership styles and so on). Other scholars working from a critical perspective have examined the gendered performance of power and leadership in public relations, how women practitioners construct gender, understanding gender as performative, and the importance of constantly pushing the feminist paradigm to be more inclusive of diverse feminisms (e.g., Daymon & Demetrious, 2016; Fitch et al., 2016; Golombisky, 2015; Place, 2012, 2015; Place & Vardeman-Winter, 2018).

Sha's (2006) research on the racionethnic dimensions of publics' avowed identities focused on incorporating multicultural identities in the situational theory for segmenting publics (J. E. Grunig, 1997). Like Aldoory's (2005) argument regarding gender, she emphasizes that cultural differences and identities should play a prominent role in how an organization communicates with internal and external stakeholders. Her work is an attempt to augment existing theory through incorporation of race/ethnicity and cultural identity scholarship. More recently, Edwards (2015) studied D&I with a focus on race in the public relations industry in the United Kingdom. Overlaps are detectable between the UK and US contexts. Melding critical theory on race, Whiteness and social theory with focus group, diary and interview data from marginalized practitioners Edwards examines the strategies and approaches these practitioners use to navigate the dominant culture and habitus of the profession. While her focus is on race, Edwards keeps an eye on other identity categories that intersect with race (e.g., class, gender). She demonstrates how power and privilege work as obstacles to diversity, inclusion and equity.

The more recent effort to incorporate the concept of intersectionality into public relations scholarship is a further move in this critical direction. The concept of intersectionality, which emerged from Black feminist and critical legal studies (Collins, 1990, 2000; Crenshaw, 1991), points out that identities and lived experiences, especially of members of marginalized groups, cannot be grasped through singular categories (such as just race or just gender). They exist at the intersections of categories and form a web of multiple interlocking oppressions for some (e.g., lesbians of color who are systemically disadvantaged by race/gender/sexual orientation) and privileges for others (heterosexual White males who are systemically advantaged by race/gender/sexual orientation) (Vardeman-Winter & Tindall, 2010). Such intersections are necessary to understand to get an accurate reading of identities and power relations as they apply to internal and external publics/stakeholders in various contexts. According to Vardeman-Winter, Tindall and Jiang (2013):

> Current public relations research and practice is limited because of the dominance of the traditional paradigm of publics' identity as comprised of discrete demographics. This limits our understanding of how multiple identities shape publics' communication behaviors. Publics are increasingly complex because they align with multiple demographic and sociographic groups, and they identify as other to traditional segments. Thus, public relations researchers and practitioners should forge more sophisticated categories based on intersectionality.
>
> *(p. 283)*

Some scholars have followed this path to look at how the intersections of gender and race/ethnicity shape the experiences of women of color in the profession (e.g., Pompper, 2004, 2007; Tindall, 2009).

Munshi and Edwards (2011) also critique the functional and singular category-based approaches to race-related diversity research which they emphasize as being organization-centric and not inclusive of issues of systemic power and inequities:

> This paradigmatic way of thinking about PR may be pleasantly logical, but imposes blinkers on practitioners and scholars in relation to race.

In this rather limited worldview, the context of PR relates to environmental factors that affect the ability to communicate messages effectively, or the realization of organizational goals. The wider sociocultural
processes in which organizations participate, remain invisible.

(p. 355)

They argue that race (and other dimensions of diversity) should not be reduced
to variables to be "managed" since this approach positions "diverse" internal and external stakeholders as "other" or different from the norm. Such
positioning, they argue, works against genuine efforts toward inclusion and
equity and "allows Whiteness to reassert its dominance by emphasizing difference, rather than similarity, as the underlying logic of diversity discourse
and practice in public relations. Thus the apparent inclusion of 'diversity' is
at best tokenistic and in fact reinforces exclusion" (p. 358) (see also Edwards,
2015; Mundy, 2016). Instead, they suggest that race, like gender, should not
be essentialized and should be conceptualized as a process and practiced and
studied "as an inherently socio-cultural, rather than merely organizational,
activity" (p. 351). Similarly, Vardeman-Winter and Place (2017) urge scholars
to develop more theoretical work on the topic and:

> ... explore the socially constructed, discursive, and cultural notion of
> diversity in public relations. Specifically, scholars need to ask the field
> and themselves about the extent to which eurocentrism and systemic
> racism have played a role in the state of diversity in the field.
>
> *(p. 334)*

In this vein, some scholars have demonstrated the value of critical race theory
and postcolonial theory in studying difference and diversity in public relations
(e.g., Bardhan & Patwardhan, 2004; Curtin & Gaither, 2012; Edwards, 2011;
Logan, 2011; Munshi & Kurian, 2005; Pompper, 2005a).

Logan (2011), for example, uses critical race theory to highlight historical
and societal power inequities that are reflected in the industry and highlights
structural and cultural changes that need to occur so that the "natural" public
relations leader is no longer assumed to be White, heterosexual and male (see
also Edwards, 2015). Pointing out that over 90% of public relations leaders
are White, she writes that "an informal racial hierarchy continues to persist
at leadership levels in public relations" (p. 442). She explains how Whiteness
is historically constituted and that it works systemically, discursively and ide-
ologically to maintain White privilege and power at the expense of racial
inequities (see Dyer, 1997; McIntosh, 1989; Nakayama & Krizek, 1995).
Consequently, invisible White norms of leadership and practice remain dominant in occupations as well, including public relations:

The White leader prototype communicates the notion that leaders in public relations are (or should be) White, which reproduces Whites as actual leaders in a self-sustaining system that makes White leadership appear normal, neutral, and natural, rather than the result of racialized practices.

(p. 443)

Logan supports her argument with a review of the racial leadership landscape of the top 25 public relations firms (as ranked by PR Week) in 2010 and the top 25 corporate communications officers of Fortune 500 companies that same year. She found agency leadership to be all White. For the companies, 19 of the 21 leaders were White (information was not available for four). She emphasizes that given this situation, it is the ethical responsibility of current leadership to diversify leadership. Aldoory (2005) has also made a similar argument tying White (male) dominance in leadership to demonstrate the flaws of the notion of requisite variety writing that "the criteria for success for practitioners of color are those created by White male norms in dominant-culture organizations. Numerical balance would not, therefore, completely remove the barriers that practitioners face when working within such organizations" (p. 674). She explains that while it is natural to follow the proportional representation logic when the actual numbers of members of underrepresented groups are so low, the system and ideologies in place continue to maintain White heterosexual male status quo. In other words, there is an expectation of assimilation, and the dominant culture in place remains undisturbed.

While gender and race/ethnicity (along with a growing argument for intersectionality) have dominated public relations D&I scholarship, attention has been paid more recently to LGBTQ+ identities. Tindall and Waters (2012) were among the first to publish on this identity group. They conducted 45 in-depth interviews with gay men practitioners to gauge their experiences:

Practitioners indicated that they enjoyed working in public relations, although they pointed out areas of dissatisfaction and suggested ways to improve the working environment for gay men. These include an increased awareness of personal lives and the gay community, reduction of stereotypes, and adopting diversity-friendly policies.

(p. 451)

Additionally, practitioners also referred to the lavender ceiling which makes it difficult to rise to leadership positions. The authors emphasize that it is not enough to focus on LGBTQ+ identities as just "markets" (i.e., the business case) but also understand them as people and their needs as internal stakeholders and as traditionally and culturally underrepresented members of the practitioner population (see also Ciszek, 2020). These authors subsequently published a collection of essays that focuses on how LGBTQ+ identities are represented within communication output and treated as internal and external stakeholders/publics within strategic communication (Tindall & Waters, 2013). More recently, Ciszek (2018) has suggested the need for queering dominant and heterosexist theory and theorizing in public relations and "to rethink the very identity, knowledge sources, and politics that define public relations" (p. 134).

Those who have emphasized intersectionality have also pointed out the limitations of the proportional representation interpretation of requisite variety logic (e.g., Pompper, 2014; Vardeman-Winter et al., 2013). Others have argued that the business case gets privileged by this logic. According to Edwards (2015), "In normative PR research on diversity, the idea of 'counting' diversity is reflected in the notion of requisite variety, where the level of diversity in the profession is determined by the variety of audiences to be addressed. . . " (p. 5). This, she critiques, makes diversity purely a business matter and commodifies diverse people (see also Aldoory, 2005; L. A. Grunig & Toth, 2006; Hon & Brunner, 2000; McKie & Munshi, 2007; Mundy, 2016). Another point is that the requisite variety approach does not keep in mind that diversity is highly contextual, impacted by geographic and cultural location, and not a static phenomenon by any means. Arguing against too much emphasis on requisite variety and a business case approach, Uysal (2013) writes that "diversity should be conceptualized as a core company value established through dialogue" (p. 8). Diverse practitioners should feel their differences are valued for reasons beyond purely commercial concerns. In other words, while requisite variety can work as an argument when there is a glaring lack of representation, it does have some clear drawbacks.

Overall, the critical turn in public relations D&I scholarship has elevated the importance of power, context and systemic issues that are historically constituted and which continue to maintain clear inequities in the profession, culturally as well as structurally. Focusing just on organizational interests without paying attention to D&I, critical scholars argue, will not bring about real change. It is necessary for those currently in positions of power, privilege and leadership to engage in strong introspection and demonstrate the genuine will to work (i.e., act on cultural and structural changes needed) toward inclusion and equity in a larger societal and social justice sense.

Most recent research describing the D&I landscape

Research on D&I in public relations has seen a slight growth in the last decade and has spanned a variety of topics within the D&I realm. As previously mentioned, research interest in the millennials as a specific category is high (along with the now emerging Gen Z entering the workforce). In her study of millennial agency-based public relations practitioners' views on

D&I, Gallicano (2013) reported "a continued trend in which public relations practitioners with dominant identity markers are less likely to identify challenges faced by diverse practitioners" (p. 60). While there is evidence that millennials value diversity more than any previous generations (see Brown, 2016; Dishman, 2015; Kochhar, 2016), this study provides evidence that those occupying more privileged social identities have a rosier perception about the state of D&I, at least in the agency setting. Also, another study found that among the millennials in public relations, women are more inclined toward issues of ethics, culture, diversity and social responsibility than men (Meng & Berger, 2017). Therefore, although we suggested earlier that there is reason to be hopeful about this general pro-D&I attitude, there is also a need to be cautious and remain on the lookout for intersectional oversights. Continuous study of the millennials and the emerging Gen Z in the public relations workplace will generate useful knowledge about how they can be involved in improving the D&I situation.

Another relatively recent study conducted by Appelbaum and Walton (2015) reported that "[w]hile some companies and public relations agencies reflect the racial, ethnic, and gender diversity of the overall population, both anecdotal experience and published research suggest an overall picture that is solidly Caucasian and female" (p. 5). This study focused on young African American and Hispanic professionals and those who recruit them (mainly White professionals). A discrepancy emerged between the perceptions of the former and the latter. Results showed that while minority practitioners were not unhappy in their positions, they reported challenges (e.g., microaggressions, low inclusion, need for better mentorship) and were less inclined to see recruitment and retention efforts as successful compared to White recruiters. A similar discrepancy between the perceptions of dominant and non-dominant identity practitioners emerged in another recent study of Arthur W. Page Society members (Jiang, R. Ford, Long, & Ballard, 2016). This study was a quantitative survey which featured responses from 82 respondents representing 80 organizations, with additional qualitative interviews with respondents who have been actively implementing D&I programs. When perception results were compared with Appelbaum and Walton's African American and Hispanic respondents, it was found that Page Society respondents (68% White) had a much rosier picture about inclusion and equal treatment of racial/ethnic minorities. Overall, results showed that 53% of the respondents were dissatisfied with the D&I efforts of their organizations. Most said they had some sort of diversity mandate and programs, but no clear sense of goals, outcomes and measurement. Slow movement, lack of accountability regarding outcomes and minimalist budget commitments for D&I efforts were reported. It was emphasized that more involvement and commitment from senior leadership is needed for real change to occur faster. While the broad nature of diversity was widely acknowledged, it was noted that in recruitment and discourse it usually comes down to the categories of race/ethnicity and gender.

Mundy (2016) conducted an extensive review of D&I literature and developed what he calls an "actionable model" for operationalization of how public relations D&I communication should be conducted, internally and externally. He emphasizes that best practices include message development and executive coaching, extensive involvement of leadership, connecting with all functions throughout the organization that are relevant to D&I, a "valuing" rather than "managing" approach to D&I and maintaining inclusive dialogue in daily organizational life. Like Hon and Brunner (2000), Mundy (2016) also makes the case for a multicultural and social responsibility approach to D&I: "Scholars have revealed the shortcomings of the business case paradigm, however and – similar to public relations research – have called for diversity to become a more substantial driver of an organization's culture and for organizations to take up the mantle of social justice" (p. 15). More recently, Laskin and Kresic (2021), Logan (2021) and Pompper (2015) have urged that in order to boost the moral case, D&I should be tied to corporate social responsibility (CSR) since the work of CSR is to improve and contribute to the societies and environments within which corporations exist and benefit from. Munshi and Edwards (2011) have argued similarly: "[T]he narrow business case approach obscures the potential role that PR could play in organizations as part of a mechanism to ensure moral and ethical organizational behavior" (p. 355) (see also Edwards, 2015). Mundy (2016), however, does not fully reject the business case and calls for a balance with the social responsibility approach writing that "the business case for D&I risks reducing diversity to a commodity, where diverse groups can be exploited" and that this leads us more toward a "managing" rather than "valuing" diversity mindset and reduces "diverse" people to mere categories (p. 16); he goes on to add though that "the business case for diversity should not be abandoned, necessarily. … there must be a balance between the head and the heart, between an organization's commitment to the bottom line and an organization's commitment to its employees' lived experiences" (p. 17).

In a study of qualitative interviews with 17 PRSA member practitioners working in-house in various organizational settings, Mundy (2015) found overall support for D&I:

> Participants explained that the value of diversity to an organization is no longer a debate – diverse organizations allow for diverse thinking, which leads to more creative and responsive decision-making and ultimately a better workplace with a competitive edge. Today's challenge, they argued, is how to shift organizational mindsets to position D&I as foundational to organizational culture, and then how to better integrate D&I values into both internal and external communication practices.
>
> *(p. 15)*

Participants said that to accomplish organizational change in favor of D&I, it is important to "pay attention" to D&I and what it means for any given company/organization, get buy-in from internal stakeholders and diversify the definition of D&I beyond traditional identity categories for the purpose of inclusion: "Employees have been told for years that diversity is important, but no one has explained in concrete terms the tangible business and cultural benefits that a diverse work force provides" (p. 27). They also put leadership in the spotlight stressing that the leadership team needs to be diverse and make D&I a part of the structure and programming. One interviewee said: "It's always leadership. There's just no replacing the fact that the leadership has to talk about diversity, has to email about diversity; they have to host events and really be driving that" (p. 17).

In a very recent online survey by the Institute for Public Relations and The Wakeman Agency investigates the role of language in D&I and how public relations and communication leaders are defining terms such as diversity, equity, inclusion and related terms such as social justice, privilege and so on (Institute for Public Relations, 2021a). The study emphasizes the powerful role language and meaning play in defining organizational D&I realities. Reiterating what we have described previously the study found that the breadth of diversity perception is limited with a primary focus on race, followed by sex/gender and ethnicity; that while diversity, equity and inclusion are the most used terms in organizational discourse, there is confusion about their meanings (e.g., there is a tendency to not understand the difference between "equality" and "equity" and to conflate "diversity" and "inclusion"); that there exists a gap between what organizational discourse states about D&I commitment and what it actually does; and that D&I is located primarily in human resources departments or is a stand-alone unit (although about 80% of the respondents reported that the communication function works closely or somewhat closely with the D&I function). This brings us to the role of D&I in internal communication.

Public relations scholars have already pointed out that D&I is an important aspect of employee relations or internal public relations and that this is an area of research that needs particular attention and theoretical development (Kennan & Hazleton, 2006; Men & Jiang, 2016; Ni, 2007; Pompper, 2012, 2020; Ruck & Welch, 2012; Walden, Jung, & Westerman, 2017; C. White, Vanc, & Stafford, 2010). Internal communication is of major strategic importance, and it is not possible to communicate effectively with diverse external publics if the skill does not exist at the internal level:

> The competitive advantage of strategic internal communication comes not only from the obvious benefits of employee satisfaction and productivity, but also from the positive contributions that well-informed employees can make to a company's external public relations efforts.

> Employees can be an organization's best ambassadors or loudest critics … Put simply, employees are the face of an organization and have a powerful influence on organizational success … Effective internal communication can enhance corporate reputation and credibility, because employees are viewed as particularly credible sources by external stakeholders …
>
> *(C. White, Vanc, & Stafford, 2010, p. 66)*

Building on Kennan and Hazleton's (2006) research on social capital, which they describe as an organization's ability "of creating, maintaining, and using relationships to achieve desirable organizational goals" (p. 322), Pompper (2012) offers a theoretical framework for understanding successful internal public relations by combining the social capital component with diversity. She states: "Like social capital, diversity is a defining feature of IPR [internal public relation] – perhaps because of widely-held opinions that managing diversity is a communication management responsibility…. diversity under the IPR umbrella requires greater attention to reveal its dimensions" (pp. 100–101). In a more recent article, Pompper (2020) further builds on the diversity prong of her internal public relations model by positioning the practitioner as a diversity advocate responsible for "holding organizations accountable and inspiring them to authentically embrace social justice beyond mere mention of the word diversity in mission/vision statements" (p. 2).

While the scholarship on diversity in public relations scholarship has rightly focused on identities, power differentials and the inequalities in place that are obstacles in the path of equity, what seems to still be missing is an understanding of D&I as a *process*. Also, *more study of how to practice inclusion and equity is needed*. A central ingredient for diversity to work in any setting is inclusion. While people/identities, context, power and difference/inequities are all key components of "diversity," no one component is equal to all of D&I, which is a human performance, a process and an effect of complex interactions across identities and power differentials in organizational and societal settings (see Chapter 3 for more on this).

The inclusion question

The "D" in "D&I" has received much more attention than the "I." In fact, as we argue in this book, the cart of diversity has been put before the horse of inclusion in scholarship and practice. The same is true for the notion of equity, which we treat as a part of the inclusion imperative (see Chapter 3 for more on the notion of equity). It has become common to lump "diversity" and "inclusion" together as though they are one and the same (Mundy, 2019; Roberson, 2006). This masks a critical point – that there is little understanding about inclusion and how to successfully *do* (i.e., practice) inclusion for the diversity process to work and produce desired outcomes. Research on inclusion in public relations is slimmer, almost non-existent, compared to the research on diversity despite the inseparable relationship between the two. Inclusion entails giving voice and opportunity to those who have been historically oppressed and excluded from societal processes (Sison, 2017). It is about creating and sustaining an organizational culture that genuinely respects difference, welcomes needed change and does not perceive diversity to be simply an "add-on" to already existing culture (Appelbaum & Walton, 2015). An interesting finding emerged from a recent study on practitioner perceptions on D&I. Blow, Bonney, Tallapragada and Brown (2021) found that while most study participants were similar in their understanding of the meaning of inclusion, they differed on their understanding of diversity. The participants mostly described inclusion in terms of empowerment, belonging and diverse voices being heard, but they were not on the same page regarding the identity dimensions that they believe constitute diversity. For example, while race was emphasized the most overall followed by gender, the data showed that race was emphasized more by Black and female participants while age and disability were emphasized more by older participants. Based on these findings, Blow et al. (2021) recommend using an intersectional lens for understanding the complexities of D&I.

Sison (2017) emphasizes that while much research on inclusion may not have been conducted in public relations, there is more research on inclusion in general which needs to be consulted (see Chapter 3). She writes that as practitioners, educators and researchers, "We have to move outside our comfort zone, experiment, and have the courage to accept mistakes" (p. 132). Berger (2007) emphasizes the importance of an organizational climate and communication culture which include the "the support of top management in words and deeds; and equal opportunities for women, men, and practitioners of diverse ethnic, cultural and racial backgrounds …" (p. 225). Without such a culture, genuine inclusivity is a difficult goal. According to practitioner and senior leader Y'Anad Burrell (2015):

> The strength of diversity is set in motion when we respect and value differences. … In order to unleash the potential of workforce diversity, a culture of inclusion needs to be established. This should be a culture that fosters enhanced workforce integration and brings latent diversity potentials to life; a culture that is built on clarified normative grounds and honors the differences as well as the similarities of the individual, self and others. Diversity is about balancing this natural tension in different organizational and cultural settings.
>
> *(paras. 1, 3)*

According to Vardeman-Winter and Place (2017), too much focus on workforce composition, which is the representation aspect of the diversity process, has pushed inclusion into the shadows of diversity discourse. While representation is obviously the first step and very important, it cannot be the only step. According to Mundy (2016), "Organizations also must understand that talking about the importance of diversity and training employees about diversity is a different challenge than creating an inclusive environment in which minorities and women know they are treated well and their perspectives respected" (p. 14). Chitkara's (2018) recent study of agency leaders highlights the inclusion challenge in the industry. The leaders in her study tended to confuse the distinction between diversity and inclusion and noted that the industry has a long way to go on the inclusion front (Sudhaman, 2017). This is a serious challenge and obstacle in the path of D&I progress.

In more than three decades of research, the topic of inclusion has received scant attention in both industry and research discourse, and the business case for D&I dominates industry discourse over the social responsibility imperative. While critical scholarship has started emphasizing notions of power, privilege and systemic inequities, and while there is an increased sense of the importance and urgency of D&I and the need to change organizational/industry culture, especially after the racial upheavals of 2020, D&I in public relations remains a work in progress. Genuine leadership engagement, support and overall vision are necessary for significant and meaningful change.

Leaders need to lead on D&I

We now turn to the matter that resides at the heart of this book – the link between leadership and D&I. Looking back at the story of D&I in the public relations industry and in scholarship reviewed in this chapter, it seems like there has been a major oversight in not spotlighting this link earlier. About 25 years ago in an attitudinal survey of public relations executives, Diggs-Brown and Zaharna (1995) found that while there was some recognition of the D&I problem, executives had very little understanding of the issues pertaining to D&I. Less than half reported having some recruitment initiatives in place, and retention efforts were almost non-existent. According to the authors, "Currently, there appears to be a wide gap between the growing diversity within the American population and workplace and the relative monocultural environment of the public relations field" (p. 115). What is troubling is that while now there is a better recognition among leaders of the D&I dilemma, the situation has not improved much since 1995 (see Chitkara, 2018). Currently, the culture of the US public relations industry is not welcoming or comfortable for most diverse practitioners (Ramaswamy, 2018). According to Cripps (2015):

> The challenge before us is to identify and remove the barriers so we can induce more diverse candidates to work in our dynamic business. A key question is why do many people of color choose to leave an agency after

only a short stint, whether to take a corporate position, open their own firm, or leave the business altogether?

(para. 4)

The answer to that question is quite obvious. As already described, about 88% of the industry is White, about 30% are men and about 70% of leadership is male (White and presumably mainly heterosexual) (Aldoory & Toth, 2004; Balta, 2015; Logan, 2011; Vardeman-Winter & Place, 2017). This is the composition of industry culture and power in a nutshell. Clearly, some deep cultural, structural and perceptual changes are needed. If leadership itself is not diverse, as is the case in public relations, then the struggle is definitely uphill despite good intentions and talk.

Public relations leaders, like other leaders in general, are in strategic positions of power to make a positive difference in the D&I realm. General research on the link between leadership engagement and D&I success has been available for about two decades (see Chapter 4), but emphasis on this relationship in the public relations industry discourse and even in scholarship is more recent and sporadic. At the turn of the century, Hon and Brunner (2000) noted that "genuine commitment from top management seems to be the best predictor of an integrated diversity strategy for organizations" (p. 334). In 2005, the PR Coalition summit report made a similar observation. More recently Mundy (2016) urged, "Organizations truly must address the expectations and interest of underrepresented groups, and leadership must be held accountable" (p. 14). And according to Jiang et al. (2016) in their survey of Arthur W. Page Society members, "Survey members emphasized consistently that leadership support and commitment is critical to implementing strategies and achieving D&I goals" (p. 19). One issue that can be gauged from past research is that there seems to be a discrepancy between how leaders and those they lead (the latter tend to be slightly more diverse) perceive and orient to the state of D&I in their organizations and in the profession. The former seem to have a more positive impression of the situation than the latter; they also seem to think they are performing better on D&I than those they lead (Bardhan, Engstrom, & Gower, 2018; Diggs-Brown & Zaharna, 1995; Hon & Brunner, 2000; Jiang et al., 2016; Mundy, 2016; "Report Card on PR Leaders," n.d.). This perception gap (which we explore further in Chapter 5), if it does exist as the research suggests, constitutes a clear obstacle in the path of overall D&I progress.

D&I in the agency setting has been particularly challenging (Ramaswamy, 2018). Chitkara's (2018) interviews with agency leaders revealed the following obstacles:

Achieving D&I goals is complicated by several factors, including the revenue and cost pressures that agencies face, client expectations, the legacy culture of public relations firms, the organizational structure of many of them, and the available labor pool.

> The barriers to entry appear varied, with layers of complexity pertaining to culture, socio-economic backgrounds, acceptance of a diverse work-force by the clients and not having the right environment to foster growth.
>
> *(p. 16)*

Other obstacles mentioned include not having a clear definition for D&I at the industry level, lack of effective metrics for measurement of D&I (including the politics of measurement and reporting, and structural constraints), little aware-ness about and/or low financial attraction for the profession among underrep-resented groups, the history of lack of diversity in industry culture, lack of industry-wide sustained effort and the amount of time and energy needed to mentor/train diverse hires. Not investing time in training/mentoring results in low retention rates and the lack of a pipeline of diverse practitioners ready to move into mid- and senior-level positions (Chitkara, 2018).

In a perceptions study of Hispanic and Black practitioners in agency set-tings sponsored by the PR Council, respondents said that while some progress has been made in the D&I realm, advancement to decision-making roles is still difficult for practitioners of color, and they often leave when they get more attractive offers elsewhere. Based on these findings, the PR Council advises:

> CEOs and leadership teams must set the vision and tone, using their influence, visibility and power to advocate for changes and put policies and practices in place. While HR professionals can provide implemen-tation support, and chief diversity officers can manage the work, efforts to increase the presence of high-performing black and Latino profes-sionals in the C-Suite depend on the active involvement of the CEO. Tie the advancement, promotion, and/or bonuses of senior leadership to the success of their team members, including specific targets around the success of underrepresented PR professionals who are part of a senior leader's team.
>
> *(PR Council, 2016, para. 7)*

According to Mundy (2016):

> There must be accountability (including incentives and rewards pro-grams) in order to ensure an effective D&I program. Leaders also must be visibly involved; studies repeatedly have argued that leaders must walk the talk. Finally, across these initiatives organizations must meas-ure. Beyond tracking recruitment and retention rates, organizations must have a sense of employee experiences, if they indeed are being

given access to leadership opportunities, and if leadership has followed through on their D&I-specific promises.

(p. 16)

The conversation clearly seems to be turning more in the direction of the need for better leadership, vision and accountability for real change.

Thus, as we have reviewed in this chapter, there is plenty of evidence that leaders in the public relations industry are not as directly engaged with D&I as they need to be. There is much work still to be done, including better reporting of industry D&I metrics for measurement. What is needed is leadership that truly understands what D&I means, is not afraid to have brave and uncomfortable conversations about persisting inequities, does not shy away from the structural and cultural changes needed, and values what D&I done well can accomplish in the world of public relations and in society. In interviews with leaders of global companies known for embracing and advancing D&I, Groysberg and Connolly (2013) report that these leaders make D&I their personal mission and attribute their success to being able to strike a balance between the moral and business case for D&I. In several cases, leaders mentioned how being excluded as outsiders in some form in the past has made them extra diligent regarding the importance and value of inclusion. This seems to suggest that inclusive leaders experientially know what it means to be different from the norm (whatever the norm may be) and be excluded. Perhaps, and in order to genuinely value D&I, the public relations industry needs more leaders who are capable of personally understanding and empathizing with what it means to be different and to be excluded.

Key takeaways

Several key takeaways regarding D&I and leadership in the US public relations industry and scholarship emerge from this chapter:

- First and foremost, and related to the main focus of this book, the role of public relations leadership in accomplishing D&I success must be heavily emphasized and further researched. Hardly any scholarship exists on the link between D&I success and leadership in public relations specifically. More systematic research on this link is needed.
- The focus on inclusion has been generally weak, in practice and in scholarship. The attention that has been paid to inclusion is very recent and has mostly followed the surge in D&I discourse in the wake of the 2020 racial and social justice upheavals. Industry discourse needs to clearly establish the relationship between diversity and inclusion and not lump them together. Recruiting diverse individuals does not automatically lead to inclusion. Research needs to better demonstrate how inclusion is *done*,

how to build inclusive organizational climates and how to accomplish organizational culture/structure change for this purpose.

- While there has been some progress on the D&I front in industry, this progress has been minimal. There is now more diversity in mid-level leadership, but senior-level leadership remains in the White male prototype zone (Logan, 2011). This is where the highest decision-making power resides and where change is almost non-existent. Leaders must be held responsible and accountable for D&I. The "comfort zone" issue at this level that Len-Ríos's (1998) research found is still a clear barrier in the way of change and parity. Senior leadership needs to diversify, senior leaders need to move out of their comfort zones and address homophily bias, and overall leaders need to lead for real change to happen.

- Diversity categories need to be described in more complex ways. Peoples' entire identities do not reside in one category (e.g., only race, or only gender, or only sexual orientation and so on). The intersectional lens should be adopted. Further, while it is useful to broaden diversity definitions to be inclusive, this should not be done at the expense of downplaying the categories of ongoing historical inequities.

- The business case for diversity is more prominent in industry discourse and scholarship emphasizes the moral and social responsibility approach. We agree that diversity should not just be thought of as something that needs to be "managed" since this approach can result in commodifying people rather than valuing them for their differences. Like Mundy (2016), we believe it is necessary to maintain a balance between the moral and the business case and that an "and/both" (rather than "either/or") approach would be a fruitful path ahead on this matter (see Chapter 3 for more discussion on this).

- Research suggests that practitioners in more privileged identity positions, along with leaders (who tend to mostly belong to this group), have a rosier picture of the state of D&I than those with marginalized identities and in non-leadership roles. This discrepancy needs to be addressed since it poses a major barrier in the path of D&I advancement. A realistic and multi-perspective understanding and genuine appreciation of D&I and what it can accomplish is necessary, especially among leaders so they can lead effectively on D&I.

- The power of Whiteness remains strong in the US public relations industry. It would behoove the industry to understand that unless some significant structural, cultural and perceptual changes occur to de-center Whiteness, practitioners will not be able to cope with client needs and communicate effectively and build relationships with increasingly diverse publics/stakeholders. The result will be that the profession which claims to build reputations for others will itself have a serious reputation and credibility problem.

Conclusion

According to public relations scholar and educator Natalie Tindall (2016), who has written the foreword for this book, "diversity is not an option. It is a mandate …" (para. 11). However, as this chapter has highlighted, the US public relations industry has a long way to go before it can start claiming it is a champion of D&I. Unless leadership diversifies and steps up to advance the process, promises will ring hollow, and the industry will struggle to remain relevant in a growing sea of diversity.

In closing this chapter, we would like to emphasize that the work of D&I is never smooth, but it is necessary and must be embraced for societal good. Further, D&I is also a matter of ethics. The public relations industry, to be an ethical member of society, must make D&I part of its DNA. Leaders need to work harder, welcome uncomfortable discussions and be open to change and power-sharing. They need to come together to develop D&I vision and convert vision into reality. That said, and along with the will to bring about change, leaders must also have the knowledge needed to guide the work of meaningful change. A central responsibility of scholarship is to provide theory that can guide practice (i.e., enable praxis or theory-informed practice). Therefore, in the next chapter, we look closely at the extant literature on the two concepts of "diversity" and "inclusion" and connect that body of knowledge to the public relations profession.

3

Diversity and Inclusion in the Context of the United States

In this chapter, we provide an overview and synthesis of the literature that exists on diversity, inclusion and equity across disciplines such as organization studies, management, communication and social psychology. We then assess diversity and inclusion (D&I) in the US public relations industry and scholarship in relation to this extant literature. We conclude with key takeaways.

A brief history

Diversity is a feature of all societies around the world, but each national context (and one can argue regional context) has its specific history which drives how people, groups and organizations produce meanings, develop policies, legislate and take actions with regard to diversity. Therefore, as mentioned in the last chapter, the D&I dilemma in the US public relations industry must be understood within the context of the larger diversity history of the United States.

The US diversity narrative has its roots in attempts to rectify the wrongs that have been committed against marginalized and oppressed groups mainly on the basis of race/ethnicity and also gender/sexual orientation. As a result, these identity categories tend to lead the diversity narrative in most contexts (as described in the previous chapter, this has been the case in public relations discourse as well). The subjugation and segregation of minority groups is older than the formal formation of the country itself, but the legal, business and moral discourse on diversity in the context of the workplace and education began to take shape mostly in the 1960s during the Civil Rights era. President Kennedy's 1961 Executive Order 10925, President Johnson's 1965 Executive Order 11246 and Title VII of the 1964 Civil Rights Act made it illegal to

DOI: 10.4324/9781003170020-3

discriminate against disadvantaged groups in employment, federal and otherwise. These legislations were propelled by the goals of equity and social justice (Kelly & Dobbin, 1998).

The rise of affirmative action (AA) and equal employment opportunity (EEO) was marked by many struggles. While policies and compliance mechanisms were developed and instituted, not all were happy with how this was done. According to Gilbert, Stead and Ivancevich (1999):

> Even though the intent of affirmative action is to ensure equal employment opportunity for all, negative perceptions, combined with poor implementation at the organization level, have resulted in a social policy which is considered ineffective and unjust by some.
>
> *(p. 62)*

Complaints came from members of dominant as well as marginalized groups (Linnehan & Konrad, 1999). Lack of clarity on compliance and enforcement policies made many employers increasingly nervous of discrimination charges and litigation. The language of quotas, and what some felt was lack of transparency in hiring procedures, led many from dominant groups to cry reverse discrimination. Others complained that compliance pressures were resulting in the hiring of unqualified individuals. Women and members of marginalized groups, in turn, were not happy with the pressures they felt to assimilate into mainstream organizational culture and, in many cases, with being pigeonholed and perceived as "diversity hires." There were heated arguments on both sides, and this climate did not do much to foster trust and inclusion in the workplace (Mazzei & Ravazzani, 2012).

While some progress was made in increasing the numbers of women and members of underrepresented groups in the workplace due to AA/EEO policies, lack of support from the Reagan administration in the 1980s and the Bush and Clinton administrations that followed did not bode well for AA/EEO efforts (Kelly & Dobbin, 1998). In the late 1980s, the publication of *Workforce 2000* (Johnston & Packer, 1987), a report commissioned by the Reagan administration Department of Labor and produced by the Hudson Institute, resulted in a significant shift in the diversity narrative. The report predicted that by the end of the twentieth century, women and minorities would enter the workforce in much larger than expected numbers and that new US-born White male entrants would drop to about 15%. Seizing this rhetorical moment and the stir that it caused, and without completely abandoning the AA/EEO roots of the diversity movement, experts began to promote the language of "diversity management" (DM). This move shifted the tone somewhat away from social justice and equity and more toward a business case for diversity (Kelly & Dobbin, 1998; Lorbiecki & Jack, 2000; Qin, Muenjohn, & Chhetri, 2014). As one senior vice president of human resources put it in 1991, "despite all our work with Affirmative Action and EEOC, we haven't yet gotten to the guts of dealing with diversity and the massive changes in corporate culture that requires. AA deals with equity. Diversity is a business issue" (Plank, 1991).

According to Bassett-Jones (2005), "The term 'diversity management' refers to the systematic and planned commitment on the part of organizations to recruit and retain employees with diverse backgrounds and abilities" (p. 170). The primary focus is on how diversity can contribute to the corporate bottom line, and according to scholars such as P. Prasad (1997) and Linnehan and Konrad (1999), this pivot in the narrative fitted well with the US culture of individualism and worked to appease the threatened dominant White male demographic. The addition of several categories of diversity, beyond the traditional equity-based categories of race/ethnicity and gender (and later sexual orientation), was on the one hand lauded as more inclusive and on the other hand it was alarming to many who saw this as a watering-down of diversity and a shift away from groups historically disadvantaged (we address this important debate in more depth a little later in this chapter). Unfortunately, like AA/EEO but for somewhat different reasons, DM discourse and practices have not helped the needle on the diversity meter move much in the last three decades, and according to Lorbiecki and Jack (2000), dissatisfactions "manifested themselves under a number of guises – male backlash, White rage, political correctness – as well as a general sense of frustration and disappointment from those who felt that diversity initiatives had failed to deliver its promise of greater equality within the workforce as a whole" (p. S22). The diversity narrative began seeking a new direction, and there has been increasing emphasis in the last decade or so on the need for inclusion/equity for diversity to work (Chrobot-Mason & Aramovich, 2013; Oswick & Noon, 2014). The racial upheavals of 2020 further propelled the narrative in this direction.

Diversity theories and models

Within the ups and downs of diversity discourse, both academics and practitioners have contributed useful theories and models to explain how differences play out in organizations and society, how intercultural dynamics manifest across groups, and how diversity may be conceptualized for better outcomes.

Theories

Diversity is about differences, cultural as well as power-related differences (e.g., gender, race/ethnicity, sexual orientation, dis/ability, age, religion, nationality), that make up group identities and lead to inequity-based hierarchies and intergroup power dynamics within and across societies. The level of the group has been the primary focus in diversity scholarship. Early academic work theorized how group-based "Us vs. Them" dynamics formed within societies as well as the workplace. In the context of the workplace, the primary focus has been on how diversity impacts team/group performance within organizations, especially since work is increasingly accomplished in teams these days (Page, 2007).

The earlier theories explaining diversity are social psychological in nature and position difference as a divisive phenomenon. They are the similarity-attraction theory (Newcomb, 1961), self-categorization theory (Turner, 1985) and social identity theory (SIT) (Tajfel, 1981; Tajfel & Turner, 1979). Similarity-attraction theory, which explains the dyadic level of interaction, posits that people are interpersonally attracted to those who are similar to them in values, beliefs and attitude. The theory also posits people tend to avoid communication with those who are different to avoid conflict and disagreements and perceive those who are similar as more intelligent and functional (Byrne, 1971; Rosenbaum, 1986; Triandis, 1959). Self-categorization theory explains how people, in the process of self-identification, cognitively categorize themselves as part of a group, or groups, they see themselves as belonging to. In turn, the view of the self is impacted by the groups one categorizes oneself into. SIT follows from self-categorization and explains how people cognitively and emotionally engage in social comparisons between in-groups (the ones to which they see themselves as belonging) and out-groups (Tajfel, 1978). Members of out-groups tend to not be seen as unique individuals and are reduced to group characteristics, and in-groups are perceived more favorably for self-esteem purposes. SIT has been popular for studying workplace biases (Lambert & Bell, 2013; Mannix & Neale, 2005; Roberts & Creary, 2013)

According to Milliken and Martins (1996):

> One of the most striking and most important findings of research on diversity is that groups that are diverse have lower levels of member satisfaction and higher rates of turnover than more homogeneous groups. This is true across a wide range of types of diversity, including age, gender, racial/ethnic background, and tenure.
>
> *(p. 420)*

The authors also describe research that shows that those who are dissimilar from their supervisors tend to receive lower evaluations. This eventually leads to the tendency within organizations to drive out difference and produce what Kanter (1977) calls "homosocial reproduction," i.e., the creation and maintenance of a homogenous top management whose realities are far removed from the more diverse workforce. Homophily sets in, especially, at the top management level. Homophily is the tendency for those sharing culturally and demographically similar characteristics to form strong communication and information sharing networks (Reagans, 2013). According to Gilbert et al. (1999), one of the outcomes of homophily is that those who are more like the dominant group are more readily accepted. One CEO explained how that happens: "People say, just hire people and the cream will rise to the top. But unless White managers are trained to work with and promote women and minorities, the cream is usually White [and] male" (Plank, 1991).

The above theories conceptualize difference in mostly clear-cut singular categories. More current theoretical work on diversity is delving complexly into identity as a multicategory concept. Identity is being increasingly theorized not as the additive result of singular categories, but rather as intersectional (see Kelly & Smith, 2014). As explained in the previous chapter, the intersectionality approach posits that the effects of identity reside at the intersections of more than one predetermined category and that in increasingly multicultural societies and an interconnected world people affiliate with or avow (and in many cases are involuntarily ascribed to) more than one identity category. Some categories, of course, could be more salient than others (e.g., race/ethnicity, gender), and salience could also shift according to context (Collier, 1989; Imahori & Cupach, 2005). Tatli and Özbilgin (2012) support an intersectional approach to diversity research and sum up the drawbacks of previous theories:

> [T]here is an overwhelming focus on a single diversity category as a stand-alone phenomenon, overlooking the role of intersectionality between multiple forms of difference in the construction of diversity categories. ... the selection of diversity categories, in single- and multi-category diversity research, lacks a sense of contextuality, i.e., temporal and geographic specificity. ... the use of pre-determined categories, irrespective of historical, institutional and socioeconomic context, leads to static accounts of diversity at work, which ignore the dynamic nature of power and inequality relations.
>
> *(pp. 180–181)*

They argue for emergent rather than predetermined diversity/identity categories that are locally defined and relevant to the context of the situation, industry or organization under study. Similarly, Risberg and Pilhofer (2018) explain how predetermined categories are unable to account for the dynamic nature of identity and result in a phenomenon called identity freezing.

Identity, as a driving concept behind diversity dynamics, requires complex theorizing. More recent studies on SIT have taken a more multidimensional approach to identity than the earlier studies by Tajfel and colleagues. On the other hand, there is also a growing critique that too much focus on the fluidity of identity can take out the critical focus on power and inequity (Powell, Jayasinghe, & Taksa, 2015). Therefore, diversity research needs to strike the right note between individual-level identity complexities, intersectional effects and power dynamics, as well as intergroup dynamics that are context specific.

Models

Along with theories, several models have been forwarded to conceptualize and operationalize diversity within organizations. Taylor Cox (1991, 1994), an early DM academic and consultant, has described three types of organizations – the monolithic, plural and multicultural organization. The monolithic organization, as the term suggests, is more homogenous and is caught up in practices of homophily. The plural organization has diversity only in the lower ranks, and difference is tolerated as something that is unavoidable. In the multicultural organization, difference is valued for what it can achieve and is integrated into the culture and strategic mission of the organization.

Ely and Thomas (2001) identified three perspectives on workforce diversity that are often cited and consulted: the discrimination-and-fairness perspective, the access-and-legitimacy perspective and the integration-and-learning perspective. The first perspective views diversity as an equity and social justice issue and does not relate it to work. The second perspective is more business case oriented. Diversity is prominent at the margins of the organization that interface with diverse customers and stakeholders, but not integrated into the core functions and leadership, especially senior leadership. The third perspective is described by Ely and Thomas (2001) as follows:

> According to the integration-and-learning perspective on diversity, the insights, skills, and experiences employees have developed as members of various cultural identity groups are potentially valuable resources that the work group can use to rethink its primary tasks and redefine its markets, products, strategies, and business practices in ways that will advance its mission. This perspective links diversity to work processes – the way people do and experience the work – in a manner that makes diversity a resource for learning and adaptive change.
>
> *(p. 240)*

The authors explain that all three perspectives have been used to motivate diversity efforts, but the third perspective is holistic and promises sustained outcomes. Similarly, Mazzei and Ravazzani (2012) make a case for the:

> … leveraging of variety that goes beyond assimilating minorities and integrating diversity. The "Leveraging Variety Model" takes into account both economic and social pressures in order to maximize the ability to satisfy stakeholders' expectations, reflect the external environment, enhance the knowledge creation potential and communicate effectively from an intercultural perspective.
>
> *(p. 59)*

Adding another perspective, the resistance perspective, Dass and Parker (1999) write that resistance to diversity is well and alive in organizations and that:

> ... there is no single best way, but that the organization's approach depends on the degree of pressure for diversity, the type of diversity in question, and managerial attitudes. Strategic responses for managing diversity are presented in a framework of proactive, accommodative, defensive, and reactive modes.
>
> *(p. 68)*

This perspective suggests that diversity ideologies within organizations can exist anywhere on a spectrum between resistance and full acceptance, and there is no singular diversity logic that fits all.

Overall, the theories which are prominent in the diversity literature suggest that historically charged inequities and reified social and cultural differences (which are the source of diversity) lead to in-group/out-group divisions, discrimination and conflict in organizations. In other words, difference is theorized in negative terms, or as a phenomenon that results in problems in organizations and settings that are not homogenous. This, we believe, is a basic issue that needs to be addressed in how we conceptualize difference, and hence diversity. The prominent models offered, on the other hand, are more open and marked by possibility; that is, they suggest that difference, when navigated successfully and addressed fairly and equitably (with attention to power) in organizational culture, can lead to positive outcomes. We now look at some of the debates and arguments that mark the current diversity discourse and scholarship.

The debates and arguments

A central debate in the diversity narrative – the moral/social justice vs. the business case for diversity in organizations – is often presented as a stalemate (Van Dijk, van Engen, & Paauwe, 2012). Related to this debate is the argument that power, systemic inequities and context should be taken into consideration more often in our theorizing and practice of D&I.

The moral vs. business case

As already mentioned, the *Workforce 2000* report produced a turning point in the US diversity narrative by foregrounding the business case. Konrad (2003) sums up the business case well:

> The business case for diversity includes three basic arguments. First, ... a more diverse U.S. labor force means that businesses desiring to attract

and retain the highest quality talent will have to recruit from all demographic categories as the traditional White male demographic shrinks in relative size. Second, a more diverse U.S. society plus a globalized marketplace means a more diverse customer base, and businesses that employ a more diverse workforce will garner market intelligence to help them sell to potential customers from a variety of cultural backgrounds. Third, demographically diverse groups can outperform homogeneous groups on problem-solving and creativity tasks because diverse groups contain a greater variety of information, experience, perspectives, and cognitive styles. The business case for diversity sold well to U.S. corporations ....

(p. 5)

Additionally, the business case invites the inclusion of more categories of difference that are not necessarily inequity based. Proponents of the business case argue this is productive and inclusive of all identities, including dominant ones that are threatened by the AA/EEO focus on women and marginalized groups (Zanoni, Janssens, Benschop, & Nkomo, 2010).

Critics of the business case, however, are not in favor of abandoning the social justice and equity argument and diluting the meaning of diversity to appease the already privileged (Beer, 2010; Linnehan & Konrad, 1999). Konrad (2003) argues that "if individual differences are all that is necessary to make a workplace diverse, then all groups are diverse by definition, and the entire concept of workplace diversity [and equity] could become meaningless" (p. 7). Özbilgin and Tatli (2011) criticize the individualistic approach "because it ignores the historical dynamics of discrimination that frame the diversity problem in a society and the corresponding advantage and disadvantage in employment" (p. 1235). Oswick and Noon (2014) are critical of how:

> ... equal opportunities/affirmative action (EO/AA) is portrayed as old, tired, failing and reliant on regulation imposed by the government, while managing diversity is new, fresh and full of potential, with an emphasis on responsible self-regulation of organizations guided by the free market.
>
> *(p. 25)*

Another critique of the business case, as explained in the last chapter, is that it creates a division and power distance between the "manager" and the "managed" and commodifies diversity and those who are perceived as embodying difference (Ahmed, 2007; Lorbiecki & Jack, 2000; Mundy, 2016; Zanoni et al., 2010). According to Kirby and Harter (2003):

> If diversity is framed as something to be managed, then the power to manage diversity remains at higher organizational levels. As a result,

managing diversity often emphasizes the interests of managers and potentially suppresses the interests of other individuals.

(p. 40)

P. Prasad and Mills (1997) have also made the point that DM is a voluntary effort and whether it is supported or not depends on the goodwill of leaders and managers who tend to be from privileged identity groups. Overall, critics argue that the DM approach masks how difference and power work in organizations and the real issues and challenges involved. According to Jones and Stablein (2006), identity and agency and how they are intertwined in organizational contexts are critical theoretical constructs for diversity that should always be kept in clear focus (see also Nkomo & Cox, 1996).

According to Bassett-Jones (2005), DM is a double-edged sword, but when done right it can foster creativity and advantage. While this is a good argument, critics of DM make an equally important point that the equity purpose should not be abandoned since organizations are a part of societies and do not fall outside of social hierarchies and tensions. Pretending these tensions are checked at the door when people come into work is not useful. But the argument need not be a stalemate, i.e., an "either/or" dilemma, and efforts can be made to strike the right note between the moral and business case (Kirby & Harter, 2003; Mease, 2012; Meyerson, 2001; Mundy, 2016; Tomlinson & Schwabenland, 2010). An ethical orientation and the genuine support of equity-seeking leadership are needed to accomplish this balance (Gilbert et al., 1999).

Power and context

Although the diversity movement in the United States arose out of the need to address historically produced power inequities between groups in society, the earlier theories mainly used to understand and explain diversity dynamics (e.g., similarity-attraction, SIT) tend not to focus on power and related macro-level systemic issues. Since the late 1990s, critically oriented scholars have been pressing for the inclusion of power relations in the study of diversity in organizations arguing that unless systemic inequities and power differentials are factored in and theorized, it becomes difficult to address certain questions – for example, why resistance to diversity continues to occur, why research continues to suggest that members of privileged groups tend to think that discrimination does not occur anymore (or have a rosier picture than those who are targets of discrimination), why homophily persists, why so many leaders pay lip service to D&I, why microaggressions and the exclusion of women and members of marginalized groups continue to be a common practice, why White heterosexual males in the United States continue to disproportionately occupy positions of power, why diversity has different meanings for different people and so on (Ahmed, 2007; Allen, 1995; A. Prasad & Elmes,

1997; Zanoni et al., 2010). Ignoring power also does not help us explain why the popular logic of requisite variety, described in the previous chapter, may not always be adequate for theorizing diversity since "increasing the numbers of traditionally underrepresented groups without altering power relations between dominants and subdominants is unlikely to improve the position of those groups substantially..." (Ely & Thomas, 2001, p. 232).

Linnehan and Konrad (1999) explain how power works at several levels – from the micro to the macro – and that power dynamics in organizations will inevitably reflect social ones. If the business case is unable to account for societal power dynamics, then progress will not be made and, according to Ahonen, Tienari, Meriläinen and Pullen (2014):

> Diversity is no longer linked to histories of discrimination ... Diversity becomes everything and nothing, a signifier without a signified. In other words, diversity becomes a highly malleable object that can be deployed for various strategic purposes and with differing and shifting meanings.
>
> *(p. 272)*

Without accounting for power, differences will not be understood, addressed and theorized in a complex enough manner, and the energy, time and financial resources invested in D&I efforts will not have desired outcomes. There will be pressure to make all diversity efforts "constructive and pleasant, include everyone and offend no one," and such pressure can only suppress, mask and fester real inequities (Kersten, 2000, p. 242). Such sanitized diversity efforts do not make good financial sense either, since much energy, time and resources are spent and nothing significant is achieved. Instead, what is needed is power sharing. As Limaye (1994) explains so well:

> We need to go beyond knowledge and sensitivity because the issue of responding to or managing diversity is not merely a matter of knowing the right things and feeling the right sentiments on an individual level but of willingness by a group to share power on an institutional or organizational level.
>
> *(p. 361)*

What is needed, then, is the readiness and willingness to recognize and give up unfair privileges. This is easier said than done and requires deep changes, including attitudinal and structural changes and a purposeful moral commitment.

How power works at different levels of analysis is intertwined with context (Ahonen, Tienari, Meriläinen, & Pullen, 2014). Joshi and Roh (2013) define diversity context as "the specific features of the environmental context that might enhance or constrain the occurrence and meaning of diversity in groups or teams and the relationship between diversity and attitudinal, behavioral, and performance outcomes" (p. 211). They further segment context into relational, structural and normative context. Relational context focuses on the quality of the interpersonal relations and interactions between organizational actors "and the extent to which these interactions are inclusive, dense, and based on trust and positive affect" (p. 211). Structural context is about the extent to which the organization is heterogenous and how this impacts power relations between dominant and non-dominant demographic groups. Normative context comprises "organizational culture, history/tradition, climate, and management practices" (p. 211). Context is key to how diversity is understood and performed (or not), and the best approach to D&I is particular rather than universal, i.e., it is important to purposefully choose a diversity logic that makes sense in a given context (Dass & Parker, 1999; Özbilgin & Tatli, 2011).

Lorbiecki and Jack (2000) draw upon the work of sociologist Zygmunt Bauman to make the point that D&I research and practices that use etic (pre-determined) categories that are acontextual are "predicated on the belief that the wild profusion of human alterity can be known and controlled" (p. S25). While this may be a comforting mindset for those who prefer certainty over ambiguity, it is useful to learn how to embrace the ambiguity that marks the plays of D&I. Emphasizing the importance of context in theorizing and practicing D&I, Özbilgin and Tatli (2012) argue that diversity categories need to be emic (developed within context) and intersectional rather than etic because an emic approach allows us to pay attention to the relations of power at play in a particular organizational setting. Also, context is especially key when it comes to the job-relatedness of D&I and the dominant industry culture of any particular industry (Pelled, 1996). However, despite its central nature, context remains an understudied aspect in D&I research (Milliken & Martins, 1996; Pringle & Ryan, 2015).

At least two central arguments are scattered throughout the research on diversity across disciplines – (a) the role, engagement and full (visible, budgetary and vocal) support of leadership is a must for D&I success, and (b) diversity cannot thrive without inclusion, which entails addressing historical and cultural power differentials and striving for equity. *Diversity work is a process. It is about making differences work. Inclusion is the intentional effort needed for diversity to work and for equity to emerge.* We now turn our attention to the literature on inclusion.

Inclusion

Inclusion is the fuel needed to drive diversity toward the goal of equity. Diversity cannot be successful without a culture of inclusion, but they are not one and the same. According to Bourke (2018):

> There has been an overemphasis on diversity, and an underemphasis on inclusion, as well as on the broader ecosystem of accountability,

recognition, and rewards. … The definition of 'inclusion' is often left to personal interpretation, and many organizations seem unclear about what it means. Without a shared understanding of inclusion, people are prone to miscommunication, progress cannot be reliably evaluated, leaders can't be held accountable, and organizations default to counting diversity numbers.

(paras. 41, 13)

According to Roberson (2006), exclusion has not been the focus of much research and it is necessary to understand the difference between what diversity and inclusion/exclusion mean as well as how they are related so that "both researchers and practitioners are better positioned to create, understand, and support changes needed to promote equality for historically disadvantaged groups as well as create organizations in which all employees can use their full portfolio of skills and talents" (p. 234). Too often, it is simplistically assumed that hiring diverse individuals will automatically lead to inclusion (Ferdman, 2014). Then, companies wonder about high turnover rates and often give up on D&I efforts. Inclusion is about the successful retention of diverse organizational members at all levels. Without an inclusive environment, diversity efforts are usually futile, and resources and energy are wasted ("Diversity fatigue," 2016).

While the focus of diversity is difference, the foci of inclusion are belonging, empowerment and full participation which can occur only through successful, fair and respectful communication and relations across multiple differences. Ferdman (2014) describes inclusion as a practice that is ongoing, dynamic and intersectional: "Rather than focusing on individuals as representatives of one group at a time and on one identity at a time, an inclusion lens highlights multiplicity and integration, in the context of empowerment and equality [and equity]" (p. 11). He emphasizes that ideally, the practice of inclusion should be systemic. According to Miller (1998), "Inclusion increases the total human energy available to the organization" (p. 151). In their review of inclusion literature, Shore et al. (2011) conclude that while there are multiple definitions of the term, "inclusion remains a new concept without consensus on the nature of this construct or its theoretical underpinnings" (p. 1263). They state that inclusion has been defined as the extent to which employees feel accepted and treated as insiders at work, the removal of obstacles from full participation and contribution, the valuing of the contributions of all employees and recognition of individual talents in the daily life of the organization, involvement of all in the mission and operations of the organization, having all voices heard, and the engagement of diverse employees in the core and not just periphery functions of the organizations. They further observe two themes that emerge from these definitions: belonging and uniqueness. Based on this, Shore et al. (2011) define inclusion as "the degree to which an employee perceives that he or she is an esteemed member of the work group through experiencing treatment that satisfies his or her needs for belongingness and uniqueness" (p. 1265). They emphasize that individuals have complex social identities and needs for belonging and uniqueness within the workplace, and that feeling included improves organizational commitment and job performance.

Turnbull, Greenwood, Tworoger and Golden (2010) describe skills needed at various relational and communication levels – intrapersonal, interpersonal, group and organizational – to build a culture of inclusion and emphasize the interconnected nature of all the levels (see also Kaplan & Donovan, 2013). Inclusion skills need to be consciously and carefully cultivated, and often organizational culture change is required. In other words, *the willingness to be inclusive is a necessary pre-condition for inclusion efforts.* Just like in the diversity literature, scattered throughout the literature on inclusion is the point that leadership support and engagement is a must for building cultures of inclusion (e.g., Sabharwal, 2014; Shore et al., 2011; Wasserman, Gallegos, & Ferdman, 2008). Another prominent theme within the literature is that inclusion is an ongoing process: it never ends because mindful work is continuously needed to build, maintain and improve cultures of inclusion/equity.

Inclusion practices need to first and foremost address historical inequities and continuing discriminatory practices at individual, group and systemic levels which have become normalized. To those who subscribe to the business case, inclusion means everyone (including members of dominant groups) needs to be part of the inclusion mix. These two approaches need not be anti-thetical to each other. What needs to be kept in focus at all times are the power differentials at play, so we do not lose sight of the equity goal. Those who are in dominant positions of power (typically heterosexual White able-bodied males in the US context) need to join the mix with the attitude of being allies, the willingness to share power, and do what it takes to bring about real change. Those who are members of marginalized groups need to work across power inequities with all to bring about needed changes and build cultures of inclusion and achieve equity within the workplace. As Nkomo (2014) writes:

> The journey to inclusion will not be an easy one … Yet scholars and practitioners have no choice but to strive for the possibility of breaking the frame and transforming our workplaces from places of exclusion to ones of inclusion.
>
> *(p. 589)*

We agree with Nkomo and subscribe to the approach that *all* must be included in the D&I conversation, although in different ways that are mindful of the power and privilege inequities involved. This is certainly not an easy process but one that must be engaged in.

Equity

According to the moral/social justice approach to diversity, equity is the over-arching goal that requires inclusion. According to Berry (2016), while diversity focuses on difference:

> Equity is understood to include inclusive participation and the removal of barriers to such participation. Diversity without the opportunity for equitable participation can lead to a form of separation; equity without diversity can lead to a form of assimilation; the absence of both can lead to marginalisation; and the presence of both can lead to a full integration.
>
> *(p. 413)*

Ferdman (2021) explains equity is "about power and access to power" (p. 13). Equity is, therefore, the constant goal in the process and practice of D&I. But it is a goal that is never completely achieved, and nor should it be. By this we mean that constant work is needed to keep equity sensibilities alive, avoid complacency and remain vigilant for new inequities that may arise or old ones that need to be uncovered.

The terms "equity" and "equality" tend to often be used interchangeably, but there is an important difference. French (2005) explains that equity in an organizational context means having in place practices, policies and processes that are developed with the goal of ensuring "fair and just treatment of diverse individuals" (p. 35). Equality, on the other hand, does not consider the fact that diverse individuals do not all share the same starting point, i.e., equality-based policies and processes are not identity conscious and do not consider the underlying social and power differentials among members of the workforce. French notes that equitable access and strategic/intentional pro-D&I interventions, rather than equal access, tend to lead to better outcomes for marginalized groups in organizational settings. Bernstein, Bulger, Salipante and Weisinger (2020) further emphasize that "equity calls for the righting of systemic and structural injustices" and that "it is important to discuss and elevate practices that can move us from diversity to equity" (p. 396). According to Espinoza (2007), "rather than striving for equality among groups of people we should work towards equitable inequalities that reflect the needs and strengths of the various groups" (p. 345). He includes the caveat that equity-based policies and decision-making are complicated because people have different interpretations of what is fair and just and adds there is not enough evidence that equity-based decisions will always have positive and desired outcomes. That, however, should not stop the journey toward equity.

Theories and models for inclusion

As already mentioned, and unlike diversity, very little theoretical/conceptual work exists on inclusion (and relatedly, on equity). Within the slim theoretical body of work that does exist is the usage of sociologist Bourdieu to understand diversity power dynamics in societies and the possibility of change. Bourdieu is popular among organization studies and management scholars. As explained in the introductory chapter in relation to the public relations profession (Edwards, 2011), professions are fields within larger overarching fields of power within societies. Fields are constituted through sedimented practices and dispositions (i.e., habitus) that heavily tilt power in favor of the privileged and dominant groups in society. This, in turn, promotes homophily. According to Bourdieu, habitus do not change overnight; therefore, a culture of inclusion cannot grow overnight either, and nor is it the automatic result of hiring more diverse people. Dispositions and practices that are normalized in favor of dominant groups and structures must first change for the habitus to change and become more inclusive. Change is slow and involves the interplay of agency, structure, power and capital. Drawing upon Bourdieu, Özbilgin and Tatli (2011) explain that D&I may be thought of:

> ... as a space of relations between different institutional actors, i.e. statutory equality bodies, public and private sector organizations, professional bodies and learned organizations, trade unions, employer organizations, consultancies and training organizations. If the first principle that defines a field is that of relationality (i.e., what makes a field is the relationships between the actors), the second are the power structures within a given field that generate position taking by the actors in it ... actors engage in competition and confrontation to conserve or transform the rules of the field in which they are located ... The relationship between the agents and their positioning in a given field is characterized by a struggle over gaining symbolic domination ... However, the symbolic monopoly is never complete and fields are constantly and dynamically generated, reproduced and sometimes transformed through power struggles between institutional or individual actors, who compete for appropriation of the power and resources through which they obtain legitimacy to impose their vision ....
>
> *(pp. 1232–1233)*

Different professions and industries are, therefore, fields within which actors must strategically and constantly work across complex power dynamics and find ways to bring about changes that promote professional cultures of inclusion and equity.

According to Bernstein et al. (2020), while inclusion has been growing in importance as a concept, not enough scholarship exists on understanding the forces that create exclusion in organizations (see also Roberson, 2006). They elaborate that while representational diversity is important because it sets the stage for inclusion, just representation cannot address how interactions across various differences actually play out in organizational settings, often generating exclusionary effects. Randel et al. (2018) have made the same point: "Simply placing individuals who differ from one another in a work group or promoting diverse individuals into leadership positions does not ensure positive outcomes" (p. 200). Bernstein et al. (2020) use an ethics and social justice lens to offer what they call a theory of generative interactions which:

> …specifies organizational practices that produce and sustain generative diversity interactions, leading to inclusion and equity. We posit that dynamics such as self-segregation, communication apprehension, stereotyping, and stigmatizing will predominate by default if not countered by other forces, thereby hampering diversity and inclusion efforts. On the other hand, we assert that particular organizational practices can mitigate these phenomena, facilitating the creation of generative diversity interactions that enhance both diversity and inclusion. … the findings on cross-functional teams suggest the importance of three relational elements being combined: bringing diverse members into frequent, repeated interaction, equal status among work group members, and collaborative interaction. … Under proper organizational conditions, then, common ingroup identity enables individuals to adopt a work group identity that transcends, but still recognizes and utilizes, the differences among members.
>
> *(pp. 397, 400, 402)*

This theory emphasizes that if sustained and normalized over time, organizational practices that counter exclusionary forces will eventually reduce prejudice and generate inclusive interactions, and hence climates; additionally, leaders within organizations can use this theory as a model to practice inclusive leadership on a day-to-day basis.

There also exist some useful models which assist with envisioning how cultures of inclusion may be developed. Mor Barak (2005, 2017) theorizes that inclusion and exclusion exist on a continuum and offers a model for workplace inclusivity which can be applied domestically and globally. This model comprises four levels – organizational, community, national and international. These levels range from the micro relational level of inclusion work required within organizations to working/collaborating across cultural/national differences. For inclusion to be conceptualized as systemic, Ferdman (2021) offers a multilevel model which comprises the experiential level, and moves outward toward the interpersonal behavioral level, group/team practices level, leaders/leadership practices level, organizational practices/norms/collective experiences level and the societal policies/practices/values/ideologies level. Pless, Maak and Harris (2017) offer a human dignity model for inclusion which supports the goal of equity. Explaining this model, they write:

> Dignity plays a crucial role as both a fundamental value and as an end state in the process of humanizing organizational cultures, workplaces and relationships … human dignity requires us to treat people as human beings rather than objects – whether in relationships, organizations, or in society.
>
> *(pp. 223, 225)*

According to the authors, dignity is a relational term. A dignity-based management model requires us to normalize difference and treat all members of society/organizations as full human beings. According to Pless and Maak (2004), two core values are required to build a "house of inclusion" (p. 131): reciprocal understanding and trust. Reciprocal understanding requires us to understand the existence of plural standpoints and be willing and open to engaging with multiple views. Reciprocal understanding is the foundation needed for trust, which is "getting people from different cultural backgrounds to work co-operatively together and to comfortably share their knowledge, experiences and viewpoints" and eventually developing an "intercultural moral point of view" (p. 134). Explaining that building inclusive cultures is difficult moral/cultural work, Pless and Maak (2004) emphasize that a long-term commitment is a must. Building inclusive diverse cultures is also closely related to organizational climate. We now turn to this concept.

Organizational culture and climate

Quite simply, changing organizational culture means changing organizational climate. According to Mor Barak (2017), organizational climate with regard to inclusion:

> … refers to the shared employee perceptions of the extent to which organizational policies encourage and reward acceptance of demographically diverse employees by (a) recognizing their unique attributes; (b) providing them with a sense of belonging; and (c) encouraging their involvement in organizational communication, decision-making processes and informal interactions.
>
> *(p. 302)*

According to Gelfand, Nishii, Raver and Schneider (2005), climates for inclusion can be measured by "employees' shared perception of the policies, practices, and procedures that implicitly and explicitly communicate the extent to which fostering and maintaining diversity and eliminating discrimination is a priority in the organization" (p. 104).

According to Shore et al. (2011):

> A climate of inclusion is one in which policies, procedures, and actions of organizational agents are consistent with fair treatment of all social groups, with particular attention to groups that have had fewer opportunities historically and that are stigmatized in the societies in which they live. The latter groups are especially likely to pay attention to the degree of inclusion that appears to be present in the organization.
>
> *(p. 1277)*

All of these definitions suggest that the manner in which an organization approaches difference determines inclusion climate and the possibility of equity.

Change happens through buy-in at all levels of the organization, effective training and support from the top, i.e., senior leadership (Shore et al., 2011). Most organizations do not usually have climates conducive to inclusion; they have to learn how to become inclusive, and this usually happens when they are pressured through environmental factors (e.g., changing demographics, pressure from clients with diverse publics and customers) and/or internal pressures (Miller, 1998; Wooten, 2008). A negative climate for inclusion is one where the environment is oppressive for underrepresented employees and microaggressions, conflict and discrimination charges are common (Chrobot-Mason & Aramovich, 2013). Miller (1998) suggests five steps for strategically building inclusive organizational climates:

1. Identify the organizational imperative – i.e., how does inclusion align with the mission of the organization?
2. Build a core of advocates for change – this group should include leaders from all levels.
3. Build on the successes of the pockets of readiness – i.e., identify and equip groups readier than others to change.
4. Coach the leaders (and diversify leadership).
5. Change the system – this involves structural changes that are pro-inclusion (pp. 152–153).

Winters (2014) suggests various relational behaviors and ways of communicating necessary for building inclusive climates. These include improving listening skills, asking appropriate questions when necessary, shifting the frame of reference when needed, developing constructive conflict management skills, recognizing unconscious bias, showing respect for interest in those who are different from oneself and aiming for meaningful interactions with them, striving to be as non-judgmental as possible and making all decisions through the lenses of culture and difference (pp. 212–214). Structural and process changes could include recruiting strategically, mentoring, sponsorships, establishing work-life strategies, employee resource and network groups, diversity councils and surveying inclusion climate on a regular basis.

For such changes to occur, however, an organization must invest in long-term efforts such as training that is strategic and aims to "establish a relational culture within which people feel proud of their own uniqueness, while becoming socially integrated into a larger group by celebrating the 'me' within the 'we'" (Chavez & Weisinger, 2008, p. 332). Barriers need to be detected and removed, and opportunities need to be built upon.

Unconscious bias: A barrier to D&I

A clear barrier in the path of D&I progress is unconscious bias, also known as implicit or hidden bias. Unconscious bias is a cognitive process which comprises behaviors and attitudes demonstrated by members of dominant/privileged groups that are discriminatory in nature. According to Miller (1998):

> Expressed in conscious and unconscious behaviors as well as routine practices, procedures and bylaws, these barriers are often rooted in the very culture of an organization. Typically, they favor people who look and act like the leaders of the organization; and to those they favor, the barriers can be as invisible as air. But to those who confront them daily, these barriers can be demeaning, discouraging and insurmountable.
>
> *(p. 152)*

According to Winters (2014):

> Unconscious bias is also a primary factor in the perpetuation of exclusive cultures … [it] can be defined as preferences based on perceptions, thoughts, feelings, and beliefs that are deeply hidden in our subconscious. Theorists believe that discriminations persist because we routinely act on our unconscious biases ….
>
> *(p. 210)*

Exclusive cultures promote homogeneity and homophily, which are barriers to D&I. Those who are in the minority are often excluded from information sharing networks, which automatically puts them in a position of disadvantage. Homogeneity is a result of attraction-selection-attrition, i.e., individuals are attracted to organizations that appear to have values that are similar to theirs, organizations tend to select those who seem similar to the dominant group within the organization, and heterogeneity perishes as a result of homophilic practices that support homogeneity and push out diversity (Mor Barak, 2017).

Lee (2005) argues that it is particularly necessary to understand how unconscious bias works in US society in the post-Civil Rights era. Since legal action is more possible now, discrimination, whether conscious or unconscious, works in more subtle ways (e.g., microaggressions) and "psychologists have found that unconscious bias is quite prevalent, often in sharp contrast to individuals' self-professed identity" (p. 484). Since it is not easily recognized, it is especially necessary to remain vigilant and detect unconscious bias because it is not just an individual or interpersonal level phenomenon; unconscious bias is systemic and impacts hiring practices, promotions, policies and many other aspects of organizational/professional cultures and practices that hurt D&I efforts (see also Kaplan & Donovan, 2013).

Unconscious bias, therefore, is the source of many behaviors and organizational/professional/systemic practices that are barriers in the path of D&I. For example, unconscious bias may not allow an organization to see the importance of investing, in terms of budget and time, the resources needed to make cultural and structural changes (e.g., developing a strategic, focused and measurable D&I plan, training employees at all levels, setting up diversity councils, employee resource groups, mentoring, etc.). Relatedly, reactive training in response to negative climates, or training not designed strategically with the specific needs, context and culture of a given organization, could further hurt rather than improve D&I. The "one size fits all" type of training as well as training that engages shaming techniques do more harm than good and can further alienate dominant members and increase dissatisfaction and anger among members of marginalized groups (Chavez & Weisinger, 2008). Finally, leaders (who are usually members of dominant/privileged groups) may not perceive D&I as a pressing issue and, therefore, may not engage visibly and consistently in D&I efforts or understand that D&I is an ongoing process which has no end point. An organization mired in barriers generated by unconscious bias will simply ignore at worst, or pay lip service at best, to D&I and no real change or action will occur beyond that. Equity and inclusion will remain unaddressed.

To develop a focused and productive D&I vision, unconscious bias must be honestly confronted. Additionally, senior leaders need to lead the charge in addressing unconscious bias by communicating clearly about how the phenomenon works, how it hurts organizational performance, how it hampers relations with stakeholders and how it can be costly because of high turnover, discrimination lawsuits and reputation damage (Brown, 2016; Chavez & Weisinger, 2008; Kaplan & Donovan, 2013; Miller, 1998; Sabharwal, 2014; Shore et al., 2011). In many cases, leaders themselves will need to be educated, and they must be willing candidates for such education (Miller & Katz, 2002).

According to Lee (2005), "social psychology research suggests that individuals are able to control their unconscious biases" (p. 486). But they must first do the hard work of recognizing their own biases, not give in to defensiveness and/or resistance, or become paralyzed by guilt. Also, according to Moule

(2009), along with "unswerving, unnerving, scrupulous honesty ... individuals need to become less focused on feeling very tolerant and good about themselves and more focused on examining their own biases" (p. 325). Addressing unconscious bias means including everyone in the dialogue, including the most privileged identity group/s in organizations despite the fact they may be resistant to D&I. Some would argue against this position; however, we align with the advice of consultants such as Brown (2016), Kaplan and Donovan (2013) and Miller and Katz (2002) who argue that privileged and dominant groups need to be part of difficult dialogues for meaningful change to occur. In the case of senior leadership in corporate America, which includes public relations, this group currently comprises mostly heterosexual White males. Leaving them out of the conversation could not be a productive approach for desired change; rather, they need to be engaged as willing allies.

Allyship and dialogue

What is most important is the attitude members of dominant groups bring to the dialogue. If they are ready to be allies, then this is good news for the organization. According to Nagda (2006), an expert on intergroup dialogue, difficult dialogues across power differentials require critical self-reflection and appreciation of difference:

> Alliance building involves relating to and thinking about collaborating with others in taking actions toward social justice ... Alliances involve a trusting, conjoint commitment toward learning and action in the context of differences and inequalities; they represent an earnest grappling with differences and conflicts in the pursuit of social justice ....
>
> *(pp. 563, 569)*

Alliances can promote "affective relationships across cultural and power differences" and produce "critical empathy" that is sensitive to inequities (Nagda, 2006, p. 570). We also believe, like Miller and Katz (2002), that heterosexual White males should not be treated as a monolithic group when it comes to allyship and D&I efforts:

> In many organizational frameworks of diversity and inclusion, white men are left out of the picture ... Some white men's resistance to diversity efforts arise from the fear that they are being excluded and diversity does not mean them. ... [engaging white men] creates an environment in which more than one type of white man can succeed and enhances white men's competencies to effectively partner, engage, manage, and interact in a more and more diverse organization.
>
> *(p. 87)*

Recent industry research shows that while heterosexual White males are in a majority of leadership positions in organizations, they are less engaged in D&I than their diverse colleagues (Brown, 2016). This needs to change for the D&I needle to move faster. According to Gilbert et al. (1999), "While the preponderance of diversity literature examines primarily women and/or people of color, management scholars have suggested that research of diversity's impact on majority members is also important" (p. 71). According to Brown (2016), "White men can learn to accept and invite difference; the rest of us need to find a way to include the dominant group …" (p. 247). Further, and this we believe is a critical point, White males with power who are dedicated to equity must work hard to educate others in their own identity group who are not.

Since members of dominant groups do not all come to the dialogue table with the same mindset, unconscious bias training could gauge the attitude, inclusion/equity temperature and intercultural competency levels of trainees. Training should also take into consideration what D&I and allyship mean for a specific organization and the baseline climate of the organization. Historically marginalized identities should be kept in clear focus at all times, intersectional and contextual dynamics that apply should be considered, and appeasement approaches must not be adopted to include dominant groups. Overall, all groups must engage in dialogue for change, and the main challenge is to work with the difficulties and discomfort involved when all are involved across different vectors of power and privilege. This challenge must be welcomed.

Assessing the US public relations industry in relation to D&I scholarship

In the last chapter, we provided an in-depth review of industry discourse and scholarship on public relations and D&I in the United States. We wrap up this chapter by assessing this review in relation to the literature on D&I discussed in this chapter. Earlier in this chapter, we explained diversity is complex and that it is best understood as a process. We described how D&I are not the same but are deeply linked. Diversity is about differences (mainly theorized at the group level in the literature) and how people from different identity groups tend to orient across cultural and power differences in the work/organizational setting (and in societies in general). The organizational context is always embedded within larger local, regional, national and often global contexts. Inclusion is related to organizational culture. It is the complex, mindful and careful everyday work needed to engage and empower diverse employees and proceed toward the goals of belonging and equity in diverse organizations. How D&I/equity are envisioned, conceptualized and defined impacts how they are practiced in any given industry. A clear vision is difficult without clear understanding, and focused action for change is unlikely without clear vision.

Envisioning D&I

The public relations industry in the United States does not offer any one definition of D&I that is commonly accepted. In the last chapter, we reviewed the definitions and descriptions provided by professional associations such as the Public Relations Society of America (PRSA), the PR Council and the Commission for Public Relations Education (CPRE). We detected an ongoing struggle to define D&I over the last decade. The word "inclusion" was added to PRSA's definition only in the last six years or so. There was a hesitation to keep the definition too narrow for fear of alienating White males who dominate senior leadership. The business case was prominent, and the recent CPRE definition is the first definition that uses moral case terms such as "power differentials" and "marginalized groups." Overall, and up until the 2020 racial upheaval, we detected a tendency to shy away from the historical inequities that continue to permeate the industry.

The racial justice upheavals and reckoning of 2020 marked a significant turn in language. A new PRSA toolkit replaced the old one and a three-year D&I strategic plan was unveiled. The following words are from the email PRSA leadership sent to members unveiling the new D&I toolkit and strategic plan: "PRSA has a lack of diversity across our membership and leadership that cannot continue if our organization is to not just grow but evolve. The time for talk is long past. The time for action is now" (T. Garland Stansell, M. Olson, & D. Peterson, personal communication, July 2, 2020). The email further describes specific actions needed:

- Improve diversity in PRSA's board of directors.
- Engage members from more diverse backgrounds on the national committees.
- Expand delegate representation.
- Deliver on the three-year strategic plan.
- Develop new programs to support new professionals of color.
- Strengthen relationships with Historically Black Colleges & Universities and Hispanic Serving Institutions.
- Launch unconscious bias training at local and national levels.
- Pledge support to the Diversity Action Alliance (DAA), a coalition of leaders and professional associations formed in 2020 dedicated to coordinating and accelerating D&I progress in the industry.

The honest admission of lack of diversity in the organization and its leadership in this email is refreshing. The following description of D&I in the new D&I toolkit replaces the 2016 language that did not mention race/ethnicity and was nervous about excluding White males:

> Diversity and inclusion are integral to the evolution and growth of PRSA and the public relations industry.

The most obvious contexts of diversity include race, ethnicity, religion, age, ability, sexual orientation, gender, gender identity, country of origin, culture and diversity of thought. However, in a rapidly changing society, diversity continues to evolve and can include class, socioeconomic status, life experiences, learning and working styles, personality types and intellectual traditions and perspectives, in addition to cultural, political, religious and other beliefs.

These defining attributes impact how we approach our work, connect with others and move through the world.

Inclusion, according to the Society for Human Resource Management (SHRM), is defined as "the achievement of a work environment in which all individuals are treated fairly and respectfully, have equal access to opportunities and resources, and can contribute fully to the organization's success."

Inclusion is not just about having that "seat at the table" but is about ensuring everyone's voice is heard and fully considered.

Diversity and inclusion are proactive behaviors.

Respecting, embracing, celebrating and validating those behaviors are integral to PRSA's DNA. Diversity and inclusion are vital to the success of our profession, our members and the communities in which we live and work. It is essential and is our responsibility as members of the Society to carry this forward.

(PRSA Chapter D&I Toolkit, 2021, p. 6)

This new language emphasizes the dynamic and open-ended nature of diversity and distinguishes between diversity and inclusion. The toolkit also provides instructions on how to build relations with Historically Black Colleges and Universities (HBCUs) and Hispanic Serving Institutions (HSIs) and includes details on unconscious bias training and several D&I resources. The business case language is not in the forefront (and is mentioned only once in the three-year strategic plan), and the social justice/moral case is more evident. Leadership accountability is clearly highlighted. The strategic plan has measurable goals related to increasing awareness of PRSA as a diverse and inclusive organization among members and external stakeholder, increasing diversity in leadership at all levels in the organization, and increasing diversity in Public Relations Student Society of America (PRSSA) chapters to form a diverse pipeline into PRSA.

A major industry-level step was taken in 2020 through the formation of the DAA. According to its website: "We are a coalition of public relations and communications leaders joining forces to accelerate progress in the achievement of meaningful and tangible results in diversity, equity, and inclusion across our profession" ("The Alliance," n.d.). The DAA aims to coordinate disparate D&I efforts in the profession and provide direction and focus, enhance D&I goal setting and measurement efforts and increase leadership accountability. The work of establishing the DAA had already begun and was expedited in 2020.

These efforts and the language of inclusion/equity and social justice approach to D&I are recent developments, and they indicate a move in the right direction. However, talk must follow walk. Inclusion must be well understood and practiced and should not be lumped together with diversity, as is still often the case (Chitkara, 2018). Inclusion is hard work and necessary for diversity to thrive. It is connected to equity, which means particular attention must be paid to power differentials and historical inequities while developing D&I programs, policies and organizational culture (the word "equity" does not appear in the above PRSA definition, but the DAA does mention it). If diversity recruitment efforts have improved but retention is poor, as is often reported, it means inclusion is still a problem, despite new language. If companies and firms keep shying away from addressing historical inequities and power differentials when discussing diversity (see Wills, 2020), then inclusion will remain an ongoing challenge despite recruitment efforts and social justice language. The wheels will keep spinning with no forward movement.

The literature reviewed in this chapter emphasizes the need for more intersectional approaches to identity, difference and diversity categories in D&I work (see Blow, Bonney, Tallapragada, & Brown, 2021). This is something that still needs to seep more into industry D&I discourse and practice. Differences are still mostly conceptualized in singular categories. The more recent critical scholarship on D&I in public relations also highlights the need to increase emphasis on power differentials and keep equity in sharp focus for the work of inclusion. Along with intersectionality, the literature reviewed in this chapter also emphasizes the importance of context, i.e., diversity needs to be sensitive to regional, demographic and others relevant intra- and supra-organizational contexts and its definition should be connected to the nature of the work involved (i.e., the industry to which it applies). Some scholars have even argued that pre-conceived categories for diversity should be replaced with emic and context-sensitive categories of diversity. Finally, organizational climate and culture are deeply tied to inclusion/equity. This means which differences get emphasized, or ignored, matters. A pro-equity organizational culture is more likely to be successful in accomplishing inclusion and, therefore, make diversity successful. These are all areas and topics which require more attention in the public relations profession's discourse and practice.

While some research is available on this topic (e.g., Mundy, 2016; Pompper, 2012, 2020), public relations scholarship needs to focus more on the various dimensions of how to build organizational cultures that support inclusion/

equity and build genuine relationships with diverse external stakeholders. D&I need to be studied more as a process; that is, diversity does not reside in people considered "diverse," it is the process of people embodying differences coming together in a common space (e.g., an organization, an industry and so on). And as we keep emphasizing, the role of leadership in supporting understandings of D&I that are equity and process-oriented and working personally to build cultures of inclusion/equity is an important area for further research.

Just business or something more?

As reviewed in this chapter, there are those who support the business case for D&I and those who critique it. As described in the last chapter, the business case is popular within the public relations professional discourse, and this is not surprising given most of the industry is for-profit. Therefore, there is a tendency to justify diversity in terms of how it can benefit the bottom line. Emphasizing only the business case, as we have already explained, does not bode well for successful genuine inclusion and equity. For public relations specifically, it also does not bode well for building relationships with internal and external stakeholders and publics across cultural and structural differences and inequities. This is an important point given that relationship building lies at the heart of public relations practice.

By foregrounding profitability, the business case makes it difficult to get at what makes diversity work – i.e., inclusive cultures and equity orientations. As some public relations scholars (e.g., Mundy, 2016; Munshi & Edwards, 2011) have rightly argued, framing diversity only in business terms is a form of commodification of important historical differences and inequities and the people who embody them. The business case suggests that those who are considered "diverse" are valued only for economic reasons and not for who they are and the many ways in which they can contribute. As Ciszek (2020) convincingly argues, trust is a key antecedent for building relationships with diverse internal and external stakeholders, many of whom have been historically marginalized and discriminated against; therefore, equating their identities with only profit works against building trust and genuine relationships. The general literature on D&I in this chapter makes the same points and adds that the business case aligns with the language of DM which tends to not consider larger contexts and discourses within which organizations are embedded. The DM approach sets up a power dichotomy between those who "manage" diversity and those who are "managed" (i.e., those who are considered "diverse"). Questions of discrimination resulting from power inequities, unrecognized privileges, practices that favor dominant group cultures which have become normalized and unconscious bias are difficult, and even uncomfortable or taboo, to address within the business case frame. However, these are issues that must be genuinely engaged with for success in D&I.

On the other hand, altogether ignoring the business case is not practical or necessary either. In our desire to enhance the moral case, we need not omit or be opposed to the business advantage. As Kirby and Harter (2003) explain:

> We see a clear need to position the appreciation of differences as important for reasons beyond mere profitability. We do not question the importance of diversity initiatives as a means to increase an organization's competitive advantage. Yet, we do not think such an approach should come at the expense of enacting diversity initiatives because they are the right thing to do. Perhaps this can be a both/and situation, where we talk about how what is good for society is also good for business.
>
> *(p. 43)*

Therefore, more nuanced discussion about how to reach a fine balance which upholds the moral case without abandoning the business one is needed (see Mundy, 2016). For example, in a recent study, Mease and Collins (2018) have made the argument that the business case should not be monolithically rejected but carefully analyzed for how differences are positioned – as an asset, a liability or as possibility. Attending to such nuances could steer us toward the fine balance and the conversations needed between the business and the moral case for D&I.

Successful D&I requires change, and change is not possible without addressing difficult questions and learning how to engage in difficult dialogue. Everyone from across the entire spectrum of privilege and disadvantage needs to participate in this process. Inclusion/equity is not about pretending all differences are equal and that everyone is equal; it is about acknowledging that power differentials are very real, that they do not get checked at the door at the workplace and that some identity groups are already ahead. Once public relations practice gets this right, the creative and business advantages of D&I will follow more naturally.

The ability to address power differentials and context

As described earlier, industries and organizations do not exist in a vacuum and nor does D&I in any given society. The movement for diversity in education and the workplace in the United States arose within the context of social/racial justice movements in the 1960s and 1970s and was geared toward addressing historical and ongoing marginalization and oppressions based primarily on race/ethnicity, gender and sexual orientation. This macro-historical context and the power differentials that constitute it reside at the heart of D&I discourse in this country and form the backdrop for every industry, including public relations. It cannot, and should not, be ignored.

As already described in the last chapter, the public relations discourse on equity and diversity began with gender, closely followed by race/ethnicity and more recently sexual orientation. The eventual addition of other categories of difference (both non-alterable and alterable)) has been an inclusive move, and this has been necessary because of the shifting nature of the US cultural landscape and D&I discourse. But as reviewed in this chapter, some question whether these additions are diluting or detracting attention from the traditional inequity-based categories. This is a complicated question and just like the business vs. moral case argument, we believe it does not need an "either/or" answer. One kind of difference does not need to be addressed at the expense of another; that is, this matter should not be treated as a zero-sum game. The macro context should always be considered along with the particular internal and external stakeholders involved for a given organization within a given industry; the understanding of context needs to be layered to include all the differences at play (local all the way up to global if applicable). Overall, historically prominent inequities and oppressions should never be ignored or forgotten as long as they exist. Instead of feeling threatened by these inequities, those in dominant positions must feel encouraged to learn how to be genuine allies in the process of pro-D&I change. Genuine D&I means those already privileged are ready to willingly share power.

Earlier in the chapter we described the sociopsychological theories (i.e., similarity-attraction theory, self-categorization theory and SIT) that are commonly found in diversity literature. While these theories cognitively explain why and how people process differences and interact with those similar and different from them, as well as how homophily often occurs as a result, these explanations do not address the macro-systemic level power inequities that form the context for these interactions and for homophily to persist. Some of the more recent scholarship on intersectionality and inclusion/equity are attending more to power. Power, from a sociocultural perspective, is the ability of a dominant identity group in society to define reality, set values and standards, decide what is right and wrong and establish policies and practices to build structures that support and maintain their power (Halualani, 2020). Applied to a profession like public relations, this means the dominant group defines the profession and its codes and culture and occupies strategic decision-making positions (Berger, 2005; J. E. Grunig, 1992). Currently, in corporate America and in public relations, this group comprises mainly heterosexual White males followed by heterosexual White females (Brown, 2016).

Furthermore, the power differentials that keep inequities in place are different for different categories of difference/identities and they intersect in complicated ways. For example, and quite recently, more women and those identifying as LGBTQ+ have been promoted to senior leadership positions in public relations. From an intersectional and critical perspective, it is important to note that race/ethnicity is still being left out as these women and LGBTQ+ leaders are still mainly White (Gupta, 2021; see also Chapter 5). As described earlier, the US public relations habitus is clearly marked by homophily, and power has resided structurally and culturally within a framework of Whiteness since the inception of the profession (Logan, 2011; Vardeman-Winter & Place, 2017). The above changes, while inclusive to a certain extent, continue to support this Whiteness frame the industry has been increasingly critiqued for. Therefore, it is necessary to address issues of conscious and unconscious bias which may be keeping inter-sectional inequities in place. For example, agency leaders in Chitkara's (2018) study cited, among other reasons, the legacy culture of the industry and not enough effort spent on retaining diverse hires as some of the reasons for the poor state of D&I. These reasons clearly suggest that unconscious biases continue to permeate industry culture and obstruct change.

Going back to the models of diversity described earlier in the chapter, organizations or industries can exist anywhere between full resistance and full acceptance of D&I. Public relations is somewhere in the middle in practice, and in the acceptance zone in the D&I language found in professional organizations and bodies such as PRSA, PRC and CPRE (see Chapter 2). It follows the plural industry model wherein diversity is seen as something unavoidable and is found mainly in the lower ranks (Cox, 1991, 1994) (it should be noted that there have been more recent increases in the middle ranks). The industry can also be described in terms of the access-and-legitimacy perspective which is a business case-oriented model wherein diversity resides outside of senior leadership and is more prominent at the margins/middle, i.e., D&I are not incorporated fully into the core functions (Ely & Thomas, 2001). The critical branch of schol-arship on D&I in public relations has been emphasizing power differentials, intersectionality, the power of Whiteness in the industry and other related mat-ters for almost two decades now. Gender-related power differentials have been studied for a much longer time. Scholarship is ahead of industry in this regard and industry needs to learn how to become more comfortable with address-ing these uncomfortable truths. What public relations scholarship can further examine is how to break up homophily (i.e., comfort zones), how to find ways to discuss difficult D&I issues across power differentials, how to share power, how to build alliances across historical differences, how to conceptualize and position difference as an advantage rather than a hurdle in public relations prac-tice and how to better confront, accept and address unconscious bias.

Leaders need to step up

Leaders need to be at the helm when it comes to supporting and advancing effec-tive D&I communication, policies and action. As reviewed in the previous chap-ter, it is amply clear that the lack of strong leadership support and engagement has been a prominent obstacle in the path of D&I progress in the public rela-tions industry. Further compounding the problem, many leaders and dominant identity practitioners seem to have a rosier picture about the state of D&I in the industry (see Chapter 5). Homophily is a clear pattern (especially among senior leadership) which, along with unconscious bias, impacts various organizational policies and practices such as recruitment, hiring, retention and promotions. The sticky floor syndrome is real, and diversity remains locked at the entry to middle levels. Overall, there is a lack of D&I accountability among current public relations leadership, and inclusion/equity remains a critical challenge. If genuine D&I/equity are desired, as the more recent communication emerging from the industry in the wake of the 2020 racial upheavals indicates, then leaders must be visibly committed to finding ways to have these complex and difficult conversations and making the cultural and structural changes needed for systemic and sustainable change. And scholarship must aid in this effort.

Key takeaways

- The US public relations industry has a long way to go when it comes to developing D&I best practices. In relation to the various extant models for D&I reviewed in this chapter, the industry is currently in the earlier phases of these models where diversity resides more at the margins/middle, is not an integrated part of the workings of the entire organization/industry and is absent especially at the senior leadership level. In other words, D&I is not yet a normalized and organic part of the industry's culture. Inclusion/ equity remains a major challenge and the industry has only recently begun discussing its critical importance.
- To advance in the realm of inclusion/equity, power differentials and unconscious bias must be honestly confronted and worked through. A thorough understanding must be gained about how unconscious bias creates perceptual barriers and keeps in place professional and industry practices that systemically exclude underrepresented groups (e.g., recruitment and hiring practices). Confronting unconscious bias requires awareness, introspection, courage, authenticity, humility and compassion. And most of all, it requires communication and a willingness to act. Only then can power sharing and alliances across power differentials emerge and D&I advance.
- A fine balance needs to be achieved between the business and moral/ social justice case for D&I in public relations. Inclusion and equity cannot be achieved if the business case is prioritized, and minoritized publics and stakeholders are equated only with profit. At the same time, the business dimension must not be ignored either.
- Context matters in how diversity and inclusion are described. While we do not recommend a fixed and static definition, since that would be antithetical to the very nature of D&I, public relations needs a clearer vision of what D&I means for the profession, i.e., how it impacts the ways the profession itself is practiced and its future viability. Relevant intra- and supra-organizational contexts (local all the way up to global if applicable) should also be considered in D&I policymaking and action.

- From a research point of view, there is a need for more theoretical perspectives on both D&I as a process. Scholars need to focus more on how organizational cultures and climates conducive to advancing D&I can be built (internal public relations, see Pompper, 2020), how power differentials need to be addressed for allyship and equity, and how unconscious biases in internal and external communication can be detected and reduced. There is also a need to develop more intersectional perspectives on D&I that can aid communication, dialogue and relationship building across differences with internal and external publics and stakeholders. Finally, the role of leaders and leadership in advancing D&I in the public relations profession needs more scholarly attention.

Conclusion

The more recent attention diversity, and especially inclusion/equity, has been receiving in public relations professional discourse is a positive development. There seems to be a stronger recognition of the problem now, but there is still much work to be done and equity-related barriers to remove. There is also a lack of clarity about how to proceed in the future. If the industry wishes to remain competitive and survive in an increasingly diversifying country and world, then the current culture of homophily and practices that promote homogeneity must be discarded in favor of genuine D&I practices and action. Unconscious biases that maintain the status quo need to be addressed head on. Overall, for D&I to be successful, not just in public relations but in any industry, there needs to be buy-in from all involved, not just those boxed into "diversity" categories. Inclusion is not likely when diversity is something only a few feel invested in or see the value of. If the majority feel D&I is an obligation, or perceive it as a threat, then unspoken resistance builds and inclusion remains a distant dream. Diversity and the work of inclusion need to be everybody's ethical mission, business and priority (Balta, 2017; P. Ford, 2017; Sha & R. Ford, 2007). Brave conversations, genuine learning and power sharing need to occur for inclusion to prosper and for allyship and the true benefits of diversity to come to life.

For real change to occur, leaders must be willing to visibly and passionately lead this charge. In so doing, they must also be willing to embrace humility and vulnerability, and this is something that most traditional leadership literature does not underscore. The "comfort zone" needs to be disbanded so difference may enter and thrive. In the next chapter we review the general literature on leadership, its relationship to D&I and the extant scholarship on public relations and leadership. This review aids in mapping what direction scholarship on public relations leadership and D&I needs to move in. It also serves as a compass for leaders, especially senior leaders, who wish to see the D&I needle move faster.

4

Leadership and D&I

Where Is Public Relations?

Leadership has been a popular subject of academic study for almost a century. There is no final word on the topic, and our understanding of leadership keeps evolving and changing with the times. In this chapter, we provide a broad overview of leadership scholarship in the fields of management, communication, organizational studies and human relations. We note overall trends and patterns in theorizing, and the place and consideration of diversity and inclusion (D&I) in leadership conceptualization and research. Next, we look specifically at how public relations scholarship has theorized leadership and its relationship to D&I. We conclude with implications and takeaways.

Leadership matters

In 2018, Sodexo, a large global food services and facilities management company that has employees from over 130 nationalities, was recognized for the tenth consecutive time for its outstanding D&I performance by DiversityInc. More than ten years ago their chief diversity officer Rohini Anand said:

> While the success of any inclusion initiative is the result of the complex interplay of several factors, I believe that leadership commitment and buy-in is a foundational prerequisite. ... Our CEO chairs the Diversity Leadership Council that sets the strategic direction for our diversity and inclusion efforts and reviews the diversity outcomes on a quarterly basis. I sit on the executive team and report to the CEO, and I ensure that the executive team engages in a series of quarterly learning experiences to enhance their awareness of and skills in diversity. ... Executive involvement has to be coupled with accountability. At Sodexo, 25 percent of

DOI: 10.4324/9781003170020-4

the executive team bonus is linked to a diversity scorecard and the CEO has committed that he will pay this bonus regardless of the financial performance of the company, as he sees the inclusion culture change efforts as a journey, not limited to a company's financial cycle.

(Dreachslin, 2007, p. 151)

This is still true for the company today. Sodexo serves as a model for how leadership needs to walk the talk on diversity and prioritize inclusion, accountability and the willingness to continuously learn. It is also an example of how to institutionalize D&I and make it an organic, ongoing and an everyday (systemic) part of organizational culture and structure.

While on the one hand there are companies like Sodexo, on the other hand there are companies that question the value of D&I or simply do not feel the urgency:

Many companies and leaders continue to question the value of a diverse workforce (and the inclusive environment in which it can thrive), even when considering the complex, connected and demographically diverse world we are living in. … So, if we know all of this, why don't we treat diversity and inclusion like a priority on par with other parts of the business? The true issue is not that we don't know what to do, but that many lack the will and courage to act on what we do know.

(Diversity Best Practices [Seramount], 2017, pp. 2–3)

We can only hope that the watershed events of 2020 and the current climate of emphatic and visible support of numerous high-profile companies and organizations for D&I will be a clear enough signal to such companies and their leaders. Leaders who still need to be convinced about the value of D&I are shortsighted and woefully behind the times.

Leaders are powerful and influential, and people take note of what they say, what they support and how they behave (Bardhan & Engstrom, 2021; Conger & Riggio, 2007; Fairhurst, 2007; C. E. Johnson & Hackman, 2018; Moss, 2019). According to a recent report in the *Harvard Business Review*:

[M]ostly it comes down to leaders. We find that what leaders say and do makes up to a 70% difference as to whether an individual reports feeling included. And this really matters because the more people feel included, the more they speak up, go the extra mile, and collaborate – all of which ultimately lifts organizational performance.

(Bourke & Titus, 2020, para. 2)

Therefore, leaders must take great care and responsibility in how they communicate about D&I. People from different cultural backgrounds make sense of the world differently and members of different groups in societies are unequally located in terms of power and privilege. These dynamics and identities are reflected within organizations. If employees feel that their worldviews are not supported or even acknowledged at work, especially by leaders, then they have little reason to remain or be attracted to a company or profession. This means leaders need to understand that recruiting diverse employees does not automatically result in retention because "diversity doesn't stick without inclusion" and "[d]iversity without inclusion is a story of missed opportunities, of employees so used to being overlooked that they no longer share ideas and insights. But diversity *with* inclusion provides a potent mix of talent retention and engagement" (Sherbin & Rashid, 2017, para. 13, emphasis in original). Leaders' words and actions must emphasize that diversity is an asset and advantage, that diversity efforts must be intentional (i.e., they will not just automatically happen) and that a culture of inclusion and equity is not an option but a necessity that everyone must work toward together with care, patience and the will to learn and unlearn.

The previous chapters have made a few things evident. First, diversity is a problem in the US public relations industry and inclusion seems to be an even bigger challenge. Second, public relations leaders just have not done what needs to be done with regard to D&I. The industry is approximately 90% White and overwhelmingly male dominated at senior levels. Women comprise almost 70% of the industry but are severely underrepresented in senior leadership (Place & Vardeman-Winter, 2018). Third, homogeneity and homophily are clear obstacles that are preventing the D&I needle from moving at a needed pace. While some urgency has been building in the trade press indicating an understanding of the severity of the problem, diversity efforts are not necessarily turning into retention and impactful structural change. Fourth, there seems to be a lack of direction in how to move forward, how to build inclusive cultures and structures and no clear sense of D&I best practices and measurement at an industry level. Strong and vocal leaders who walk the talk are rare, and accountability on D&I is clearly missing. This is a case of leadership failure.

There has been a notable surge in the D&I discourse and language emanating from the industry after the 2020 racial and social unrest. Promises are being made and urgency is being expressed. The ride ahead is still uphill, and bold and courageous leaders who are genuine and passionate about D&I, in talk and in walk, are needed.

Leadership theory

Many decades of scholarship have given us much insight into the topic of leadership. However, given the complexity of the topic and the increasing complexity of the world we live in, leadership research continues to unfold and inform. According to C. E. Johnson and Hackman (2018), the various definitions of leadership can be thematized around three foci: (1) who the leader is/should be (traits), (2) how the leader acts/should act (behavior) and (3) how the leader works/should work with others (relationship building). The bulk of leadership scholarship positions the leader-follower dualistic relationship as the core focus of study and conceptualizes leadership in individualistic ways. More recent scholarship since the turn of the century has been moving toward more relational, dispersed, dynamic and dialogic conceptualizations of leadership which are needed in an increasingly complex, diverse, unpredictable and interconnected world; models that presume stability are no longer sufficient (Ferdman, 2021; Moss, 2019).

Earlier theories

From the 1940s to the early 1960s leadership research revolved around two aspects of leadership: task focus (authoritarian style focused on getting work accomplished) and interpersonal focus (concerned with people and building relationships). Certain distinct patterns or schools of thought on leadership emerged. First, there was the traits approach which assumed that leaders are born and that natural leaders have certain traits, i.e., cognitive and psychological abilities, skills, status, education, physical characteristics and so on. This perspective has been challenged since the late 1940s since first, no consistent pattern of traits could be identified that differentiated leaders from followers and second, traits research only focused on leaders and ignored the impact of followers (Berger & Meng, 2014b; Gill, 2011). There also arose a situational leadership body of work which investigated how situational factors (e.g., nature of the task/work, the quality of leader-follower relations, context, etc.) impact leadership effectiveness. Situational leadership emphasizes leader flexibility and prescribes that based on the situation, the leader should adopt directive or supportive behaviors with the prime goal of developing followers (Northouse, 2022).

The above approaches focus on the traits of leaders and followers. Another approach that followed was functional leadership, which studies the behaviors of leaders and the quality of the relationship between leaders and followers and how that, in turn, impacts the productivity and satisfaction level of followers. Leader-member exchange theory is one prominent line of research that focuses on the leader-follower relationship. Another approach developed by Robert Greenleaf in 1970 was the servant leader style. Servant leaders put those they lead before themselves and see follower empowerment and development as their primary mission. While this is a good model for non-profit leadership, several for-profit companies (e.g., Southwest Airlines, Aflac) have also adopted this approach successfully (C. E. Johnson & Hackman, 2018).

In the 1980s, fueled by much enthusiasm and inspired by the work of James McGregor Burns (1978), a body of scholarship focusing on transformational (as compared to transactional) leadership began to develop. While transactional leadership treats the leader-follower relationship as primarily a transaction (i.e., work done for expected reward), the transformational approach focuses on change through leaders who aim to appeal to the higher order and intellectual needs of their followers. Related models are the visionary and charisma models where the focus is on a heroic and charismatic leader who brings about great (and much needed) organizational change; leaders and followers are both elevated through their relationship (Gill, 2011). Leaders who aim for transformation and follower empowerment, according to Kouzes and Posner (2017), need to (1) model the way, (2) inspire a shared vision, (3) challenge the process, (4) enable others to act and (5) encourage the heart. A more recent stream of transformational leadership research is the notion of the authentic leader. An authentic leader is self-aware, performs with relational transparency (genuineness), engages in balanced processing (fair decision-making considering multiple perspectives) and has an internalized moral perspective. In other words, authentic leaders "are self-regulating leaders who are positive role models for their followers because they behave in accordance with their morals and values despite contradictory pressures" (Boekhorst, 2015, p. 246; see also Cottrill, Lopez, & Hoffman, 2014; Gardner, Avolio, Luthans, May, & Walumbwa, 2005).

Other foci in leadership scholarship have included vision, strategy, ethics, conflict management, leadership during crises, power, influence, leader development and cultural intelligence (C. E. Johnson & Hackman, 2018; Northouse, 2022). While D&I has received some attention, its importance in relation to leadership began to be emphasized in scholarship only a little over a decade ago.

More recent turns in scholarship

With the speeding up of globalization since the 1990s, what it means to be a leader is also changing. Universal definitions are not suitable for different leadership phenomena and contexts. The world itself has become more interconnected and unpredictable and we are living in an age of cultural dynamism and "complex connectivity" (Tomlinson, 1999, p. 2). According to Connerly and Pedersen (2005), "Complexity is our friend and not our enemy because it protects us from accepting easy answers to hard questions" and allows us to enhance our leadership scholarship to stay in pace with changing times (p. 28). Complexity exhorts us to look at leadership as a process and emphasizes the importance of ethics and D&I in a world where trust in leadership is waning (Edelman, 2013; Maak & Pless, 2006a; Maritz, Pretorius, & Plant, 2011).

The main critique of the earlier scholarship on leadership is that the heroic "great man" theories it generated are too leader-centric and individualistic and do not pay enough attention to the phenomenon of leadership itself, which is a complex and dynamic process involving many stakeholders, contexts and actors (Bolden 2011; Gill, 2011). Avolio, Walumbwa and Weber (2009) specifically point out:

> Perhaps one of the most interesting omissions in theory and research on leadership is the absence of discussions of followership and its impact on leadership. Leadership researchers treat follower attributes as outcomes of the leadership process as opposed to inputs ….
>
> *(p. 434)*

Fairhurst (2007), who takes a social constructionist and discursive approach in her research on leadership, argues that leadership is a "distributed phenomenon" and that these earlier theories grant an "exaggerated agency" to leaders which results in a "rather unsophisticated leader-follower dualism" (p. 13). She emphasizes that more attention needs to be paid to the relationship between the leader and the organization and the process of organizing. Others following the distributed leadership line of inquiry have theorized leadership as more emergent (and less leader-centric), with open boundaries where a variety of needed expertise are distributed across many rather than concentrated in a few (Bolden, 2011; Gronn, 2002). Such critiques and "post-heroic" theoretical moves around the turn of the century set in motion various strands of scholarship that focus more on leadership rather than on individual leaders; leadership scholarship over the last two decades has been examining leadership as a process, focusing more on the relational and dialogic aspects, delving into complexity and highlighting the importance of leadership responsibility and accountability in a complicated world. Context, organizational culture and stakeholders have been centered more to understand leadership as a process.

Given the move toward studying leadership as a "shared phenomenon constructed across people" (Chrobot-Mason, Ruderman, & Nishii, 2013, p. 317), individualistic theories are turning into more process- and stakeholder-oriented theories emphasizing responsibility and accountability. Some scholars are paying more attention to leadership as a communicative, dialogic and discursive phenomenon (e.g., Fairhurst, 2007; Fairhurst & Connaughton, 2014; Fairhurst & Grant, 2010; Fairhurst & Putnam, 2004; Gergen & Hersted, 2016; Grint, 2005; Holladay & Coombs, 1993; C. E. Johnson & Hackman, 2018; Uhl-Bien, 2006). Arguing that communication lies at the heart of leadership in their popular multi-edition textbook, C. E. Johnson and Hackman (2018) provide a communication-based definition of leadership: "Leadership is human (symbolic) communication that modifies the attitudes and behaviors of others in order to meet shared group goals and needs" (p. 12). Others are even arguing that the very popular transformational theory belongs to the past, especially since it does not include the component of responsibility (Avolio et al., 2009; Moss, 2019; Pless & Maak, 2011). As Voegtlin (2011) explains: "Transformational leaders lead by advocating a powerful vision of the future, by setting challenging tasks or by proposing intellectually stimulating ideas. In contrast, responsible leaders create arenas where all stakeholders can engage in mutually beneficial dialogues" (p. 59). The rise in the concepts of responsible, dialogic and relational leadership, specifically from a social constructionist perspective, has been a prominent outcome of these shifts in scholarship.

Relational and dialogic leadership

Uhl-Bien (2006) makes the point that while the study of relationships in relation to leadership is not new, the explicit focus on relationships is rather recent. She describes two perspectives on studying leadership and relationships:

> … an entity perspective that focuses on identifying attributes of individuals as they engage in interpersonal relationships, and a relational perspective that views leadership as a process of social construction through which certain understandings of leadership come about and are given privileged ontology.
>
> (p. 654)

She leans toward the social constructionist approach which emphasizes the interdependent and intersubjective nature of relationship building and "centers communication processes as the vehicle in which self and world are in ongoing construction" (p. 659). Terming it a "process approach" to the study of leadership she explains that the relational approach "moves leadership beyond a focus on simply getting alignment (and productivity) or a manager's view of what is productive, to a consideration of how leadership arises through the interactions and negotiation of social order among organizational members" (pp. 672–673).

Similarly, Cunliffe and Eriksen (2011) utilize a social constructionist and relational lens to counter the drawbacks of heroic and individualistic models of leadership (see also Bushe & Marshak, 2016; Gergen & Hersted, 2016). They emphasize the importance of moral accountability and dialogue in this ontology of leadership. They describe dialogue as action and not just the pre-condition for action and elaborate that dialogue emerges through the everyday mundane interactions and communication of organizational life. Drawing upon Russian philosopher Mikhail Bakhtin's notions of polyphony (multi-voiced nature of dialogue, many stakeholders) and heteroglossia (merging and diverging meanings and ideologies that intersect in dialogue) and French philosopher Paul Ricoeur's notion of ethical selfhood (moral accountability, how we treat others), Cunliffe and Eriksen (2011) position "leadership as non-hierarchical, distributed throughout the organization as a relational practice of collaboration, empathy, trust, empowerment, etc.: something that collaborating actors 'do' within social interactions and networks of influence to construct realities…" (p. 1430). They emphasize that dialogism is intersubjective and never complete, i.e., it is ongoing and emergent in nature, and that it values "respecting differences and shaping new meanings and possibilities for action from those differences" (p. 1435). Similarly, paraphrasing Bakhtin for the workplace context, Raelin (2016) writes that "we derive truth not from our heads but from our interactions with others as we search for it" (p. 6). Elaborating on dialogue, van Loon and van Dijk (2015) explain that a dialogue:

> … is a form of conversation through which we examine and question ourselves and others on points of view, values, visions, and opinions. For individuals this means self-reflection, discovering why one thinks, feels, wants, or does something. Doing so with others implies opening up to other people's ideas and *together* arriving at a different and often new vision on a topic.
>
> *(p. 66, emphasis in original)*

They note that those wishing to engage in true dialogue should be mindful of not letting power struggles obstruct the potential of dialogue to generate new and creative meanings. To be in tune with the socially constructed reality of an organization is as, if not more, crucial than being on top of its business performance figures (Bushe & Marshak, 2016).

Endorsing the dialogic relational leadership ontology, Sugiyama, Cavanagh, van Esch, Bilimoria and Brown (2016) add that leaders need to dialogically attend to identities and intersections of identities as they play out in their organizations on a day-to-day basis to build inclusive climates. Such social capital building, or the building of inclusive and rewarding relationships, involves embodied and co-created learning. Gergen and Hersted (2016) explain that dialogic scenarios can be sustaining, generative or degenerative; the first type of scenario is not consequential in that it maintains the status quo, the second one produces new and enhanced organizational realities, whereas the third one produces negative realities and relationships that harm the organization's health. The role of inclusive and authentic leaders is to assist in the production of generative dialogue, and as Agger-Gupta and Harris (2017) write, make "the workplace a center of dignity, meaning, and community" by "forging new directions" through "profoundly respectful appreciation for and engagement of all organizational stakeholders across diversities" (p. 3). They further explain that inclusion-oriented change can only come about when those who are impacted the most are involved in the dialogic process, and when leaders are open to possibility, welcome different perspectives, are ready to move away from degenerative ways of thinking and are eager to create new knowledge dialogically along with the combined wisdom of all organizational stakeholders.

Noting that the dominant narrative of the stable organization and the heroic leader is in the past and that we now inhabit a diverse and interdependent world marked by complexity, ambiguity, uncertainty and volatility, Bushe and Marshak (2016) endorse what they call the "dialogic mindset" as the suitable way forward (see also Raelin, 2016; van Loon & van Dijk, 2015). Embracing the social constructionist view of organizational reality and meaning production, they emphasize:

> The Dialogic Mindset assumes that what happens in organizations is influenced more by how people interact and make common meaning than by how presumably objective factors and forces impact the organization. This also means that attending to, listening to, and including marginalized or excluded voices is critical for innovation in a diverse world with a complex array of factors, influences, and stakeholders.
>
> *(p. 45)*

Taking a narrative view on socially constructed organizational realities, they make the case that dialogic leaders help develop, not impose, new storylines or narratives to make sense of and work through emerging complexities and new realities. Furthermore, they write that:

> … the leader may have to encourage disruption to existing narratives and patterns of meaning-making to create the necessary stimulus for innovation and adaptation. In the latter case, the leader is, in effect, doing the very opposite of the visionary narrative. Rather than show people the way forward, the leader shows them that the current way is no longer tenable and must be thrown out.
>
> *(p. 49)*

As new narratives collectively emerge through generative dialogue, the role of the leader is to help shape new behavior and action. Change occurs when people start talking and communicating differently to produce new realities (Bardhan & Engstrom, 2021; Raelin, 2016). Instead of solo-authoring heroic and grand visions, the dialogic and inclusive leader helps create conditions and spaces that unleash needed change and allow newness and new meanings to emerge.

True dialogical leaders are able to transcend their egos in that they are able to merge with the collective without losing their sense of self and leader identity. Raelin (2016) terms this form of non-leader-centric and intersubjective leadership "collective agency." Such leadership does not focus on any one individual but on what can be invited, enabled and unleashed collectively by people working together:

> Once participants to dialogue make this connection, they acquire intellectual humility, empathy, and courage to challenge standard ways of operating ... agents would model such behaviors as tolerance of ambiguity, openness and frankness, patience and suspension of judgment, empathy and unconditional positive regard, and commitment to learning. Learners themselves would "learn through" their own problems, while the change agent would offer resource suggestions, alternative framings, as well as reflections on "learning how to learn."
>
> *(pp. 26, 29)*

This form of agency does not extinguish the individual, instead it merges the individual into a collective "we" that is embedded in a specific social context and confident in what can be accomplished collectively across power and other differentials.

Responsible leadership

Responsible leadership is a combination of research on social responsibility and leadership (Waldman, 2011). Influenced by leadership scholar Joanne Cuilla's work on ethics and leadership, Nicola Pless and Thomas Maak started developing the concept of responsible leadership which shifts the focus from the individual as leader to leaders in relationship with stakeholders (see Cuilla, 1995, 1998). They write: "Responsible leadership is a specific frame of mind promoting a shift from purely economistic, positivist and self-centered mind-set to a frame of thinking that has all the constituents and thus the common good in mind too" (Maak & Pless, 2006b, pp. 1–2). A responsible leader needs to work with "relational intelligence" (Maak & Pless, 2006c, p. 105) and be able to think through multiple ideological perspectives (Waldman, 2011).

Maak and Pless (2006c) explain how stakeholder theory itself has changed with time since its inception in the 1980s. It has morphed from conceptualizing stakeholders as "means to corporate ends" and taken on more moral tones, is less instrumental and more normative, and its "underlying individualistic and masculine assumptions" have been challenged from a feminist perspective which emphasizes the quality of interactions and relationships (p. 102). This transformed version of stakeholder theory informs the scholarship on responsible leadership. They further explain:

> Leadership legitimacy does not come with position, status, reward or coercive power. It is only in and through the stakeholder relations that

leadership legitimacy can be earned from stakeholders as followers. And it is only in a process of co-creation of all parties involved that commonly shared objectives can be achieved.

(Maak & Pless, 2006c, p. 104)

In this form of leadership scholarship, the leader is considered a stakeholder in the larger mix who has the added responsibility of building relational (i.e., social) capital (Jones, 2014). A responsible leader is "a good *weaver* in the web of humanity" (Maak & Pless, 2006a, p. 50, emphasis in original) and is able to perform a "gestalt" of the following roles: a steward who navigates complexity, uncertainty and change; an active citizen both inside and outside the organization (private/organizational and public spheres); a visionary who is able to engage stakeholders in building realistic and achievable visions; a servant who puts the community and stakeholders before personal fame and gain; a coach who is able to motivate, affirm and bring together people from diverse backgrounds so they can achieve their best; an architect who enables an organizational culture and structure that supports ethical performance; a storyteller and meaning enabler who aids in the creation and communication of joint sense-making (and meaning-making) and relational processes between internal and external stakeholders with both business success and the common good in mind; and a change agent who mobilizes and guides stakeholders in the process of responsible change in complex times (Maak & Pless, 2006c, pp. 108–112).

Several scholars have now produced fruitful research on responsible leadership (e.g., Miska, Hilbe, & Mayer, 2014; Voegtlin, Patzer, & Scherer, 2012) and as Maak and Pless (2006b) point out, this shift from focusing on just the organization to including stakeholders inside and outside at micro, meso and macro levels is what makes this line of research distinct from previous leadership research. Also, this broader level approach is better equipped to embrace the complexity of leadership which entails "balancing external pressures of conflicting stakeholder interests with leaders' internal tensions of having to lead coherently and consistently with integrity across multiple contexts" (Miska & Mendenhall, 2018, p. 118). Relatedly, another recent line of research is that of complexity leadership. According to Uhl-Bien and Arena (2017):

In today's environment, complexity is occurring on multiple levels and across many sectors and contexts. Although many forces are driving it, the underlying factors are greater interconnectivity and redistribution of power resulting from information flows that are allowing people to link up and drive change in unprecedented ways. Complexity is transforming entire industries, with many organizations ill prepared to respond to these threats ....

(p. 10)

The authors explain that the traditional leadership response is to try and control complexity with order. However, order, which follows old logic, does not enable adaptability and can stifle creativity and needed change. Therefore, complexity leaders need to learn how to enable adaptive spaces. They must know how to work with "the collective intelligence of groups and networks" to enable emergence (p. 11).

Overall, modern leadership theories can be organized into four paradigms: classical, transactional, visionary/transformational and organic. We say "modern" because the concept of leadership has been with us since ancient times, but its formal study in our contemporary world is more recent (see Grint, 2011). The first three paradigms uphold the concept of the solo or heroic leader. The organic paradigm, which is most reflective of our times, is post-heroic and dynamic and theorizes leadership through ideas such as complexity, networks, stakeholders, collaboration, responsibility, change, inclusion, dialogue, emergence and so on. It conceptualizes leadership as a process and distributed phenomenon and pays close attention to stakeholders, social responsibility and relationships (Gill, 2011).

One current critique that needs more attention is that extant leadership theories have a definite North American bias (Eagly & Chin, 2010). All theories involving human relations develop in cultural contexts and the same applies to leadership theory. Leadership theories and knowledge cannot be taken as universal, i.e., we cannot assume that leadership styles and concepts that apply in North America will work all over the world (Ensari & Riggio, 2021). We live and work in a hyperconnected world, but this does not mean that differences have disappeared. In fact, we engage more with difference now than ever before. If we are going to emphasize the importance of D&I in leadership theory, then diverse leaderships theories from various cultural and societal contexts must be developed and included in the repertoire of leadership theory in order to avoid imperialism in the realm of knowledge production on the subject. We now turn to the matter of leadership theory and D&I.

Leadership theory and D&I

Popular textbooks on leadership state that D&I is an ethical imperative connected to social justice and that leaders need to see it as such (e.g., C. E. Johnson & Hackman, 2018; Northouse, 2022). However, research at the intersection of D&I and leadership is fairly recent within the long history of research on leadership (Chin, 2010; Chrobot-Mason et al., 2013; Gallegos, 2014). According to Chin (2010):

> Although leadership theories have evolved and reflect changing social contexts, they remain silent on issues of equity, diversity, and social justice. Theories of leadership need to be expanded to incorporate diversity if

they are to be relevant for the 21st century amidst new social contexts, emerging global concerns, and changing population demographics.

(p. 150)

It is harder to lead in more diverse environments rather than in more homogenous ones, and our theorizing has not sufficiently grappled with this complexity yet (Dreachslin, 2007). Creating goals and visions across differences, especially inequity-based differences, is not an easy task, and leaders increasingly must be able to do so at individual, relational, organizational and societal levels (Chrobot-Mason et al., 2013; Ferdman, 2021; Gallegos, 2014; Mor Barak, 2017).

Being in a leadership position means one has more power/authority and privilege compared to other organizational members. Leaders' "position as decision and policy makers, as well as organizational role models, places leaders in an unparalleled position to guide the diversity management efforts of their organizations" (Offermann & Matos, 2007, p. 280). Therefore, from an ethics and responsibility perspective, leaders must remember that what they say and do (or do not say and do) impacts others and have societal consequences (C. E. Johnson, 2007). Another ethics-related matter is that many organizations are talking the D&I talk but are not necessarily walking the walk. According to Gallegos (2014):

> Unfortunately, many organizations today have gotten on the bandwagon of celebrating diversity and including language to that effect in their mission statements without doing the deeper work to make their organizational reality align with their [espoused] aspirations. They – and particularly their leaders – need to pay attention to consistency between espoused values and demonstrable behaviors in organizations.
>
> *(pp. 196–197)*

The lack of leaders who are trained to effectively and genuinely engage diversity and foster inclusive climates is a problem that could, and does, give rise to scenarios of unauthentic communication. When words seem insincere, then leadership credibility is put in question (Mor Barak, Luria, & Brimhall, 2021; Simons, Leroy, Collewaert, & Masschelein, 2015). Leaders today, instead of neglecting D&I, must realize that how they orient toward diversity makes a significant difference. For example, in a study of the relationship between diverse teams and leadership, Homan and Greer (2013) found that considerate leadership is preferred by diverse teams and improves team functioning. Leaders also need to be open to learning from diverse employees, who may be at more subordinate and junior levels, so that they can see how taken-for-granted organizational structures and practices tend to favor the already privileged. They must be open to making some real cultural, structural and systemic changes (Gallegos, 2014; Offermann & Matos, 2007).

The responsibility of scholars is to theorize the relationship between leadership and D&I in ways that will aid movement in this direction.

Inclusive leadership

Inclusive leadership is a necessary leadership skill and priority in increasingly diverse workplaces. It has been categorized as falling within the relational approach to leadership (Mor Barak et al., 2021; Roberson & Perry, 2021) and has been receiving more academic attention in the last two decades and especially in the last ten years. In the past few years, there has also been a surge in the popularity of the topic of inclusive leadership in the popular trade press. However, organizations are lagging when it comes to practicing inclusion (Chitkara, 2018; Chrobot-Mason & Roberson, 2022).

Thompson and Matkin (2020) conducted a search through Ebscohost for scholarly articles on inclusive leadership and found 133 articles between 2000 and 2009 and 421 articles between 2010 and 2019. The scholarship on inclusive leadership, however, still needs to align more with diversity scholarship since, and as mentioned earlier, practicing inclusivity in more diverse workplaces is more challenging than practicing inclusivity in more homogenous settings not marked by high levels of identity and power differentials (Chrobot-Mason & Roberson, 2022; Dreachslin, 2007). The scholarship that engages diversity with inclusive leadership has begun but still has a long way to go. As Mor Barak et al. (2021) put it, "researchers have a narrow understanding of the process in which inclusion climates emerge," and that while the idea that leaders shape organizational climate is an old notion, little is known about how they can, in everyday practice, marshal diversity to create inclusive climates (p. 2).

According to Ferdman (2021), "inclusive leadership serves a pivotal role as a fulcrum or force multiplier to foster and magnify inclusion at micro and macro levels and to connect micro and macro aspects of inclusion" (p. 5). Emphasizing the layered micro/meso/macro continuum (see also Mor Barak, 2005), he states the work of inclusive leadership is an active process that values a form of human/social capital that values people *because* of their differences and not *despite* their differences; inclusive leadership is anti-homogeneity, challenges what is accepted as normal, and calls out and addresses structural and cultural inequities in the workplace. Several scholars have pointed out the need for what van Knippenberg, van Ginkel and Homan (2013) call a "diversity mindset" and emphasized that instead of just focusing on building climates devoid of discrimination the focus should also be on how to build synergy out of diversity; leaders with diversity mindsets value the benefits of diversity and work actively to create climates where diversity thrives (Leroy, Buengeler, Veestraeten, Shemla, & Hoever, 2021; Mor Barak et al., 2021; Nishii & Leroy, 2020; Shore & Chung, 2021; Shore, Cleveland, & Sanchez, 2018; van Knippenberg & van Ginkel, 2021).

Mor Barak et al. (2021) explain that one of the main obstacles in the path of building such climates is when senior leaders develop policies and processes to reflect their D&I values but do not ensure these get enacted throughout the organization. The authors state that when such decoupling of words and actions (or a policy-practice gap) occurs, those who are already privileged tend not to notice but those from marginalized groups notice right away (see also Shore & Chung, 2021). They write: "We argue that both forms of inclusive leadership, leaders who create inclusive workplace policies and leaders who carry out the day-to-day practice of inclusion, are critical to fostering a work group climate for inclusion" (p. 9). Inclusive leaders are accountable for implementation, responsible for clearly explaining the diversity values/needs/purposes of their organizations and working on aligning the workplace with the same (Creary, 2021).

While still much research is needed on how to build more inclusive workplace climates, a more recent line of inquiry offers useful theoretical insights for leaders. In the last chapter, we explained that inclusive climates require that people in organizations feel like they belong and are also valued for their uniqueness in their contributions to the work of the organization (Brewer, 1991; Shore et al., 2011). Shore et al. (2011) have heuristically applied Brewer's (1991) optimal distinctiveness theory to the concept of inclusion. Optimal distinctiveness theory explains that people feel the need to be connected to groups through feelings of similarity, symbolic attachment and belonging and that they simultaneously also feel the need for uniqueness and individuation (i.e., not be lumped altogether into a group identity). This dual and dialectical need must be recognized and valued by inclusive leaders, and they must understand their role in how to accomplish and maintain this balance and productive tension. Shore et al. (2011) do point out that depending on context, one need may be greater than the other, and define inclusion "as the degree to which an employee perceives that he or she is an esteemed member of the work group through experiencing treatment that satisfies his or her needs for belongingness and uniqueness" (p. 1265). They describe feelings of inclusion and exclusion as existing on a continuum (high belonging/high uniqueness – low belonging/low uniqueness) (for a similar continuum approach to inclusion-exclusion see Mor Barak, 2005). The unique contribution of this approach to inclusion is that it points out the need to balance opposite seeming feelings rather than focusing on just belonging (which can lead to glossing over important differences). According to DiTomaso (2021), inclusion is the ability to work together and connect on a superordinate identity without erasing or downplaying social and cultural identities. The approach of Shore et al. (2011) foregrounds the important role that differences can play in creating climates of inclusion – the key is to develop a positive attitude toward how differences can work creatively to produce belonging.

In another recent study, Randel et al. (2018) also highlight the lack of theory building on inclusive leadership and point out that the scant scholarship that exists focuses primarily on belongingness. They build on social identity theory and optimal distinctiveness theory to explore this dual dynamic of inclusive leadership and offer behavioral advice on how to achieve this balance (see Chapter 7 for more details). The authors emphasize that inclusive leaders serve as role models for others and should strive to make such practices and behaviors a normal part of the organizational culture. Several recent studies that have followed in the footsteps of Shore et al. (2011) and Randel et al. (2018) offer more support for the important role of balancing belonging and uniqueness in creating climates of inclusion (e.g., Mor Barak et al., 2021; Shore & Chung, 2021; van Knippenberg & van Ginkel, 2021). Even more recently, Chrobot-Mason and Roberson (2022) offered another theoretical model for inclusive leadership with the aim of developing more conceptual clarity. This model has three components: (1) antecedent conditions (leader characteristics, group diversity cognitions, organizational policies and practices), (2) behaviors (inclusive leader behaviors) and (3) outcomes (e.g., psychological safely, creativity and innovation). They state leaders must be self-reflexive, open to learning the skills they lack, and not resist the challenges of building diversity mindsets and inclusive climates: "Seeking out challenges often forces leaders outside their comfort zone; yet this is exactly what must happen for them to become more confident and capable of fostering inclusion" (p. 338).

So how do leaders create and institutionalize inclusive environments in increasingly diverse organizations? What must they believe, know, communicate and do? Scholarship has started enumerating the skills and qualities needed for leaders to genuinely engage in pro-diversity inclusion efforts. First and foremost, inclusive leaders must be advocates of the moral case for D&I, be very aware of the various asymmetries and power differentials (especially historic ones) in society and specifically within their industry/organization and work reflexively through a pluralistic lens (DiTomaso, 2021; Roberson & Perry, 2021; Smith, 2021; van Knippenberg & van Ginkel, 2021). According to Shore and Chung (2021):

> Marginalized employees have backgrounds and experiences that are quite different than those who are privileged, and the expectation that majority member norms should be operational, inflexible, and unchanged in an organization, that all members should know and effectively follow the 'rules of the game' is both unrealistic and unfair. … By implementing equitable practices, recognizing that not everyone has had the same advantages, opportunities, or experiences, the leader can ensure a more welcoming and inclusive environment that facilitates the experience of being an insider for all members of the work group.
>
> *(p. 21)*

They add that inclusive leaders should also constantly seek feedback to make sure those they are leading are treating others inclusively.

It is necessary for senior leadership to be personally involved in D&I. According to Shore, Cleveland and Sanchez (2018), "In sum, the research on organizational inclusion practices emphasizes the role of top management in building and supporting an environment in which members of all social identity groups can be authentic while also being treated fairly and respectfully" (pp. 180–181). Leaders must work to build a diverse pipeline at all levels, take responsibility for structural and cultural changes that support retention and equity, work to reduce status differences between group, diminish the leader-follower duality without losing their sense of leader identity, build accountability structures for themselves and others, address subtle discriminations, humanize all employees, help build psychological safety and empowerment and leverage diversity for business enhancement (Gallegos, 2014; Mor Barak et al., 2016, 2021; Nishii & Leroy, 2020; Roberson & Perry, 2021; Shore & Chung, 2021; Shore et al., 2018)

How leaders communicate about D&I matters a lot (Bardhan & Engstrom, 2021; C. E. Johnson & Hackman, 2018; Shore et al., 2018). Wasserman, Gallegos and Ferdman (2008) write that inclusive leaders must create a "meta-narrative" or story of what inclusive culture means and how to accomplish it. Inclusive leaders must communicate that diversity is an opportunity. Too often, diversity gets narrated as a problem, and this creates a negative frame for D&I efforts. According to Chrobot-Mason et al. (2013), "Leaders are unlikely to be successful at creating an inclusive climate for diversity unless they convey a convincing narrative that focuses on the opportunities afforded by successful management of diversity" (p. 330). While leaders should not suggest that the work of D&I is easy, clear communication of its purpose and benefits must be communicated so that the challenge is accepted willingly.

Inclusive leaders must be role models. They are the architects of organizational climate and culture. While they are not solely in charge of climate building (and should not be either, according to relational and dialogic models of leadership), they are instrumental in shaping perceptions and meanings (i.e., they do occupy positions of power and responsibility). Boekhorst (2015) states that leaders who visibly demonstrate inclusive behaviors help others learn this behavior and that such behavior, when emulated, should be rewarded; in other words, "Organizational reward systems that reward inclusive behaviors are positively related to vicarious learning of inclusive behaviors by followers" (p. 253). Inclusive leaders must also avoid boxing people into simple identity categories and instead treat them "as unique combinations of values, preferences and needs" (Offermann & Matos, 2007, p. 288). They must understand that identity is not static, not essentialize identity, emphasize and not erase complexity, and work to create alliances across identities at all levels (Smith, 2021). This helps in checking pigeonholing, stereotyping and reducing the complexity of employees' identities and promotes intersectional mindsets.

Inclusive leaders must engage in the creation of climates that embrace standpoint plurality which, in turn, can aid in building relational/social capital with internal and external stakeholders and allow for the continuous and dynamic emergence of viewpoints (Booysen, 2014). Finally, inclusive leaders must possess the humility to recognize privilege, and the courage to make necessary changes to entrenched (normalized) practices that maintain inequities. According to Smith (2021), "What makes something a form of institutional inequity is when it limits access, success, or participation by individuals or groups who would otherwise be successful" (p. 294). According to Gallegos (2014): "The adaptive work of inclusion needs to be broad enough to encompass the heart and the head, and to develop strategies and practices that challenge dominant organizational paradigms and redress ways of being long held as sacrosanct" (p. 179). Inclusive leaders must also recognize that the work of D&I is never fully done and that it is an ongoing process.

A recent study conducted by Deloitte identified six traits of an inclusive leader (most of which overlap with the skills and traits enumerated above): commitment to D&I, curiosity or the desire to understand different viewpoints, courage to challenge the status quo, cultural intelligence, cognizance of bias and the ability to collaborate across difference for greater creativity and innovation; additionally, some of the primary characteristics associated with these traits are humility, openness, adaptability, the ability to cope with ambiguity and belief in fair play (Dillon & Bourke, 2016). A more recent study building on the six traits asked those who rate leaders what they consider to be the most important qualities for inclusive leadership; raters responded that inclusive leaders should constantly challenge their own biases and learn from those around them and that they should demonstrate humility, perspective-taking skills and genuine empathy (Bourke & Titus, 2020). Additionally, a Catalyst study of inclusive leadership in six countries found four key elements across all countries: inclusive leaders (1) help those who report directly to them feel empowered regarding their performance and career enhancement, (2) display humility, are able to admit mistakes and limitations and are willing to improve by learning from criticism and alternate viewpoints, (3) are courageous and do the right thing even in the face of possible negative consequences and (4) help build accountability at all levels, including leadership (see Bommel, Shaffer, Travis, & Foust-Cummings, 2021).

Overall, the work of inclusive leaders must be intentional, and they must pay attention to the role of identities and power differentials on the micro to macro continuum. Employees do not stick around in organizations where they do not feel welcome, i.e., diversity just does not work without inclusion. Leaders who pay attention to D&I purely for compliance reasons are not true champions of D&I; genuine belief in the value of D&I is necessary (Chrobot-Mason et al., 2013). Winters (2021) explains the importance of creating brave spaces, which she says is one step forward from creating safe spaces. Brave spaces are spaces where people can learn how to engage with discomfort knowing they will be cut some slack because the goal of these spaces is for diverse individuals who are there willingly to listen and learn from each other and attempt to find some common ground and purpose across differences. Inclusive leaders must be able to work with diversity in ways that help create such spaces.

Theorizing leadership through the lens of D&I

While it is important to identify leadership skills and attitudes that aid in building diversity and fostering inclusion, that is not enough. Traditional leadership theories themselves do not account for diversity (Chin & Trimble, 2015; Gallegos, 2014; van Knippenberg & van Ginkel, 2021). That is, D&I must be an inherent part of the theorizing process itself, and not treated as an add-on to existing leadership theories which are assumed to be universal. According to Chin (2010), "Attention to diversity means paradigm shifts in our theories of leadership so as to make them inclusive; it means incorporating explanations of how dimensions of diversity shape our understanding of leadership" (p. 150). That is, our understanding and theorizing of leadership should be guided primarily by D&I.

Chin and Trimble (2015) question dominant (North American) models of leadership that are presented as universal but are based on research that has excluded the experiences of non-dominant identity leaders and employees; such theories are based primarily on the experiences of the "power elite" (White, heterosexual, Protestant male leader prototype) (p. 10) (see also Ensari & Riggio, 2021; Logan, 2011). According to these authors, in our increasingly diversifying societies around the world, traditional leadership theories "remain silent on issues of equity, diversity, and social justice" (p. 40). They elaborate that a D&I paradigm for leadership theory needs to do several things:

- Position difference (rather than homogeneity) as the starting point or lens for developing leadership theory. Developing D&I-focused leadership theory does not mean adding D&I onto existing models and theories; rather "it means incorporating how dimensions of diversity shape our understanding of leadership" (Chin & Trimble, 2015, p. 22).
- Take into account the cultural contexts in which leadership is enacted since it deeply impacts leadership performance.
- Take into account how experiences of inequity, oppression and marginalization shape the leadership styles of leaders of non-dominant identities.
- Take into account how interactions across various types of differences and inequities impact workplaces and how leaders need to lead ethically and inclusively in such environments. Emphasize that leaders need to be multiculturally competent to lead within diversity.

- Take into account the workings of power differentials, privilege and marginalization (e.g., how marginalization can restrict access to senior leadership positions, the challenges faced by leaders from marginalized groups who lead in dominant identity settings).
- Emphasize that leaders need to be change agents who value diversity and promote inclusion and equity through a "power with" (or empowerment, power sharing) rather than "power over" (top-down) approach.

In sum, new leadership theories that organically account for D&I and use D&I as the primary sense-making lens are needed. Some of the more recent dialogic, relational and responsible leadership scholarship is moving in this direction.

There have been convincing arguments in favor of the transformational leadership model as being best suited to D&I since transformational leaders are able to (or at least expected to) inspire all employees across differences, value what each individual brings to the organization and generate team spirit (e.g., Chrobot-Mason et al., 2013). However, as explained earlier, current theorizing on leadership is moving away from individualistic and leader-follower dualistic models of leadership (Eagly & Chin, 2010). While transformational leadership certainly does emphasize follower empowerment, the model is still individualistic and adheres to the leader-follower dualism. This puts it in the more traditional leadership theory category (Gallegos, 2014). According to Uhl-Bien, Marion and McKelvey (2007), the drawback of traditional leadership theories is their focus on influential acts of individuals and not on the fact that these acts are embedded within larger and complex interactions of many forces. The more relational and dialogic stakeholder-oriented models that conceptualize leadership as a distributed and shared phenomenon and emphasize responsibility and complexity are more suitable springboards for theorizing the intersection of leadership and D&I. As Booysen (2014) states, "Inclusive leadership thinking falls squarely in the relationship-based process and follower-focused, less-dominant way of leadership thinking" (p. 303). While the leader's role and support are no doubt instrumental for D&I success, the very nature of D&I necessitates that the leader cannot be the sole architect and visionary when it comes to an organization's D&I journey: both D&I and leadership are distributed phenomena and must be theorized as such.

Leadership models conducive to D&I also need to have a social justice, accountability, equity and complexity focus (Roberson & Perry, 2021). The responsible, relational and dialogic leadership concepts described in the previous section lend themselves to this focus. According to Maak and Pless (2006a): "Insight and foresight, empathy and listening skills, self-knowledge and a sense of community, moral imagination and a morally sound values base are among the hallmarks of a responsible leader" (p. 12). Such leaders are not heroic individuals standing above others but enmeshed in a web of stakeholders in which the emphasis is on weaving inclusive relationships across similarities and differences. The leader is not assumed to be an autonomous individual contained within a vessel but an effect of intersubjective interactions and communication with all stakeholders. Uhl-Bien (2006) writes that the relational approach "changes the focus from the individual to the collective dynamic" and "leadership is an *outcome* of relational dynamics" (p. 662, emphasis added). Diverse organizations are complex and marked by rich connectivity which means that when two things interact, they can change each other in unexpected ways (Uhl-Bien & Arena, 2017). Such dynamic environments are full of potential for the emergence of new and creative possibilities and solutions to challenges. However, to allow the outcomes of rich connectivity to emerge, we need complexity leaders who can enable adaptive spaces. Therefore, any theorizing on leadership and D&I must take complexity into account. Old logics, assumptions and ideas of order and leadership cannot be imposed on emerging realities if we want D&I to flourish and grow.

Our final point about theorizing leadership through the lens of D&I is the need for an intersectional approach so that our understanding and practice can be synchronous with the complexity of diverse identities in a hyperconnected world (Chin, 2010; Ferdman, 2014). As emphasized in the previous chapters, this is the direction scholars of D&I and those working on D&I and public relations are also urging. Identity is a complex phenomenon, and we do not live our lives through singular identity categories. While one or more categories may be more salient than others in particular contexts, we are a. gestalt and interplay of several identity categories that we perform in complex and dynamic ways in various settings. Our theorizing on leadership and D&I needs to reflect this intersectionality so that we can "move away from the etic treatment of diversity as a static and pre-determined notion that transcends time and place" (Tatli & Özbilgin, 2012, p. 181). However, while the identities of leaders and stakeholders are intersectional, D&I programs in organizations continue to conceptualize identity in compartmentalized ways. This does not match lived reality and can, in fact, have an adverse impact when peoples' complex intersectional identities are force fitted into simple boxes (Kelly & Smith, 2014). This outdated way of thinking about difference, identity and D&I needs to change. Approaching leadership theory through an intersectional lens is one way of shifting the paradigm on how we theorize the intersection of leadership and D&I (Chin, 2010).

Intersectionality is emphasized by two more recent leadership studies conducted by Deloitte (Kelly & Smith, 2014; Smith, Turner, & Levit, 2018). Both of these studies emphasize that one of the primary reasons behind the push for the intersectional approach is that newer generations (Gen Z and millennials) and increasing diversity are making D&I a more complex phenomenon in US society and around the world and that older models of diversity simply do not work anymore. The millennials, who will constitute about 75% of the workforce by 2030 and who are increasingly moving into leadership positions, "are generally more focused on being valued for the multiplicity of their identities – their *whole self* – as opposed to just those conventional delineations to which they belong" (Kelly & Smith, 2014, p. 3, emphasis in original). As discussed in Chapter 2, along with Gen Z, they comprise the most diverse generation in the history of the United States, they are highly dedicated to social justice issues, they expect the organizations they work for to be involved in social activism, and they believe that D&I should be an organic part of the work environment (Diversity Best Practices [Seramount], 2017). Therefore, how they understand and enact D&I needs more attention in leadership theory. According to Kelly and Smith (2014):

> To respond to these changing expectations, organizations must fundamentally change and, potentially, reject old models of diversity, and focus instead on the multiplicity of employee experience and identity. This requires a drastic shift in the expectations and competencies of leaders and the cultures they create.
>
> *(p. 4)*

The good news is that millennials overwhelmingly perceive D&I in terms of possibility and have a high level of "connectional intelligence" (Smith, Turner, & Levit, 2018, p. 5). This is a distinct shift from past generations and their tendency to frame D&I as an obstacle to overcome. Additionally, "millennials are more likely to define diversity as pertaining to the individual mix of unique experiences, identities, ideas, and opinions. Older participants, on the other hand, frame diversity in terms of demographics, equal opportunity, and representation of identifiable demographic characteristics" (Smith, Turner, & Levit, 2018, p. 4).

Overall, leadership scholarship needs to continue foregrounding D&I in ways that highlight accountability, intersectionality, responsibility, equity, dialogue, relationality, complexity and the moral imperative that drives the D&I charge. Against the backdrop of this leadership literature, we now review how leadership has been theorized in public relations scholarship specifically.

Theorizing leadership for public relations

The body of research on leadership and public relations is slim but growing. While concepts related to leadership (e.g., management, strategy, relationship building) have been studied for a while, the direct study of leadership itself is more recent (Aldoory & Toth, 2004).

Two of the earliest studies (Aldoory, 1998; Aldoory & Toth, 2004) focused on leadership through the lens of gender. In a qualitative in-depth interview study that explored language use and the behavioral intentions of women public relations practitioners and educators, findings showed that the respondents viewed vision and compassion as important aspects of leadership (Aldoory, 1998). They reported using both two-way and one-way communication and interactive (power-sharing and participative management) approaches and being capable of assertiveness as well as sensitivity in communication depending on context and situation. Aldoory described them as "situational" rhetors and as possessing the qualities of transformational leaders. Soon after, Aldoory and Toth (2004) conducted a study of leadership and gender to examine what style of leadership is best suited to public relations and if there are any gender differences in perceptions. Findings from a quantitative survey and focus groups showed a strong preference for transformational over transactional leadership style as being more suitable for public relations leaders with some support for situational leadership. Transactional leadership was perceived as more masculine (i.e., top-down, task-oriented) and transformational leadership as more marked by traits considered to be feminine (e.g., empowerment, focus on relationships). Several respondents reported women make better leaders in public relations even though in practice men dominate senior leadership.

In a more recent article that reviews the state of leadership research through the lens of gender, Place and Vardeman-Winter (2018) note the continued lack of attention to the subject:

> Additional discursive, critical, and feminist inquiry is necessary in order to examine the implicit biases and assumptions associated with the concept of leadership in public relations and how they hinder women's advancement. It must also address the socially constructed and cultural expectations or stereotypes surrounding leadership in public relations.
>
> *(p. 169)*

Also, as described in Chapter 2, Logan (2011) has applied critical race theory as a lens to study industry leadership and convincingly demonstrated that the normalized leadership standard is White, male and heterosexual. There is some good news though on the gender and leadership front. Public relations firm Ketchum conducted a global leadership study over five years (2012–2016) and gathered data from over 25,000 respondents spread across five continents; they found that women are outperforming men on four of five key leadership attributes: leading by example, communicating transparently, admitting mistakes and bringing out the best in others. Additionally, feminine styles and values of leadership are projected to be the preferred models/styles for the future (Ketchum Leadership Communication Monitor, 2014, 2016). The study also found that there are glaring leadership crises in all sectors. In this overall scenario, business leaders fare the best and political leaders the worst. Leaders are not viewed as taking responsibility when falling short of expectations and not communicating effectively enough. The 2016 study added another clear finding and pointed out the existence of "stark barriers blocking equal access to leadership opportunities as a result of race, gender, disability and sexual orientation" (Ketchum Leadership Communication Monitor, 2016, p. 2). There is also a clear leaning in the findings toward non-hierarchical and dispersed (i.e., title-less) leadership. These results indicate a trend toward conceptualizing and performing leadership as a more shared and less individualistic process.

Recently, Meng and Neill (2021) undertook a thorough investigation of public relations leadership and women. They write:

> In general, women in public relations feel less engaged, less satisfied with their job status, and less optimistic about their future career development. … Being successful in the field is still a challenge for women as reflected in the actual pay gap, the limited leadership advancement opportunities, as well as the ongoing battle to be involved, heard and respected in the organizational decision-making process.
>
> *(pp. 5, 15)*

In a book length study, the authors specifically look into the top issues and the attitudinal, structural and social barriers that obstruct women's progress into leadership positions, the role of influence for women in the path to leadership, work-life balance issues and the role of mentorship in leadership advancement. The results from 51 in-depth interviews with women public relations leaders (middle and senior management levels) and a largescale survey (N = 512) of female practitioners show that while there have been some gains in leadership advancement for women, especially at the middle management level, advancement beyond that is very difficult. The top constraints observed were workplace structures, the dual pressure of balancing home and professional life and social attitudes toward women leaders. The lack of mentoring and professional networking opportunities was also noted.

In general, support for the transformational style of leadership has consistently emerged in various studies. In a study that focused on internal communication and the relationship between transformational leadership, symmetrical communication and employee attitude, Men (2014) found that "transformational leadership positively influences the organization's symmetrical communication system and employee – organization relationships" and that "symmetrical communication demonstrates large positive effect on the quality of employee–organization relationships, which in turn leads to employee advocacy" (p. 256). Previously in another study, Men and Stacks (2013) demonstrated that relationally oriented transformational communication leadership results in employee empowerment which, in turn, leads to employees viewing internal reputation favorably. Making the link between two-way symmetrical communication (which has long been the normative model for excellent public relations communication with mainly external publics; J. E. Grunig, 1992; L. A. Grunig, J. E. Grunig, & Dozier, 2002) and internal communication, Men (2014) emphasizes the important parallels between transformational leadership and two-way symmetrical communication and also recommends that this link should be further examined by taking other factors such as organizational, culture/structure and diversity into consideration. She notes that the "limited studies on leadership in public relations have primarily focused on examining the leadership styles and traits preferred by public relations leaders" (p. 257) and that there is a need to work more toward building more comprehensive theories and models (see also Meng & Berger, 2013).

Also supporting the transformative model and foregrounding the role of communication within leadership, Gregory and Willis (2013) describe the public relations leader as a strategic communicator who "is involved in all aspects of organisational life including its structures, processes and systems" (p. 101), possesses contextual intelligence, factors in all stakeholder concerns and builds relational and reputational capital for the organization. They elaborate that public relations leaders need to ensure the organization's values, link it to wider society and contribute toward building shared internal identity and community; the leader is an educator and cultural guide who "helps to set the tone and style of communication within the organisation" (p. 137) and ensures the words and behaviors of leaders and other organizational members align with espoused values, and sometimes this means playing the role of an internal activist (see also Holtzhausen, 2012) who is unafraid to point out uncomfortable truths in order to serve as the conscience of the organization.

The Plank Center's role in developing leadership research

The Plank Center for Leadership in public relations has played a prominent role in building the body of research on leadership and public relations. Established in 2005 at the University of Alabama, the Center is named after Betsy Plank who was an alumna of the university and a legendary leader in the public relations industry. Not only was she the first woman to become president of Public Relations Society of America (PRSA), she shattered the glass ceiling in many other capacities as well. One of the main goals of the Center "is to build a research-based foundation of knowledge regarding the values, qualities and dimensions of excellent leadership, mentorship and diversity and inclusion in PR" (The Plank Center Mission, n.d.).

Since its establishment, several leadership studies have been funded and supported by the Plank Center. In a qualitative interview study of senior public relations executives, Berger, Reber and Heyman (2007) found that interpersonal communication skills, internal and external networking and relationship building skills, diverse experiences and positive and proactive attitude emerged as some key leadership values in public relations. Choi and Choi

(2009) conducted a quantitative survey of PRSA members that examined leadership behaviors and found that providing employees with vision and acting as change agents were behaviors strongly associated with public relations leadership. Jin's (2010) national survey of public relations leaders found that emotional intelligence and empathy are considered top leadership skills and that there is strong support for transformational leadership. However, findings also showed that the larger the organization the more the tendency to engage in transactional leadership. Another study which surveyed PRSA members also found evidence for transformational, inclusive and participatory leadership which entails inspirational communication, innovative risk-taking and shared decision-making and problem-solving (Werder & Holtzhausen, 2009). Lee and Cheng (2010) conducted a qualitative study that showed that communication leaders are guided more by personal rather than professional codes of ethics and that followers are influenced more by leaders advocating and modeling rather than through workshops and trainings they may participate in.

According to a study by Meng, Berger, Gower and Heyman (2012) which examined the perceptions of 222 mid- and senior-level public relations executives, the top three qualities of leadership in public relations which emerged were strategic decision-making capability, problem-solving ability and communication knowledge and expertise. Other points noted were diverse on-the-job experiences, individual initiative and desire and the availability of role models. Furthermore, about half of the respondents reported that public relations leaders differ from leaders in other industries in three ways: "They must hold a compelling vision for communication, possess comprehensive understanding of media and information systems, and effectively develop and implement strategic communication plans" (p. 18). The participants also supported the practice of pluralistic leadership in public relations and perceived "leadership in the field as a dynamic activity that encompasses individual traits, attributes, behaviors, values, and context" (p. 34). Some Plank Center supported studies have examined how public relations educators teach leadership. While very few offer full courses on the topic, educators do advocate for leadership and emphasize communication knowledge and skills, strong ethical orientations and problem-solving skills as being key components of leadership education (Erzikova & Berger, 2011, 2012).

Based on a meta-analysis of leadership research initiated and supported by The Plank Center, Berger and Meng (2010) proposed that excellent public relations leaders:

1. Lead by example, engage in two-way communication and demonstrate exemplary behaviors worthy of modeling
2. Participate in strategic decision-making in organizations
3. Demonstrate a strong ethical orientation, professionalism and a propensity for doing the right thing at all times

4. Possess complex communication and rhetorical skills
5. Possess self-knowledge that guides successful interactions and relationship building and aids in further self-development
6. Possess a strong desire to lead
7. Demonstrate transformational and inclusive leadership styles that are sensitive to context/environment as well as to individual needs/differences
8. Possess passion for the profession and are able to inspire others
9. Serve as change agents capable of creating open communication environments and organizational cultures

(pp. 428–430)

In addition to distilling the above nine leadership qualities, Meng and Berger (2013) further pointed out that a lack of a "widely recognized theoretical framework of excellent leadership exists within the public relations and communication management literature and most of what has been written about leadership has its basis in practice, rather than in theory construction" (p. 142). In a move to address this theoretical gap, and based on extant research on public relations leadership, they offered a definition:

> Excellent leadership in public relations is a dynamic process that encompasses a complex mix of individual skills and personal attributes, values, and behaviors that consistently produces ethical and effective communication practice. Such practice fuels and guides successful communication teams, helps organizations achieve their goals, and legitimizes organizations in society.
>
> *(p. 143)*

They developed The Plank Center integrated model for public relations leadership comprising seven dimensions: self-dynamics, team collaboration, ethical orientation, relationship building, strategic decision-making capability, communication knowledge management capability and, finally the organizational culture and structure (i.e., the internal context) that influences the work of the leader. The self-dynamics dimension has two prongs: self-insight and the ability to inspire shared vision and project a clear path for the future. The relationship building dimension also has two prongs: internal and external relations (Berger & Meng, 2010). Additionally, in a survey-based study of senior US public relations executives, Meng (2014) further found that there is a reciprocal relationship between organizational culture and excellent public relations leadership.

In a book that applies this integrated model to 23 countries/regions including the United States, as well as probes into issues impacting public relations leadership and leader development, Berger and Meng (2014c) further describe leadership as a sense-making, sense-giving and sense-negotiating process. That is, leaders gather and make sense of information, issues and events from their internal and external environments, they help followers understand the meanings of these issues and events, and finally, sense negotiation is the "interplay of the leader's preferred meanings, and the views of other organizational members who have their own interpretations" and the leaders' attempt to "negotiate some collective understanding as the basis for subsequent decisions and actions" (p. 7). Berger and Meng (2014b) summarize past scholarship on public relations that has implications for leadership and highlight certain skills and traits necessary for effective leadership in the industry: these include the possession of a managerial worldview, diverse experience and assignments, strong communication and rhetorical skills, strong coalition building, networking and interpersonal skills, the willingness to take risks on the job, and the ability to recognize and address gender and other inequities. Past research also suggests that in-house public relations leaders need to be part of the dominant coalition, participate in strategic decision-making, understand how power relations influence organizational culture and climate, the contingent nature of leadership and the importance of context (e.g., Berger & Reber, 2006; Cameron, Cropp, & Reber, 2001; J. E. Grunig, 1992).

In the US portion of the global study (Berger, Meng, Heyman, Harris, & Bain, 2014), findings showed that public relations leaders see the need for talent, the growing complexity of the digital revolution and globalization, and the changing nature of stakeholders to be the top three challenges for the industry. These issues, leaders explained, are what they invest a lot of their time and energy in. They also emphasized the need to change organizational cultural to better engage employees, practice more transparency, strengthen internal communication which is currently considered too tight for a complex world that requires flexibility, and better understand and strategically use digital technology and social media. Some of the main barriers to effective leadership noted were internal politics, functional silos, lack of empowerment, a culture of slow decision-making, CEOs who are too controlling, and the negative history of public relations as a weak function (p. 286). It was also noted that future leaders in public relations will be better educated, will come from diverse economic backgrounds and will be more economically savvy. They will be adept data users/analyzers, bolder and more culturally aware. For all 23 countries combined, the digital revolution and the importance of soft skills (e.g., emotional intelligence, cross-cultural sensitivity and communication skills, good listening, change management and conflict resolution skills) emerged as major themes as did the fact that leaders see their own performance as much better compared to how followers view them; furthermore, across all countries, it was noted that there will be more women leaders in the future, that future leaders will be more courageous, ethically and globally minded, digitally savvy, better educated, comfortable with taking risks and committed to transparency (Berger & Meng, 2014d).

In addition to the above studies and projects, a survey developed by The Plank Center has been used to produce ongoing "report cards" (2015, 2017, 2019) of US public relations leaders to gauge organizational culture, level of employee engagement, employee satisfaction, trust in organization and leadership performance (including how they lead on D&I). Over the course of the three surveys conducted so far, the grade for all of these factors has dropped from B– to an overall C+ grade; specifically noted were increasing job disengagement among top leaders and women and increasing concern among women and men regarding two-way communication, organizational culture, diversity and shared decision-making ("Report Card on PR Leaders," n.d.). More recently, in a study that compared the views of millennials with those of managers who manage them, Meng and Berger (2018) found that millennials prefer open and positive organizational cultures, organizations that are socially responsible and committed to D&I, and that they have a strong passion for leadership. The study offers useful suggestions on how to better engage and prepare millennials for leadership positions. The Center continues to invest in and support studies that advance the body of knowledge about public relations leadership.

Support for the transformational style of leadership

As described earlier, the extant scholarship on public relations leadership shows a good amount of support for the transformational style of leadership. This growing research evidence and support for transformational leadership is a positive development in our understanding of public relations leadership; however, as some scholars (e.g., Men, 2014; Willis, 2019) have already suggested, more focus is needed on D&I. Also, along with internal organizational dimensions and culture, scholarship on public relations leadership needs to pay more attention to the environment external but connected to the organization/industry, especially given that the work of the profession is to build mutually beneficial relations with mostly external publics and stakeholders (see Mundy, 2016). This is also a crucial point when it comes to D&I since one of the ongoing critiques of the industry is that the demographic make-up of the profession does not reflect the diversity of the environment in which it exists (especially at the level of senior leadership). Conceptualizing internal and external organizational environments as being connected will help foreground the clear link between the profession and the society within which it exists and leadership's role in ensuring the two align in terms of D&I. As described earlier in the chapter, scholarship on inclusive leadership is also emphasizing the importance of factoring in the layered micro-meso-macro continuum and contexts of leadership (e.g., Ferdman, 2021; Mor Barak, 2005)

Additionally, trust and responsibility are important factors given that lack of trust in leadership is a clear problem in today's world, including the public relation profession (Edelman, 2013; Ketchum Leadership Communication Monitor, 2014, 2016; Meng, Berger, Heyman, & Reber, 2019; "Report Card on PR Leaders," n.d.). This means the role of introspection for public relations leaders/leadership (or the self-dynamics dimension of The Plank Center leadership model) needs more scholarly attention. In this vein, in a recent study based on interviews with senior public relations leaders in the United Kingdom who believe empowerment should be a central outcome of leadership, Willis (2019) emphasizes the importance of detecting the contextual constraints that prevent leaders from consistently leading in ways they would ideally like to. Arguing for more reflexivity (i.e., self-confrontation and acknowledgement of structural and cultural constraints, or what he calls "contextual intelligence"), Willis proposes that future leadership scholarship in public relations should address the complexities and nuances of leadership environments in addition to prescribing models and traits. The struggles between structure and agency faced by leaders, according to Willis, need more attention for a more enhanced and holistic understanding of the culture, practices and paradoxes of the way power works in the public relations leadership process. Adding that diversity dimensions also need to be addressed in future studies in this direction, he encourages scholars and practitioners to confront the reality that leadership is a "messier" phenomenon than normally described in literature (see also Pless & Maak, 2011). He emphasizes that through ongoing reflexivity, leaders can be more honest with themselves and others about the constraints in the path of inclusive and empowering leadership practices and devise ways to address and overcome them.

In sum, there is a clear need for further theorizing public relations leadership through the lens of D&I. Transformational leadership, while it gets much support in the profession's discourse, still maintains an individualistic focus and a leader-follower duality and scholarship has not sufficiently addressed the D&I dimensions of this form of leadership. These matters must be addressed through scholarship. While we do not recommend abandoning the goal of transformation, which is essential for D&I-oriented leadership, there is a need to move toward less dualistic and individualistic and more context and process-oriented, stakeholder-centered, dialogic and D&I-focused conceptions of leadership that emphasize responsibility, inclusivity, empathy, ethics, relationality, accountability, complexity, reflexivity and intersectionality (see Chapter 7). Such a direction aligns well with the current trends in scholarship in leadership and D&I.

Key takeaways

Leadership is a popular topic for research and a vast amount of scholarship accumulated on the subject for almost a century is available. However, the work of scholarship is ongoing. As times change, the meanings of leadership change, and new challenges and realities arise in a hyperconnected and increasingly diverse world. Following are some key takeaways from this chapter:

- Early leadership scholarship focused on traits and then moved on to models and styles (e.g., situational, transformational). The transformational style has received much attention in leadership research, including public relations leadership research.
- Research over the last two decades, which coincides with the speeding up of globalization, hyperconnectivity and the digital revolution, has increasingly focused on leadership as a process and shared phenomenon in attempts to move away from the leader-follower dualism. Stakeholders, both internal and external, are being moved more into the spotlight. Relationship building, communication, humility, inclusivity, dialogue, self-awareness, equity, empathy and other leadership values and traits considered to be feminine are rising in importance and there is a move away from individualistic "great man" theories of leadership.
- Success in D&I is impossible without leadership support. We reiterate this takeaway from previous chapters because it gets at the heart of this book. Leaders need to lead with a focus on D&I, and more research is needed at the intersection of leadership and D&I. The research that exists is quite recent and there is still a long way to go.
- Recent leadership research suggests there is a need to move away from old ways of thinking about identity and difference when it comes to D&I. There is an emphasis on intersectionality which requires us to conceptualize more than one difference at the same time. Additionally, millennials, who now comprise the majority of the workforce and are emerging as leaders, think about D&I in more intersectional ways and resist being boxed into singular categories. Also, inclusion, which has received less attention compared to diversity, needs to be foregrounded in leadership research.
- Overall, D&I should not be simply added on to existing leadership models; theorizing that approaches leadership primarily through the lens of D&I is needed. Furthermore, such theorizing must recognize that leadership engagement with D&I is ongoing and never completely done.
- Scholarship on public relations leadership is growing. Like the early general research on leadership, it has been mainly traits focused and there has been a growing interest in the relevance and applicability of the transformational style of leadership. A few scholars have offered theoretical propositions, definitions and models that are specific to public relations leadership and a few global level studies have been conducted (e.g., Aldoory & Toth, 2004; Men, 2014; Meng & Berger, 2013). The research also shows that the path to leadership for women and members of marginalized groups is fraught with various structural, social and attitudinal obstacles (Meng & Neill, 2021). While there is a recognition of the cultural complexity of

society and the work environment and an acknowledgement that future practitioners will be more culturally aware, there is no concerted focus on D&I in the scholarship on public relations leadership. This is a clear gap that needs to be addressed.

Conclusion

A few committed public relations leaders are becoming more vocal about their commitment to D&I and recognizing not only the moral imperative involved but also that our ability to see opportunity often gets buried under the negative framing of D&I as a problem and challenge. The PRSA leadership language used to unveil the 2021 D&I toolkit and strategic plan reviewed earlier suggests a turn toward valuing the moral case for D&I. Such language needs to be sustained and turned into practice, and more senior leaders need to publicly voice their support for D&I and put resources into initiatives.

On the scholarship front, more research is needed to understand the intersection of public relations leadership and D&I. According to Place and Vardeman-Winter (2018), there has been "a lack of support and prestige associated with scholarship on 'diversity issues' in public relations (compared to broader business or management issues)" (p. 166). It is fine to focus on the more functionalist and business aspects of public relations work as long as we do not ignore the other equally pressing matters that form the larger social and cultural context that shapes the stage on which we perform the many dimensions of public relations work. Diversity impacts every nook and cranny of this stage. We must recognize its importance and prioritize it in research and practice.

Overall, D&I must be a deliberate effort, it must be institutionalized, and public relations leaders need to play a major role in this charge. In order to be genuine change agents, leaders must have an accurate sense of the state of D&I in the industry and their own performance and accountability in this effort. Finally, leadership (especially senior-level leadership) itself must diversify.

5

Mind the Gap

The Story of Lackluster D&I Leadership in Public Relations

So far, we have described the main arcs and nuances of the industry narrative of public relations leadership and diversity and inclusion (D&I) and that of scholarship. We have also traced the trajectories of D&I and leadership scholarship both across disciplines and specifically in relation to the public relations profession in the United States. Several key takeaways have emerged in the process. We now add two more chapters to this narrative – based on the data we gathered for this project – before offering our D&I and leadership model for public relations in Chapter 7.

According to public relations scholar and former practitioner Paul Elmer (2011), the story approach remains underutilized in scholarship about the profession. He writes: [T]he stories that practitioners tell, about themselves, their work, their organizations, their clients and working relationships ... [are] a potentially rich source of information about the occupation" (p. 48). Or as the late essayist Joan Didion (1979) put it, "We tell ourselves stories in order to live" (p. 11). As we explained in Chapter 1, the story is a powerful form of communication and sense-making. We organize and make sense of our lives and realities in various domains (work, social, private, public, etc.) through the story form. Communication scholar Walter Fisher (1984, 1987), who is credited with developing the narrative paradigm of communication, has described human beings as storytelling creatures or homo narrans. In response to Elmer's point and to harness the insights stories can provide about D&I and leadership in public relations, we developed a narrative methodological design to collect, analyze and present our data in this and the next chapter. In this chapter, we present the results of an online survey

DOI: 10.4324/9781003170020-5

of practitioners which we conducted to delve mainly into two important questions related to public relations leadership and D&I:

1. What can we surmise about public relations leadership and D&I from the stories practitioners tell? What is the overarching narrative?
2. How do leaders think about D&I and their own performance versus those they lead? Is there a perception gap? If yes, what is the nature of this gap?

The survey data were analyzed using a narrative approach which we explain shortly. The findings formed the springboard for in-depth interviews with public relations leaders, the results of which are presented in the next chapter.

A perception gap?

A few studies on D&I and public relations over the years have collectively indicated that leaders seem to have a rosier picture of the state of D&I in the industry compared to those not in formal leadership positions; they also seem to have a more positive sense of how they are performing on D&I and a lower sense of urgency regarding D&I than those they lead (e.g., see Diggs-Brown & Zaharna, 1995; Hon & Brunner, 2000; Jiang, R. Ford, Long, & Ballard, 2016; Mundy, 2016; "Report Card on PR Leaders," n.d.). The complaint that there is more lip service than actual action from leaders on D&I is also a common theme in these studies, further suggesting that there may indeed be a perceived disconnect between leaders' words and deeds; the lip service theme has also been recurrent in trade discourse (see Institute for Public Relations, 2021a). The fact that clients are now increasingly demanding that agencies provide more diverse teams if they want to gain or maintain accounts has been a wake-up call to senior leadership (see Chapter 2). The racially charged events of 2020 and the surge in support for D&I in the workplace has, hopefully, been an additional eye-opener.

Citing research in psychology, Mundy (2016) explains:

> [H]igh status groups [leaders] often assume their organization is fairer and more inclusive, simply by virtue of the fact they have active D&I programs focused on the recruitment and retention of diverse employees, and developing provisions such as diversity policies, diversity training, and diversity awards. As a result of having specific D&I mechanisms in place, however, majority groups become less sensitive to workplace discrimination and react more negatively against minorities who claim discrimination.
>
> *(p. 4)*

The current senior leadership in public relations in the United States is highly homogenous (mostly heterosexual White males) and it is likely what Mundy explains applies to them as an overall group. What we can surmise then is that the lived and perceptual world of senior leaders is more culturally homogenous while that of other employees is less so. The perception gap could be an effect, therefore, of (more homogenous) leaders being out of touch with the experiences of their somewhat more diverse employees' worlds. If they have D&I policies and goals in place, perhaps they are not checking to see if they are working and just assuming they are. Maybe leaders (consciously or subconsciously) feel that admitting their organization or agency is not doing a good job on the D&I front would be an admission of inadequate leadership. It could also be the case that these senior leaders are not paying enough attention to the fast-changing societal demographics, and assuming organizational homophily will not be an obstacle in the path of building successful relations with increasingly diverse publics and stakeholders, their own and those of their clients. That is, they do not seem to be grasping (or are perhaps ignoring or not prioritizing) the business and moral cases for D&I.

If the perception gap indeed exists as the research suggests, then we must ask more pressing questions. For example, is privilege playing a role in obstructing senior leaders from embracing D&I and understanding the reality on the ground? Is unconscious bias aiding in maintaining the status quo (Locke, n.d.)? Hon and Brunner (2000) have explained that in public relations it has been common practice for a long time to assign D&I to human resources and that "[t]his may be particularly true when, ... top management itself is not diverse" (p. 334). Could this be another critical issue, embedded in the taken-for-granted practices of the profession, that contributes toward this likely perception gap? Why do so many senior leaders in public relations, as the research suggests, not see the need to be personally engaged with D&I? Perhaps the culture in a predominantly White industry lends itself to seeing D&I through rose-tinted glasses? While Gallicano (2013) did not interview senior leaders, in her study of millennials' perceptions of D&I in agencies, she found those from dominant groups had a rosier picture compared with those who identified as being from underrepresented groups; the latter expressed concern that "they will never reach senior positions in their agencies because no one at the top looked like them" (p. 60). While millennials are known for being more pro-D&I, even within this group, it seems like there is a perception gap between practitioners from dominant and non-dominant identity groups.

As we noted in Chapter 2 the PR Council (2016), among others industry voices, has emphasized that it is the responsibility of senior leaders to develop the vision and set the tone for D&I if there is to be any meaningful progress. It is of course common practice for senior leaders to set the vision for organizations and industries; however, if these leaders are to set a clear vision, then they must have an accurate sense of what they are setting the vision for, as well as their own role and accountability in vision accomplishment. The one major obstacle already in place is that senior leadership currently itself is trapped in homophily. The task before us, therefore, is to dig deeper into this matter, which is what we did. Along with the perception gap issue, we also delved into the larger question of the relationship between leadership and D&I in the US public relations industry. We utilized a narrative approach to do so because this approach emerged out of the communication studies/rhetoric field and public relations is a communication and rhetorically-oriented profession. We now explain this approach.

A narrative and qualitative approach to leaders' views on D&I

From a social constructionist perspective, stories are reality (Berger & Luckmann, 1966). According to Fisher (1984), storytelling is "symbolic action that creates social reality" (p. 353). In professional contexts (such as public relations), it is through the telling and sharing of stories that taken-for-granted professional practices, professional identities and cultural norms and values are formed and perpetuated (Meyer & Rowan, 1977). Story is used to express emotions and convey beliefs about how things should be. What information is selected into stories, what information is left out and how information is understood in relation to existing narratives can be revealing. Therefore, as Elmer (2011) has noted, the stories public relations practitioners tell are a window into their professional world/culture and its values and practices (including those pertaining to D&I).

The storied approach is not new to public relations scholarship; however, it is underutilized despite its potential for useful applied and scholarly work. Back in the early 1990s, using the narrative paradigm, Vasquez (1993) wrote that "human beings are social storytellers who share 'fantasies' and thus build group consciousness and create social realities" (p. 202). A communication- and story-centered approach, according to Vasquez, can be used to effectively understand the realities of organizations and their publics and to develop strategic public relations messages. Vasquez combined the situational theory of publics with the narrative approach to develop a homo narrans paradigm for theory-based and story-centered investigations of organizations and their publics. More recently, Kent (2015) wrote: "Organizational goals, histories, heroes, and informational and persuasive communication, are often communicated via myths and stories" (p. 480); he emphasized that storytelling and the narrative paradigm need to be utilized more effectively in client work and in public relations theory building. Thus, the narrative paradigm has good value for understanding, theorizing, diagnosing and practicing professional culture and relationships with all levels of stakeholders, external as well as internal. Specifically, with regard to D&I, an analysis of the stories currently being told can provide clues about and explain entrenched professional cultures/practices and realities and diagnose how to change undesirable aspects of those realities by changing future storytelling practices (Bardhan & Engstrom, 2021).

Kent (2015) explains that good stories have recognizable structures. How an author narrates a story matters since choices are made during emplotment. Drawing on Fisher (1984, 1987), Kent explains: "Stories need to be rational [narrative rationality], or make sense, and should be believable [narrative probability], or resonate with an audience's beliefs [narrative fidelity]" (2015, p. 483). For a story to resonate, its audience must be able to identify with it. Stories also have plots comprising antenarratives, timelines, main characters (or actors) and events which are impactful and shape the story. A kernel in a story is a major event or turning point in the direction of the narrative (e.g., the racial justice upheavals of 2020 and the significant shift in the D&I narrative) (see Sarup, 1996). Antenarratives are fragmented, non-linear, unplotted, incoherent collections of details that need to be plotted (Boje, 2001). Emplotment, according to Kent, is arranging the details in a story to build the larger narrative theme. He writes that "a plot is not about a single event, or a 'scene,' but a series of interrelated and coherent events" (p. 484). Kent describes 20 masterplots that are common in the narrative paradigm and focuses on five that tend to be relevant in professional communication practice: quest, adventure, rivalry, underdog and wretched excess (see Kent, 2015, for detailed descriptions of these masterplots).

With the above conceptualization of story and narrative in mind, and in order to gather antenarratives from practitioners, we developed an online survey questionnaire which was administered to a targeted segment of US-based public relations professionals. (Note: this survey was completed before the racial upheavals of 2020 and the sharp surge in D&I discourse in the industry and in corporate America.) From the data collected, we compared the views of those who reported being in formal leadership positions with those who reported not being in formal leadership positions to further explore the D&I perception gap described earlier. We asked a filter question to categorize respondents as "practitioners" and "leader practitioners." Questions were a mix of directed response (quantitative) and open-ended (qualitative) items. The latter were designed to elicit qualitative input in the form of explanations, anecdotes and personal accounts (or antenarratives) and focused primarily on (1) how respondents understand the meanings of D&I in relation to the US public relations industry, (2) how they perceive the relationship between D&I progress and leadership engagement, (3) the types of communication and D&I storytelling and story-sharing leaders as well as other employees engage in and how that shapes organizational culture and (4) what changes the respondents perceive are needed to improve the state of D&I in the industry. We anticipated that responses would be brief, so we included Likert-type questions to obtain additional insights about how leaders view themselves versus how practitioners not in formal leadership positions view leaders (e.g., as empowering, disengaged, inspiring, homogeneous or diverse). We also collected demographic information regarding gender, sex, age, career length, organization type and so on. Out of a total 112 responses, 102 were usable. We consider this to be a valid number of responses given the qualitative nature of this survey.

Following data collection, we did several things. We first examined our narrators' cultural identities. Rather than give respondents a directed-choice option for their cultural identity, we asked them to describe their identities in their own words. We made this decision to allow respondents the freedom to choose their own words and identity/diversity categories. We then thematized all the qualitative responses by coding the perceived sentiment (i.e., tone) of the qualitative responses as positive, negative or neutral toward D&I. Sentiment analysis is a popular qualitative research technique in marketing communication (Gaspar, Pedro, Panagiotopoulos, & Seibt, 2016). A positive statement demonstrated an excited or enthusiastic tone toward the question, a neutral statement was generally pro-D&I but not enthusiastic (e.g., "Our organization defines D&I as supporting all individuals regardless of their difference" or "our leadership seems to support D&I"), and a negative statement demonstrated hostility or frustration with the topic (e.g., "I don't believe in nationality and culture"; "They [leaders] don't address either [D&I]. Ever."). We then categorized responses from leaders and practitioners according to gender identity (if shared), urban and rural, early career or late career, agency or organization unit and so on. We next analyzed the responses pertaining to how our narrators understand the definition of D&I in the industry. This enabled us to set the context for our analysis. Finally, keeping our two guiding questions in mind, we plotted the antenarratives to develop narrative themes.

Majority of the respondents were in organizational settings (non- and for-profit, government, education, other) (86%) and the rest were in agency settings. Forty-two percent were leader practitioners (in formal leadership positions), and 58% were practitioners. Seventy-five percent were female and 25% male, a breakdown that closely resembles US industry statistics. Sixty-six percent of the male respondents were leaders, compared to 57% of the female respondents. The average age of the respondents was 41.7 years; the youngest respondent was 23-years-old and the oldest was 72-years-old. The median age of respondents was 41 years. Seventy respondents worked in urban centers, 32 in rural areas. Of the 102, 13 respondents (13%) identified as belonging to traditional diversity identity categories (race, ethnicity, gender, nationality and sexuality). This too is a close approximation of industry diversity statistics. Of these 13 respondents, two were leader practitioners and 11 were practitioners. (Table 5.1 summarizes demographic data segmented by leader practitioners and practitioners.)

TABLE 5.1 Respondent demographic data

	Leader practitioners	Practitioners
Gender		
Female	28	49
Male	15	10
Non-binary/transgender	0	0
Organization Type		
Corporate (in-house)	16	26
Agency/firm	7	7
Non-profit	8	9
Education	4	5
Government	7	10
Other, legal/manufacturing	1	2
Career Length		
< 1 year	3	1
1–5 years	18	11
5–10 years	13	9
10–20 years	15	9
20–30 years	7	11
More than 30 years	3	2

The story of lackluster D&I leadership

In the following analysis, we focus on the cultural identities of narrators (respondents), narrators' sentiments (positive, neutral, negative) about the state of D&I in the US public relations industry and the definitions and value of D&I according to our narrators. This is followed by the four primary narratives plots that emerged from our analysis regarding the relationship between leadership, communication and D&I. Secondary plots are also described. Comparisons between practitioner and leader practitioner stories were made whenever evident and relevant.

Narrators: Cultural identity

Most respondents opted to describe their identity first by race or ethnicity and then by other factors (e.g., gender, nationality, religion, sexual orientation). The majority identified as White (practitioners: $n = 47$, 79.6%; leader practitioners: $n = 40$; 93%), writing responses such as "white female" or "white American." For the few who indicated a religious or spiritual preference, leader practitioners and practitioners collectively noted Christian ($n = 9$), Catholic ($n = 6$), agnostic ($n = 2$), atheist ($n = 1$) and Quaker ($n = 1$). For those who indicated a political orientation or philosophy, leader practitioners and practitioners collectively noted liberal ($n = 4$), progressive–liberal ($n = 2$) and conservative ($n = 1$). Words describing sexual or gender orientations other than heterosexual, straight, male or female were gay ($n = 1$), bisexual ($n = 1$) and cisgender ($n = 2$). Race/ethnicity and gender were the main categories of differences and identity reflected in these self-descriptions.

Overall, practitioners (as compared to leader practitioners) provided more nuanced cultural descriptions of themselves: "Cuban born American citizen, multicultural fluent in Spanish and French"; "I'm Salvadoran but I use the term Hispanic or Latina when referring to my cultural identity." Millennial respondents, in particular, tended to be more descriptive. For example, one 30-year-old practitioner wrote, "upper middle class, white suburbanite; moderately liberal; family-oriented; cat-lover"; another 34-year-old practitioner wrote, "white, single, female, straight, upper middle class, American, liberal/progressive." A 37-year-old leader practitioner, just at the intersection of Generations X and Y, wrote, "I'm white, cisgender woman, bisexual."

We also observed that respondents from traditionally underrepresented groups within the industry (11 practitioners; two leader practitioners), whether in a leadership position or not, tended to be more responsive to questions, reflective of organizational/industry D&I practices and observant of the stories (or their lack) supporting D&I. Although only a handful ($n = 6$; 14%) among the leader practitioners, six respondents were noticeable in their animosity or disinterest toward the question, with responses like "prefer not to answer," "I don't spend much (any?) time thinking about how I would describe my cultural identity" and "old white guy." Nevertheless, as explained in the next section, overall sentiment among all respondents was supportive of D&I.

Sentiment: Feelings regarding D&I

Respondents demonstrated an overall positive sentiment toward D&I efforts as a principle and the need to share stories of success and communicate effectively about D&I. More than 80% of the responses were coded as neutral or positive. Statements like the following reflect positive sentiment:

- "Industry leadership should encourage D&I through talent recruitment, diversity training programs, and tracking diversity goals across the industry." (practitioner)
- "As a Limited English proficiency level program manager, I bring to the office stories about how D&I is critical to effectively reach out to disaster survivors. These success stories are shared with senior leaders as an example of how possible it is to replicate internally for employees. I fight." (leader practitioner)

These positive sentiments are also somewhat demonstrated in this neutral-sentiment statement, which we further unpack for its complexity:

- "I think D&I is really important in today's culture because the political and social environment is continually moving towards increasing and embracing diversity. In my company, there is some diversity but I would say it is predominantly white/Caucasian people. However, my company does have a wide variety of sexual orientations and continually supports LGBTQ initiatives in the local community. One of our top executives is gay and also of Indian descent, which shows that the company is open-minded and non-judgmental (for the most part)." (practitioner)

From a narrative perspective, "One of our top executives is gay and also of Indian descent" is noteworthy because it is unique in its wording (and hints at tokenism while attempting to be positive). We coded this example as neutral because it suggests that a leader who identifies as gay is promoting lesbian/gay/bisexual/transgender/queer or questioning+ (LGBTQ+) issues. Perhaps the leader is a champion for more groups, but this is not reflected in this anecdote. A key point about antenarrative statements is that what is excluded in a statement shapes the narrative which, in turn, shapes reality. Working from the fragment alone, it fits in with a plotline that individuals of an identity group tend to champion primarily their group. We recognize that this is important: When given the opportunity, an opportunity long denied, it is necessary for underrepresented groups to advocate for *their* group. However, pro-one's-own-group is not necessarily pro-inclusion of other groups and could in fact result in silo mentality and obstruct allyship and relations across differences. Pro-one's-own-group and one-dimensional diversity statements emerged time and again in both leader practitioners' and practitioners' responses (see also Blow, Bonney, Tallapragada, & Brown, 2021).

Generally, there were not many negative accounts related to D&I as a principle, but there were negative feelings toward the state of D&I in practice, particularly directed toward organizational leadership and industry leaders. The key takeaway from the sentiment analysis is that both leader practitioners and practitioners support D&I in principle; however, they have different sentiments regarding practice (see narrative plot 1).

Context: Definitions of D&I

As described in Chapter 2, the US public relations industry does not have one clearly agreed-upon D&I definition (although one could argue that the Public Relations Society of America (PRSA) definition is the most formal one available); the lack of a clear definition could be an obstacle to progress on D&I (see Chitkara,

2018). Therefore, we asked the following open-ended question: "How does your organization define diversity and inclusion (D&I)?" We coded responses as consistent with Equal Employment Opportunity (EEO) language, as demonstrating organization commitment, or as showing lack of D&I commitment.

Of the 59 practitioner responses, 30 (50.8%) provided an EEO-like response, such as: "At my corporation, diversity and inclusion means valuing and respecting people, across a spectrum of experiences, viewpoints, and talents, to bring out the best in everyone" or "it [organization] does not discriminate based on age, race, creed or gender." Sixteen (27.2%) responses, mostly from respondents in agency settings, showed a lack of organizational commitment: "I have no idea. No mechanisms that I am aware of and no particular goals in that area" or "I don't think our company has ever formally provided a D&I definition and goals." Thirteen (22.0%) respondents, mostly working in government, educational and corporate settings, provided a definition that reflects a deep organizational commitment to D&I. They provided thorough explanations of D&I, as highlighted in this in-house practitioner's response:

- "Yes, we have a D&I team that manages issues around diversity and how our organization measures up with the competition. We also have a platform that is specifically to elevate the gender parity conversation that is quite extensive and is separate from D&I, however related. Meaning, it does not fall under the auspices of D&I, although our teams work quite closely on some initiatives and programs."

Leaders mostly narrated their D&I initiatives in EEO language ($n = 29$; 67.4%) and a few responses were negative or resistant ($n = 8$; 18.6%) with answers such as: "Prefer not to answer," and "I've never really thought about D&I." Six respondents (14%) provided responses that demonstrated an organizational commitment to D&I. The fact that only 14% of the leaders were able to describe D&I with commitment (compared to more generic EEO-type responses and even negative responses being minimally higher at 18.6%) is concerning and in keeping with the larger narrative of lackluster leadership when it comes to D&I.

Narrative plots

From our analysis, four primary narrative plots emerged regarding the relationship between leadership, communication and D&I. In addition, we noted three secondary plotlines from the antenarrative accounts.

Narrative plot 1: A perception gap exists

The perception gap we set out to explore was supported overall. Supporting findings of previous studies, a clear narrative plotline which emerged was the lack of agreement between how practitioners view leaders and how leaders view themselves with regard to D&I commitment. The difference of views is most clearly captured by comparing responses to the directed-choice (Likert-Type) question regarding the practitioners' and leaders' perceptions of leaders' support of and engagement with D&I (see Figure 5.1).

Practitioners, who in this survey are more diverse as a group of respondents, see leaders as *less capable* of handling D&I initiatives than leaders (more culturally homogenous) see themselves. Responses indicate that leaders rank themselves higher in D&I skills and abilities (see questions 1–5 in Figure 5.1). Personal engagement of leadership in D&I efforts and their ability to create shared vision within the organization were rated the lowest by both groups (questions 2 and 3). While the perception gap is evident for all five questions, the largest gaps were noted for questions 1 and 5 (leaders are supportive of D&I and able to bring about positive change within organization). The smallest gap

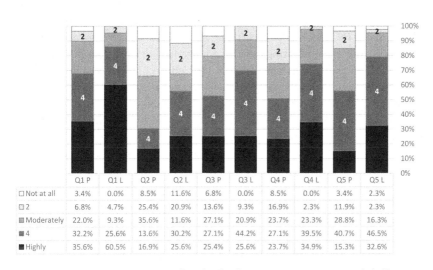

	Q1 P	Q1 L	Q2 P	Q2 L	Q3 P	Q3 L	Q4 P	Q4 L	Q5 P	Q5 L
☐ Not at all	3.4%	0.0%	8.5%	11.6%	6.8%	0.0%	8.5%	0.0%	3.4%	2.3%
☐ 2	6.8%	4.7%	25.4%	20.9%	13.6%	9.3%	16.9%	2.3%	11.9%	2.3%
▥ Moderately	22.0%	9.3%	35.6%	11.6%	27.1%	20.9%	23.7%	23.3%	28.8%	16.3%
▨ 4	32.2%	25.6%	13.6%	30.2%	27.1%	44.2%	27.1%	39.5%	40.7%	46.5%
■ Highly	35.6%	60.5%	16.9%	25.6%	25.4%	25.6%	23.7%	34.9%	15.3%	32.6%

FIGURE 5.1   Perception gap regarding leadership D&I engagement and skills

P: Practitioner (59); L: Leader Practitioner (43)
%: Percentage of responses for group

Questions:
P: The leadership in my PR Agency/PR Unit is ...
L: As a leader in my PR agency/PR unit, I am

Responses:

Q1. Supportive of D&I efforts
Q2. Personally involved in D&I initiatives
Q3. Able to create a shared vision within the organization
Q4. Able to challenge the status-quo if necessary
Q5. Able to bring about positive change within the organization

was for question 3 (leaders are able to create a shared vision within the organization). The more in-depth responses indicate leadership commitment to D&I is perceived as relatively perfunctory and surface level. That is, those providing statements with a critical tone focused primarily on the fact that organizational-level leaders and industry leaders are not doing enough to improve D&I:

- "Our leaders are moderately diverse, but they talk the talk at best and provide lip service at worst. I would like to see more diversity." (practitioner)
- "Our leadership team is mostly white men. I believe leadership should be accountable for D&I, and should reflect the same values." (practitioner)
- "Organization D&I efforts are token gestures; i.e. mixed race families in photos but not REAL commitment to represent the world as it is." (leader practitioner)

Practitioners feel that not enough effort is being made and that leaders should do more than pay lip service; leaders were mostly neutral or somewhat uncomfortable discussing the details of D&I. Overall, leaders see themselves as supportive of D&I, with only five indicating they are not involved in D&I and two indicating the leadership team is not supportive of D&I efforts. Thirty-four percent (*n* = 20) of practitioners indicated their leaders are not personally involved in D&I and only 10.2% (*n* = 6) indicated that leaders are not at all supportive of D&I in their agencies/organizations. In short, D&I is a feel-good idea, but does not seem urgent enough to leaders to make concrete cultural and structural changes.

Another noteworthy point evident in the language of both leaders and practitioners is the "managing" (rather than "valuing") approach to D&I which views diversity as an add-on to the norm rather than a part of the norm (see Mundy, 2016). This view, as explained in previous chapters, tends to privilege the business case, commodify underrepresented identities and equate them mainly with profitability. As we have explained already, this is not a healthy recipe for building inclusive cultures.

Narrative plot 2: Gender in relation to D&I

An ongoing inequity in the US public relations industry is that about 70% of the industry comprises women, but men dominate senior leadership (Place & Vardeman-Winter, 2018). Gender diversity emerged as a major plotline in leader and practitioner responses; 87 respondents (85%, both groups combined) referenced gender at least once in relation to diversity initiatives. This was so overwhelming that it was notable that references to non-gender-related diversity efforts or successes were largely absent in the responses. References to other underrepresented identities were made to point out the fact that these groups are missing in leadership teams. We believe this observation reveals a central narrative plotline; a few respondents explicitly pointed to this observation themselves: "I think we need to start by talking about it [D&I]. There's a recognition that it's important and desirable ...We are good at gender and LGBTQ+ although we could do better. Less good at race, socioeconomic, etc." Public relations leaders and associations are making progress in promoting more women into leadership positions and are *slowly* looking to diversity initiatives for other underrepresented groups (see narrative plot 3). The following antenarrative accounts highlight the theme of gender against the backdrop of a lack of focus on diversification of leadership teams with other historically marginalized and underrepresented groups:

- "I do not see company leaders taking part in D&I initiatives other than for gender; however, our office is very much welcoming to all races, religions and creeds. ... it is completely unacceptable to not be socially diverse." (leader practitioner)
- "The PR management team talks about how nice it would be for the open C Suite positions to be filled with woman or diversity. For the past 4 years, it's been nearly all white middle aged men. Now we have a Persian female COO who worked her way up over 20 years." [a single instance reflects the rarity of such occurrences] (practitioner)

We fully agree that diversifying boards and senior leadership with women is a laudable goal; however, as one respondent noted, this one-dimensional approach to diversity does not mean that diversity has been adequately addressed. It is just the beginning and much more inclusion of other underrepresented groups in senior leadership needs to occur.

Additionally, absent in the accounts from respondents is a unified vision around inclusion in general, and stories or examples of inclusion of traditionally underrepresented groups in particular. As one practitioner ironically noted, "Inclusion is a big word that's still confusing to corporate leaders." This observation supports the D&I literature (see Chapter 3) which indicates that much work remains to be done in the realm of inclusion and that there is a tendency to conflate "diversity" and "inclusion" in discourse and practice.

Narrative plot 3: Slow pace of change

Narrative pace is the rate at which a story moves. Respondents' accounts suggest that there is some progression toward the goals of D&I; however, real change is slow. For example:

- "Our sector is not as diverse as it is committed to being. So it is a work in progress. We have D&I local committees. But often times they are mostly white allies. And we can't get complacent and feel that just because we have a D&I taskforce that checks a box and make us diverse." (leader practitioner)

- "The diversity is improving. ... [however] It was often awkward to see the one woman or one black person in the room tasked with convincing everyone else we were doing better." (practitioner)

These antenarratives highlight a few issues that may be stifling a more accelerated rate of change within the industry. First, resistance to change can be masked by lip service about D&I, something that has been highlighted in industry discourse as being a problem (see Cohen, 2014). Second, the discussion about D&I still seems to focus primarily on race/ethnicity and gender (e.g., "white allies" and "often awkward to see the one woman or one black person in the room tasked with convincing everyone else"); while race/ethnicity and gender are important categories of difference, there is a need to develop more complex and intersectional approaches and thinking about D&I (the literature on D&I clearly points in this direction). Third, the D&I effort seems to stop once a threshold is met (i.e., "check box marked," therefore it is resolved). This is evidence of a continuing compliance mentality which works against genuine and ongoing diversity efforts and the building of inclusive organizational cultures. The work of D&I is an ongoing process and no organization can ever say its D&I work is complete.

While the pace of change has indeed been too slow, it must be noted that some respondents said there are a few leaders who are demonstrating engagement and genuine commitment. These leaders are the few outstanding actors in the narrative. For example, one practitioner described how leadership "recently instituted a program of all-employee webcasts for the first time. Leadership makes it a priority to communicate personal stories, as well as examples that serve as proof points for the values and behaviors that we want to model." Unfortunately, such examples and efforts are few and far apart, and not enough for setting a better pace for change.

Narrative plot 4: Leaders pass the buck to human resources (HR)

The fourth plotline that emerged pertains to responsibility for D&I initiatives. Practitioners in non-leadership roles noted that leaders are not taking much responsibility for D&I and leaders confirmed this point with responses like: "My firm really goes by the HR book – and defines a diverse culture in terms of equal opportunity and hiring for diversity/Not much else." This plot seems to be motivated by a not uncommon understanding that D&I functions belong to HR (see Hon & Brunner, 2000; Mundy, 2016). In other words, there is a tendency to pass the buck to HR. Sample accounts that support this narrative plot are:

- "We have agencies specifically designated to do that. Shaping my organization's culture of D&I does not fall under our area of responsibility." (leader practitioner)

- "Our HR team would manage this. It is not a focus and there are no formal programs I am aware of. Our leadership team is not diverse." (practitioner)

This plotline shifts the responsibility for organizational culture and D&I to HR, ignoring the important fact that buy-in and active support, communication and engagement from leadership shape organizational cultures, structures and conversations. For example, three practitioner respondents specifically noted the importance of leaders setting up employee resource groups or committing resources to D&I. However, the sentiment seems to be tilted toward lack of dedicated resources, with more than ten practitioners stating something like the following:

- "They do want to promote an environment of diversity, but sometimes are unwilling to devote the resources to them. A lot of the talk isn't as backed up by the resources that they allot to them." (practitioner)
- "If there is no buy-in from executive leadership, then the investment is not there. You need to have the investment from the top in order for the time and resources to be provided." (practitioner)

Unfortunately, some leaders expressed that D&I efforts and resources can be put off until later: "Our organization is a start-up so not many of these initiatives have come in to play yet. In the future, we plan to be diverse." This last account denies the importance of D&I for the present; rather, it is deferred to the future as something that can wait. Such accounts and attitudes toward D&I significantly slow down the pace of the story as well as real change.

Passing the D&I buck to HR seems to be a common overall problem in corporate America. As we were wrapping up the manuscript, a study of talent recruiters with a focus on D&I showed that while intentions are good, the needle on hiring more diverse professionals does not move much because of the lack of clear process for doing so; neglect, lip service (or policy-practice gaps), lack of accountability and the tendency to make D&I purely a HR function instead of a core business function are the culprits (Moody, 2021; see also "Institute for Public Relations, 2021a). Reiterating the lack of the involvement and support needed from senior leadership, this study showed that only 22% of senior leaders have been engaged in developing clear process and strategy to recruit and hire for diversity and only 15% of hiring managers have strategically tied compensation to hiring goals (Ternynck, 2021).

Secondary plotlines

In addition to the four main narrative plots, we noted several antenarrative accounts that lend evidence for the quest, underdog and transformation plotlines (Kent, 2015).

Quest plots involve a search for something elusive. Several antenarratives suggested the public relations industry has been chasing the D&I unicorn for over three decades. A quest is generally a positive storyline but can also tire if the plot advances too slowly or the main characters become complacent. Several respondents indicated that they are feeling external pressure to change (i.e., client pressure); however, a quest is more motivating when it is driven by internal desires (Kent, 2015). Also, the quest plot seems to have more support from practitioners when compared to leader practitioners. Underdog plots tell a story of overcoming, such as this account from a cisgender woman leader practitioner: "I share with my younger colleagues, stories about struggles I had moving up in the industry … and give them advice on how they can grow." Several accounts supported this secondary plotline of the underdog fighting against systemic odds and industry culture. Transformation plots emerge when something life-changing occurs, such as a professional crisis. No doubt increasing external pressures from clients serving diverse publics, and kernel events such as the #MeToo campaigns and the racial justice upheavals of 2020, will continue to impose change on industry practices and the D&I story. But practitioner respondents' accounts illustrated a yearning for transformation to occur morally and intrinsically among all levels of leadership within the industry without the compulsion of external pressures: As this one practitioner respondent emphatically stated: "Lead by example, by including diverse individuals in upper management, and down throughout the organization. Place more diverse individuals in leadership roles, including associations, as well as key role players in the organization."

Key takeaways

The key takeaways from the first step of our empirical investigation align with much of what we have already discussed in earlier chapters, further confirming the state of D&I in the US public relations industry:

- Most of our respondents, even though they were asked to describe their identities in their own words, led with the diversity categories of race/ ethnicity and then gender. This indicates the primacy of these historically underrepresented and marginalized categories in the US diversity story. Millennial respondents tended to be more descriptive and used primary (non-alterable) as well as secondary (alterable) categories of diversity to describe their identities. Respondents who identified as belonging to underrepresented group were more responsive and engaged in answering the open-ended questions.
- Unfortunately, only a small percentage (approximately 20%) of respondents described their organizations as being deeply committed to D&I. Majority of the respondents used EEO-type generic language and six leader practitioners were openly negative and/or resistant.

- It is clear from the results that practitioners not in formal leadership positions (a more diverse group in the study) think leaders are not doing a good enough job with D&I. They feel inclusion is a real problem that needs a lot of attention and that overall, the D&I needle is moving too slowly and not keeping up with the changes in larger society. They emphasized the need for concrete changes and for leaders to move beyond lip service.

- Leaders (mostly White in this study) do seem to have a rosier picture of how they are performing on D&I. The perception gap was supported by the results, especially when it came to questions of leaders being supportive of D&I and being able to bring about positive organizational change.

- Differences/diversity still seem to be conceptualized as separate rather than overlapping identity categories, and this could further promote silo mentality and obstruct intersectional thinking on D&I.

- Gender (women) as a diversity category is getting more attention when it comes to promotions to senior leadership positions; however, the same cannot be said for race/ethnicity and other diversity categories (minus perhaps sexual orientation, as some accounts seem to indicate). As described in Chapter 2, this indicates Whiteness is still strongly entrenched in the culture of US public relations leadership (see Gupta, 2021; Logan, 2011; Vardeman-Winter & Place, 2017).

- Leaders tend to pass the responsibility for D&I to human resources perceiving it as the latter's "job." This compartmentalized "job" approach to D&I is an obstacle in the path of building organization-wide authentic and inclusive cultures which are necessary for diversity to flourish.

- Successful D&I currently seems like an elusive quest, with a few stories of underdog successes here and there. There is a strong desire for transformation among those who identify as belonging to underrepresented groups and among those who are not in formal leadership positions (mostly millennials). However, and according to most respondents, there seems to be no industry-wide collective momentum in place.

Conclusion

When viewed through a narrative lens, it seems like the story of D&I in public relations has achieved narrative rationality and probability (that is, the lack of D&I in the industry is talked about now as a clear problem). However, there seems to be a real gap between talk and walk (as was pointed out by many respondents), and the story does not seem to have risen to a level of high fidelity (i.e., urgency) for senior leadership which holds the power to make significant changes geared toward moving the D&I needle faster. High fidelity narratives resonate deeply with audiences (leaders in this case) and catalyze change. The diversity category of gender is receiving more attention than other categories, and there is a need for a more intersectional approach to diversity.

The responses suggest that leaders still seem to think that D&I and organizational culture are the responsibility of human resources. This is not a good sign.

We conducted our survey before the killing of George Floyd in 2020 and the racial upheavals that followed which significantly elevated the topic of D&I in society and the business world. This sharp increase in focus on D&I made us wonder if these kernel events were impactful enough to have radically changed the D&I narrative and sentiments in the public relations industry. But it seems like more than two years after this surge, the story has not shifted much. A recent survey of 1,046 communication professionals working in the United States (75% of respondents) and Canada (25% of respondents) conducted by the Plank Center (Meng, Reber, Berger, Gower, & Zerfass, 2021) shows that a little over half of the respondent believe that organizational leaders carry the biggest responsibility for advancing D&I. On the other hand, only about 40% of leaders among the respondents agreed on this and shifted the overall responsibility for D&I to all communication professionals. While we agree that D&I is everyone's responsibility, this finding suggests that there is still a lack of understanding about the important link between D&I success and strong leadership support among practitioners, especially senior leaders. In another recent study by Deloitte focusing on the marketing profession showed that spending on D&I rose only 8.8% between February 2020 and 2021 (Crater, 2021). And just as we were wrapping up this manuscript, a webinar panelist from Seramount (a company that conducts, among other things, research on organizations and D&I) said that even after the surge in D&I consciousness since the events of 2020, there are senior leaders who are not committed enough and some even think that D&I is an overblown topic (The Museum of Public Relations, 2021). Additionally, a sobering report from Hue (an equity focused non-profit organization) and The Harris Poll ("Unsafe," 2022) just released shows a large disconnect between Black, Indigenous and people of color (BIPOC) views regarding D&I efforts and those of HR departments which, like leaders, seem to think they are doing an effective job with D&I, that an alarmingly low percentage of senior leaders are BIPOC, that there has actually been an increase in discrimination and microaggressions against BIPOC since 2020 and that many are considering changing or have changed employers, *and that women BIPOC and those in professions such as marketing, communications, advertising and design are faring the worst in all the above issues.* Additionally, of the nearly $50 billion pledged by US businesses since 2020 to address racial inequality, more than 90% are in forms which generate profit for the donor (e.g., investments, loans, mortgages) rather than direct grants. According to John Gerzema, CEO of The Harris Poll, this report is a loud call to leaders at all levels to back their words with action. Such findings and reports make us wonder how much structural and cultural impact the events of 2020 are having on D&I in corporate America in general and in public relations specifically.

A recent trade press article spotlights a handful of CEOs of companies who, after the events of 2020, are earnestly working toward concrete change (Prince, 2021) and walking the talk. Such stories are heartening, but the article is quick to remind us that the D&I needle is "tough to budge," the argument that working to enhance D&I is the right thing to do (moral case) is not motivating enough for most leaders and that most "management teams have not figured out why they need diversity in their organization" (paras. 7, 8). While the public relations industry is making many D&I promises, we need to be vigilant and hold leaders accountable in the near future since there is little evidence for these promises. Also, the evidence that we and others have found on the perception gap should not be taken lightly.

6

Digging Deeper

Practitioner/Educator/Student Leaders Elaborate on D&I

In this chapter, we report the results of 30 in-depth interviews we conducted with public relations leaders in industry (senior leaders) and education (student leaders and educators). We included students and educators to highlight the important link between the profession and public relations education and to investigate this pipeline from the perspective of diversity and inclusion (D&I). These interviews allowed us to dig deeper into the D&I and leadership relationship in public relations, and we were also able to make comparisons between the results of the survey and the interviews.

Practitioner leaders elaborate on D&I

The D&I narratives that emerged from the survey served as a platform for developing a qualitative questionnaire for conducting in-depth interviews with leaders in the public relations industry, specifically senior leaders who have a track record of dedicating themselves to D&I through personal engagement. (Note: two interviewees did not strictly qualify as senior leaders, but we interviewed them because of their stellar D&I-related contributions and accomplishments early in their careers.) We used our professional contacts and received assistance from The Plank Center in recruiting interviewees. While developing this purposive sample, we kept in mind the need to recruit from different types of settings (agency, in-house, non-profit, government). We also did our best to ensure that our interviewees themselves comprised a diverse group of individuals. The dedication of each leader we recruited to D&I work was gauged through a review of their history and accomplishments in the D&I space measured in terms of awards and other career recognition. Our interviewees comprised four women and six men who have worked in various settings. The years

DOI: 10.4324/9781003170020-6

of work experience ranged between 6 and 40 years. We asked the interviewees to describe their cultural identities in their own words (see Table 6.1). We use pseudonyms to protect the identities of the interviewees.

An in-depth interview is a "conversation with a purpose" (Lindlof & Taylor, 2011, p. 172) which aims to get at the reality of social actors' experiences. According to Castillo-Montoya (2016), a key criterion for developing sound interview protocols is to design and order questions in a manner that encourages conversation and in-depth perspectives. Following this advice, we developed a semi-structured questionnaire. We started each interview with a broad question about the state of D&I in the US public relations industry. This enabled us to set the tone for more specific questions. The first set of questions probed into how the interviewees understand the concepts "diversity" and "inclusion" and the relationship between them, and we asked if they think the industry needs a clear definition of D&I. The next set of questions focused on

TABLE 6.1 Practitioner leader interviewee identities

Pseudonym/years of experience/setting	Identity statement
April/27 years/Agency and in-house	"I identify as a Black woman."
Lara/28 years/Agency and in-house, some non-profit	"I don't feel like I am one thing" (Lara is from Brazil and has worked in several countries. She resides in the United States. She explained she has a hard time coming up with definite labels for her cultural identity)
Henry/28 years/Agency and in-house	"I'm a father, husband, Christian, purpose driven leader, White, Gen X and adopted."
Mike/12 years/Agency	"I am a fourth generation Japanese American who grew up in Idaho."
Cheryl/40 years/Agency, some in-house, non-profit and government	"I am an African American woman."
Dorothy/30 years/Agency	"I am Asian American, no hyphen. I am also the daughter of immigrants and from the American South. I am a mom. I am a wife. I am a woman of faith."
Barry/25 years/Government, some agency	"I'm a hybrid" (Barry came to the U.S. from Vietnam in the 1970s, grew up Buddhist and said he is a member of the LGBTQ family. Like Lara, he too said he struggles with claiming clear cultural identity labels)
Mark/6 years/Agency and in-house	"I am a young African American man. I grew up in a single parent home."
Andrew/40 years/In-house and agency	"I am a White gay male."
Gary/31 years/Agency, some government	"I consider myself Japanese American. I was born in a small Eastern Oregon town, but I grew up in Los Angeles."

what obstacles interviewees see as standing in the way of faster D&I change. We also shared the finding from previous studies and our online survey that leaders seem to think they are doing a better job at leading on D&I than those they lead; we asked interviewees to share their thoughts on this important perception gap. The next set of questions delved further into the topic of leaders and leadership – we probed into what role interviewees think leaders should be playing in advancing D&I in terms of setting vision, taking personal responsibility, engaging in particular types of communication/messaging with internal and external publics, concrete action and so on. We also asked interviewees to share any D&I best practices they may be aware of. We wrapped up each interview with questions about each leader's personal journey (how long they have worked in the industry, in what settings and so on) and asked if they wanted to address anything we had not covered with regard to D&I. We also asked them to reflect on their own cultural identities and how that has impacted their professional journey (see Table 6.1).

There are various suggestions regarding how many in-depth interviews are sufficient for a study. The most common argument is that interviews can be stopped when saturation point is reached, i.e., when no new information is forthcoming from the interviews. Typically, this point is achieved anywhere between 10 and 20 interviews (Charmaz, 2006; Crouch & McKenzie, 2006). While saturation point was satisfactorily reached around the seventh and eighth interviews we conducted ten for a round number. All interviews were conducted over the phone, recorded with permission, and then transcribed for coding purposes. Interviewees were ascribed pseudonyms for confidentiality and data reporting purposes. (Note: all except two interviews were conducted before the racial upheavals of 2020; the responses of the two leaders interviewed after May 2020 were obviously influenced by the conversations that emerged in the industry discourse after the killing of George Floyd.)

Open and axial coding of the interview transcripts is a common approach to analyzing qualitative interviews. Strauss and Corbin (1990) explain that researchers following this approach to qualitative data analysis seek to "uncover certain conditions" (the D&I and leadership condition in our case) and "how the actors under investigation actively respond to those conditions, and to the consequences of their [or others'] actions" (p. 419). Open coding is "an interpretive process by which data are broken down analytically. ... event/action/interaction, and so forth, are compared against others for similarities and differences; they are also conceptually labelled. In this way, conceptually similar ones are grouped together to form categories and their subcategories" (p. 432). Axial coding is the process of identifying the relationships between the open coding categories and subcategories and collapsing them to develop themes that describe and explain the phenomenon/condition under investigation. We conducted a line-by-line examination of the interview transcripts and engaged in open coding to develop categories and subcategories. Next axial coding was conducted to develop overall themes and subthemes. We also kept a diary where we noted unique comments which seemed significant and resonated with the literature on D&I and leadership. These notes were incorporated into the themes. Four primary themes emerged: (1) a broad approach to diversity, (2) inclusion is a crucial issue, (3) still a long way to go and (4) lack of leadership engagement and accountability.

A broad approach to diversity

It was evident that all respondents were aware of the difference between the concepts of D&I and saw the clear need for the two to go hand-in-hand for overall D&I success. They took a broad and flexible approach and emphasized both primary (non-alterable) as well as secondary (alterable) dimensions of diversity when they explained their understanding of the term in the context of the industry. They also made it clear that D&I is *both* a moral and a business imperative.

An evolving concept

According to Barry, diversity is about representation that reflects the "richness and the vibrancy that we are as a human family." Dorothy was more specific:

> [W]hen I think about the term diversity, to me it is really any dimension of identity. So I know [people] very commonly think about race and ethnicity, gender identity, gender expression, disability, but I also believe that diversity means many other things … including socioeconomic status … our work styles, … veterans status ….

Gary observed how the differences that have been the focus of diversity in the profession have changed over time:

> [W]e keep adding things to the diversity spectrum. I mean, before it was women and now it's Black and White, Latin X and, and gender identity, the LGBT community veterans, people that live in rural communities, people that live in urban communities, educational or socioeconomic factors, and that list keeps getting bigger and bigger and bigger. And as people start to self-identify. … the conversation around diversity is constantly evolving.

All of the interviewees were unanimous on the point that the public relations profession needs to reflect national diversity dynamics. As Cheryl put it, the "profession needs to reflect the country, … [it's a] rainbow, not monolithic."

Several interviewees were of the opinion that D&I is both a business and a moral imperative and that these two imperatives should not be seen as antithetical to each other. Public relations, according to them, is a profession and the role that D&I plays in it needs to be in conversation with the business side (we address this point again in a later theme focusing on leadership and vision).

Need for a flexible approach

While none of the interviewees were in favor of having one fixed definition of D&I for the industry, they all seemed to agree that some commonality or baseline agreement on what the industry is working together toward is needed to focus the efforts, which they think have been erratic so far. As Mark put it, there should be some "pillars" in place but not a definition that is "glued down." Noting that diversity is an evolving phenomenon, Mike said that "in order for it [a definition] to be meaningful, it also needs to be open to future challenges." According to most of the interviewees, another reason the understanding of D&I should be flexible is so that organizations can define D&I in a more focused manner according to their own specific contexts within the larger definition. April said:

> There should be a baseline definition that the industry should adopt and then it … has to be somewhat left to the individual companies and agencies on how they bring that definition to life in their organization.

Lara elaborated it is necessary to consider local diversity dynamics and the clients being serviced by an organization and other contextual matters. She explained that, for example, an agency in a smaller and mainly White town and one in a much larger and diverse city such as Los Angeles or New York City, would not have the same diversity needs and dynamics, internally as well as externally. Cheryl was the only interviewee who argued in favor of a more fixed definition stating: "I don't believe you should leave it open because when you do, it leads people to miss the mark. As far as I'm concerned, you may feel you have a diverse environment because it's based on your definition and not something that's held across the industry."

The definition of D&I, interviewees elaborated, should connect the profession with the society it is a part of, be goal oriented and useful from the perspective of accountability and tracking progress. Mike emphasized the need to abide by agreed-upon approaches and that a definition is meaningful only if all in the profession are "living it and putting it into action, making it apply and making it part of our everyday routine."

Organizational culture matters

All the interviewees agreed that the success of diversity depends primarily on organizational culture. Henry summed up the sentiment of the interviewees in these words: "[I] just think diversity should be embedded into an organization, not just as something that we do or believe in, but as core to how we operate."

Gary explained that the D&I mix is about balancing both differences and similarities in work environments. He described his approach: "I always want people to start off with the things that bring us together and then kind of celebrate and appreciate, and kind of affirm the things that make us unique and different." He offered the analogy of a symphony:

> When I think of diversity, the first thing that pops into my head is all the different instruments that you need to have to have a symphony orchestra. You need the woodwinds, you need the percussions, you need the keyboard, you need the string instruments. … you need the breath and each one of these instruments brings something unique to the symphony. So then the inclusion part really is making it work. Everyone playing their instrument and fitting in and addressing their differences and focusing on the things that make themselves unique.

Discussions of organizational culture led inevitably to the topic of inclusion.

Inclusion is a crucial issue

It was when the conversation shifted to the topic of inclusion that the interviewees seemed particularly energized.

Inclusion is the real challenge

All interviewees expressed the pressing role of inclusion for diversity to succeed. There was a general sense that there is an increasing focus on recruitment but not enough on retention. Dorothy explained the situation well:

> I think [earlier] diversity pursuits were more cosmetic and therefore we didn't have the retention. We didn't have the sense of inclusion within the organizations and therefore we've had to create that kind of add on term [inclusion] to make sure that we are very intentional about … this element of diverse diversity as well. … I think that it really is a failing of how we've pursued diversity in the past that we've had to create these additional terms to hold us perhaps more accountable ….

Dorothy was the only interviewee who delved into why she thinks the term inclusion has emerged more recently, while the others emphasized repeatedly that inclusion is a must. Everyone also agreed that inclusion is something the industry is clearly struggling with, and several interviewees critiqued the tendency to assume that inclusion (and equity) will somehow automatically follow successful recruitment of diverse employees. Inclusion, according to the interviewees, requires deliberate and hard work. As April described:

> I define inclusion as displaying or fulfilling behaviors and social norms that make people feel accepted and just welcomed, you know, ... feel like they're part of something ... you can bring all the talent you want in the door, but if they don't have a great experience when they get there, they're just going to turn around and leave.

Henry said that inclusion means a culture where everyone feels they can "bring their whole self to work." Such a culture, he said, is an everyday effort and requires "ongoing work" to produce an "inclusive environment where everyone feels a sense of belonging, a sense that everyone ... [is] contributing ... I think it's absolutely critical." Mark and Andrew elaborated that once individuals from underrepresented groups are recruited, they need to be at the table, feel like they are heard and that their voices matter. Mark said they should be encouraged to be their authentic selves rather than feel like "when you enter the door into the office, everything else outside of the work in the office stops at the door. ... Once you get the folks in the room ... what intentional steps are you taking to make people feel a part of the room? What are you doing?"

Ingredients for inclusion

Some behaviors needed for the creation of inclusive organizational environments were emphasized. Stressing the importance of mindful and inclusive communication at an everyday micro level, Henry shared a story that illustrates how mundane seeming forms of communication not even noticed by members of dominant identity groups can feel exclusionary to underrepresented colleagues. He shared a story that one time in an agency setting he noticed that in a team comprising mostly White women and a few individuals of color, the topic of conversation was often a television show that was popular among the White members of the team. While they excitedly engaged in conversation about the show, they failed to notice that they were leaving out their colleagues of color on the team who did not happen to watch this particular show:

> But if you were showing up for a meeting and you were watching everyone getting along with the leader of the meeting and the group ... and the people who weren't watching the shows started saying, ... "Do we have to watch this show so that we could participate because the leader of this team seems to be really into the show?" ... I know this is kind

of maybe not the most strategic example, but I think what it illustrates though, and what I've taken away from this is, you really do have to think broadly about how to be inclusive.

Henry added that another behavioral obstacle in the path of creating inclusive cultures is the tendency of not wanting to admit mistakes; he emphasized that vulnerability is an important quality for leaders and all practitioners to cultivate. The need for D&I efforts and behaviors to be "intentional" came up repeatedly. The terms "respect" (for differences) and "belonging" also came up often as interviewees shared their views on the challenges of practicing inclusion.

Gary emphasized an important point. He said that the work of inclusion is never fully done, and nor should it be, i.e., it should not just be another box to be checked off:

> [I]t's an ongoing process. It's never going to end. And if we think that there's an end to this idea around inclusivity, equity, and representation, then we're going to be frustrated. And so I think the process is something that we have to continue to evolve and discuss. And the best way to do this is to, is to keep that conversation going and then to make changes incrementally. ... in the immediate past, we just created a checklist. We tried to rush to do diversity and impose diversity and inclusion on people. And it doesn't work that way. ... it has to be a process. ... that process is a journey that will never end. ... [it] is kind of like what Phil Knight [of Nike] said .... There is no finish line. Diversity will always be part of our narrative and we should continue to always have those conversations.

Gary was the only interviewee to talk in depth about the concept of equity in relation to inclusion (two other interviewees mentioned the term but only in passing). He said that we might want to believe that all people are created equal, but we have to realize that "our circumstances as we grow up are not."

Still a long way to go

Similar to the results of the survey, the sentiment that there is still a long way to go when it comes to D&I in the US public relations industry was clear from all the interviews. While interviewees acknowledged that some positive changes have occurred, they described several obstacles that still stand in the path of genuine progress. Two interviewees noted that when it comes to D&I, the public relations industry is a reflection of corporate America, which also has a long way to go.

A lonely place

The public relations industry was described as a lonely place for beginners from underrepresented groups. With little cultural overlap with members of dominant identity groups, April said "they really struggle to find their niche or place on the team in an organization." Cheryl shared the story of an "extremely impressive" African American young man who was recently recruited into an agency. He started at the agency to find that he was only one of two African Americans at this place. She elaborated:

> ...it was the loneliest he'd ever felt in his life. ... [then] the Charlottesville incident happened. ... Could he talk to about it at, at work? ... there were feelings that were bottled up in him that he felt he could never release during the course of a day. And that's a bad situation to be in.

Mike explained that the lack of diversity in the profession means that there is a lack of more senior people who can mentor and understand the needs of diverse recruits. According to Mark, the reason minority employees have such a hard time is because they are surrounded by:

> ...folks [who] have become so comfortable being comfortable ... [they] don't have the cultural understanding to work with different people and it's ... easier quite frankly, to work with people who you have everything in common with.

According to several interviewees, such environments and homogenous organizational cultures are a primary reason that retention of employees from underrepresented groups has been an ongoing problem, especially at agencies, despite increases in recruitment efforts.

Unconscious and conscious biases

Several interviewees mentioned homogenous (mainly White) organizational environments are also marked by unconscious (implicit) as well as overt biases. Barry and Andrew used terms such as "complacency," "racism," "bigotry" and "stereotypes" to explain some of the problems in these environments. Elaborating on bias and racism, Cheryl (who identifies as an African American woman) shared the story of an interview experience:

> My gray hair had started to come in, you know, I have a gray streak ... my hair was beautifully done with the exception of this streak ... the leadership of the agency had to check in with another African American

colleague … to make sure that the streak in my hair wasn't a gang sign …
Now anyone African American interviewing and talking to me would
have viewed it as a style statement. … as opposed to being fearful…

She offered a second story:

When I shared with a White well-respected PR industry leader, that
my passion was in multicultural marketing and that therefore I wanted
to work at an agency which specialized in that … His reply was, 'Don't
Cheryl. You're extremely talented. You're too good for that.'

Dorothy explained how some implicit biases have become systemic. She
offered the example of some writing tests that are routinely used for hiring,
elaborating that some of these tests may very well be culturally biased toward
dominant and educationally privileged identity groups. She also said when
times are financially tough, D&I efforts tend to fall by the wayside and are not
considered a priority.

Several of the interviewees noted that while more women seem to be getting
promoted to senior positions now, there is still a bias when it comes to people
of color. In other words, the women being promoted are mainly White. Biases,
according to Henry, whether unconscious or conscious, are major obstacles in
the path of embedding D&I in the culture of public relations. He said these biases
could very well be a primary reason why people often talk the talk but do not
walk the walk on D&I, particularly senior leadership. He said there is a difference
between saying something is important and acting on it with true commitment.

Change is slow

Mike's words summed up the sentiments of all the interviewees on the pace of
D&I change: "It's a slow, difficult process." Dorothy said that D&I "remains a
unicorn in the industry today … it just needs to get much better." In addition
to the issues of problematic organizational cultures/climates and unconscious
and conscious biases which obstruct inclusion and equity, interviewees noted
some other factors that slow down change.

According to Dorothy, a very real systemic issue is the lack of awareness
about public relations as a career choice among underrepresented populations.
She said students do not usually learn about public relations until sometime
later in college and that more efforts to increase awareness among underrepresented groups must be made at the high school level to create a stronger flow
to college and then to the profession.

Gary brought up a point that one of the primary reasons for the slow pace
of change is that people have not yet figured out healthy ways to talk about

differences at work. He explained that they are often too afraid to speak honestly and are overly afraid of offending:

> [A] lot of people are thinking things in a room and want to say something, but they're afraid that someone's going to think that they're racist or sexist, or they're not sympathetic or empathetic. ... And they hold back and say nothing.

This fear and hesitation, according to him, actually works counter to building inclusion and healthy communication climates.

Several interviewees said that while there has been some increase in diversity in junior and mid-levels positions, they see the senior level as being the problem. They explained that recently there has been an uptick in the promotion of women to more senior positions, but the glass ceiling is still firm at the CEO level. Lara, Andrew and Henry also pointed out that there is a misperception, which could also be interpreted as a bias, that there is not enough diverse talent to recruit from, especially at the senior levels. Cheryl said that she does not see this problem at multicultural agencies:

> I've never, ever had a problem finding talent, strong talent that has helped me put together major award winning, results-oriented campaigns for clients, right? So if I'm able to find good talent, and I know that there are a thousand out there who have not landed on their feet.... Why aren't you able to find good talent?

Instead of giving in to this misperception/bias about lack of talent, Henry and Lara said that recruitment strategies and hiring practices need to be checked for systemic bias and reformed as needed to speed up change. Another point several interviewees made about the slow pace of change is that due to its homogenous nature, the industry has become too comfortable with doing things a certain way and that it needs to open up to new, different and more inclusive professional values and practices. Finally, several interviewees said it is difficult to make progress unless clear goals are put in place and performance/outcomes are measured. As April put it: "I'm a big believer in you move what you measure."

The response of one leader interviewed after the racial upheavals of 2020 was more optimistic. Mark said that unprecedented calls for racial and social justice were making him "very optimistic and hopeful for the future of our industry." He said he was observing that conversations that were needing to happen for a long time finally seemed to be happening. Gary was more cautious stating that "organizations are somewhat unsure about what direction they should take. And part of it is caused by, you know, the changing situation, not only in our country, but around the world." He added that along with the 2020 upheavals, the fact that currently there are five generations in the workplace, each with different approaches to D&I, leadership and other issues, means it is a little difficult to accurately predict the future.

Lack of leadership engagement and accountability

All of the interviewees lamented the lack of senior leaders' direct engagement in D&I efforts and stressed the need for more accountability if the industry wants to see any significant change. They said leaders are not doing enough to embrace societal changes and elaborated on various dimensions of leaders' role and responsibilities with regard to D&I.

Lack of commitment and lip service

The issue of lack of senior leadership commitment to D&I ran as a clear theme through all the interviews. While some said there are a few leaders who genuinely care about D&I and are involved personally in this effort, they said that such leaders are few and far apart. April did not mince her words:

> I really hate to say this, but I think that the biggest obstacle is that there are still so many leaders at the top that don't truly believe in or support D&I. They know it's a good thing to do, but they personally, their value systems aren't aligned with actually doing it. ... I just don't think they get it ... they don't see the business value of it. And they just don't put their money where their mouth.

Lara said she thinks many leaders are fearful, have "personal insecurities" and avoid "including certain minorities due to concerns for image, reputation, acceptance."

Henry said those at "the very top of these organizations" must "walk the walk and talk the talk ... I don't think we've always seen that. ... nobody says they're not for it." Confirming findings from our survey, he and Andrew elaborated another problem is that due to the lack of commitment, senior leaders tend to outsource the responsibility of D&I, usually to human resources divisions, and this prevents D&I from becoming an organic part of organizational culture. Henry said one clear way of fixing this problem would be to increase diversity in senior leadership.

The effects of rose-tinted glasses

We asked interviewees to share their thoughts on the findings of some studies, including our online survey, that leaders seem to think they are performing much better on D&I than those who are not in formal leadership roles. We received some insightful responses.

Cheryl said that leaders see a few leadership positions filled by people of color and think that the work is done. She elaborated:

> I think they're looking through rose-colored glasses and wanting to see the best possible scenario. That is not the reality. ... you know, we're in a business where very often we're developing the most optimistic story. ... We look at the glass half full, never half empty, ... So we're wired to really see the optimistic end of the same set of facts from which someone else might derive a very different story. So I think we are spinning our own story in a way that makes the leadership feel that they do have this covered and that we are moving forward.

Similarly, April said: "I think they [leaders] look around their offices and they see diverse faces and they think that they've achieved their goals .... And then they pat themselves on the back." She said, "people see what they want to see ... and they kind of rest on their laurels." What they do not see, she said, are the day-to-day struggles that underrepresented employees face in their attempts to feel included. Mike offered another reason explaining that leaders set the vision and that "they may be just focusing on their vision more than the actual reality of what's on the ground." The latter is what the others live on a daily basis and hence the discrepancy, he explained. Henry and Andrew said that since there is a tendency to pass the D&I responsibility to human resources, leaders think the work is getting done. Henry explained that there are some D&I events that employees participate in regularly (e.g., Pride Parades, Black History Month) and then there is an excited social media buzz about it and "they [leaders] think it's great." He added that "diversity shouldn't be an initiative. It should just be embedded in an organization."

According to Barry, these leaders who are out of touch are "living in a bubble." Gary described this disconnect as follows:

> I truly believe that the grass tops are quickly losing touch with the grass roots. And I see that gap growing... the leadership believes that they're doing everything because they have a little checklist... leaders need to step outside occasionally... they're not paying attention to the data. ... people are checking off the boxes, ... but what they're not checking off [to see] is are those people matriculating in our organization or are we retaining them? Are they in the pipeline for the senior most positions?

Mark said: "You know, I'm going to say this – the best leaders know that there's always [more D&I] work to be done to be better." And according to the interviewees, these types of leaders are rare.

Dorothy said this perception gap is "honestly ludicrous" because the data (which leaders should be aware of) tell the truth:

> I really think that a certain dose of humility is required here because we need to kind of see the situation for what it is, not what we wish it would be, in order for us to make significant progress."

Elaborating that senior leaders are surrounded by likeminded individuals she said the effect is there are no "truth tellers" around to help them see and think differently. Gary emphasized:

> All anyone has to do is look at the statistics of our country to see how diverse our country has become and how diverse the world is becoming in order to understand the critical importance of diversity and inclusion in our organizations ….

He said not being able to incorporate this change at the very highest levels of the organization (and industry) is a failure of leadership.

"Well, that's the role of the leader, to be a visionary, right?"

The above words are from Lara, and all interviewees agreed a leader's primary responsibility is to set a vision for the organization, and that this should include vision for D&I (including what the future of D&I should be in the industry). Cheryl said: "It has to come from the top down and they've got to recognize the importance of this [D&I]." According to Lara, if the leader includes D&I in the overall vision, then this will "just permeate the entire organization. … [and] everyone [will know]… that it is their responsibility to incorporate diversity into their own teams." Mike elaborated that a vision entails setting clear goals. Three of the interviewees gave the example of one global public relations firm that set the clear goal to increase women in senior leadership positions to at least 50% and according to April, "they have truly moved the needle." They said such clear goals should be set for other dimensions of diversity as well.

Andrew, Mark and Henry emphasized that in order to set a progressive vision, leaders must embrace vulnerability and be open to change. Henry said it is not enough for leaders to just have good D&I-related intentions, and that they must be bold and willing to take some risks (to think and do things differently) in order to learn. He explained that mistakes may be made along the way, but these are sometimes necessary for change to occur and for leaders to be able to step out of the "true-and-tried" box that may be obstructing D&I. Both Mark and Henry specifically mentioned senior leaders must be willing to learn from junior colleagues and younger generations when necessary (i.e., be open to reverse mentoring) and be in touch with the cultural pulse of society in order to, as Mike put it, "steer the ship in the right direction."

According to Cheryl, Andrew and Dorothy, D&I vision should be a collective industry effort and larger than any one organization. Cheryl said leaders who can make a difference should come together to create a "roadmap" for where we are going and develop measurements for accomplishments. She added that everyone may not agree on this, but that she is a "big proponent" of leaders' bonuses being tied to D&I goals. Gary also agreed that D&I should be "a mandate that is tied to compensation and promotions."

Several of the interviewees emphasized that D&I should be envisioned as a business imperative as well as "the right thing to do" (Henry) suggesting both the business and the moral case for diversity are equally important. They explained that it is the leader's responsibility to help others see how the two cases are intertwined rather than separate. According to Dorothy, "I think we have to be super intentional about … [the vision we] want to create … [it should be] both a moral imperative, as well as a business imperative."

Some of the interviewees spoke at length about the current lack of D&I vision in the industry. Cheryl said that US society is changing so fast: "This is unstoppable. So I'm just surprised that some people don't see it." April added:

Yeah, so we all know it starts at the top. And if the CEO is not an authentic advocate for it [D&I], then [other] PR leaders can create a vision, even separate from the CEO. I think they can have an impact. … We have a layer of leaders that are truly, truly committed and see the value of D&I and are working hard towards it no matter what level they are at, because they will ultimately be the CEO of agencies, the chief communications officers of companies. And we need to have finally created a generation that actually gets it and embraces it.

Lara had a similar view and said that if the vision and impetus from the very top is not there then the effort "has to be bottom up so the next generation is equipped."

Leader communication matters: Words must align with action

How leaders communicate matters, but several interviewees made a distinction between words and action since they believe leaders' lip service to D&I is an ongoing problem. Gary said, "demonstrate it [words] in action," and elaborated emphatically:

Back it up. … executives get up all the time and say, we're gonna do this, we're gonna do that. …but we need to see concrete action …

action being taken at the top. So if they're very serious about this, they're going to take specific steps to be more inclusive and be more diverse at that level. .... That has to happen from the top. ... so that people feel empowered at all levels to be able to make change and be engaged in diversity and inclusion. If that doesn't happen, then it doesn't matter what the executive says ....

Dorothy noted that "communication should be in both, word and deed," and Mark said that for leadership to communicate genuinely about D&I, they should make it an everyday and organic part of their communication, a lens through which they view the profession and society, and not just talk about D&I when something positive happens.

The interviewees said that internally and externally, leaders should clearly communicate the organization's D&I commitment to stakeholders and publics and according to April, their messages should be "delivered clearly," consistently and "with conviction." Along with it being the right thing to do, Lara explained that furthermore at the internal level, it is necessary for a leader to be able to communicate and explain clearly why D&I is important for the profession so that employees can understand hiring decisions and policies: "It needs to make sense in terms of the business ... It needs to be part of the messaging. It needs to be part of the strategic vision of the business." April also emphasized that employees need to understand that D&I "has tremendous business impact. It truly does. ... you have companies now going to agencies and telling them, if you don't give us a diverse team, we're not going to let you even pursue the RFP." She also said it is the leader's role to explain this impact clearly at the internal level.

Henry spoke at length about the need for leaders to engage in D&I training and change their approach to leadership, i.e., leaders should not see the need to learn and admit they may not know everything as a weakness: "We need some environments where we can train up some people, and people need to feel comfortable with being a little bit vulnerable." He gave the example of The CEO Action for Diversity and Inclusion (an initiative that grew out of PricewaterhouseCoopers in 2017), which is currently the largest CEO-led initiative for advancing D&I in the workplace in the United States. He described some of his workshop experiences:

And so I would hear some questions that were perhaps a little cringe-worthy, right? But that was the setting. These were individual leaders who have moved up because they were great line managers who became a great GM of a business, a whole business unit, then became a great leader in the C-suite and then became the CEO, but maybe they were never trained in diversity and inclusion anywhere along the way. Then once they became CEO, everyone expected that they were going to be an expert in that, in addition to balance sheets and income statements and working with Wall Street and everything else.

He said more such spaces and initiative are needed where leaders wanting to learn can feel it is okay to ask the "cringeworthy" questions without being judged.

Mike pointed out the connection between internal and external communication. He said that to build strong internal D&I cultures, leaders need to make sure internal D&I communication is clear, goal-oriented and measurable, just like in "regular campaigns." He explained:

> What that does is it then creates an internal audience of brand ambassadors that can go out and talk about what the company is doing .... Employees are the most trusted voice because, you know, they spend the most time in an organization and they end up being the best ambassadors.

Similarly, Cheryl and Andrew said that leaders need to communicate, both internally and externally, that D&I is an integral part of organizational culture. But the most important thing, according to them, is that they should check regularly to make sure the internal reality matches with the external communication. As Cheryl put it, "you have to practice what you preach" for communication to be authentic.

Across all the interviews, insightful advice was offered on what leaders can do to move the D&I needle faster in the near future and turn talk into walk. Much of what needs to be done could be surmised from what the interviewees said is currently not being done (or done well enough). "Advice for the future" did not emerge as a stand-alone theme in the coding process, and we report all the advice collectively, along with our own suggestions, in the Conclusion chapter. We now turn to D&I in public relations education, which directly impacts the college-to-profession D&I pipeline and preparation of future leaders.

Tracking D&I from college/education to profession

The public relations students of today are the practitioners, and eventually leaders, of tomorrow. According to public relations scholar and educator Donnalyn Pompper (2005b), "The status of public relations practice is directly linked to public relations education" (p. 299). According to Brown, Waymer and Zhou (2019), "Diversity must start at the classroom level in order for emerging practitioners to embrace diversity at the professional level" (p. 19). Practitioners also seem to agree. For example, according to Natalie Flores, president of Inspire PR:

> I think change needs to start at the university level. Faculty who are teaching PR should weave DE&I into the coursework from the start.

It is not only about one case study, one class or one semester. It should be part of every communications class that we teach to PR students.

However, this often does not happen. Therefore, by the time you get into the profession, your brain is already wired. We could change that and provide professors with tools to teach PR a little differently.

(Luque, n.d., paras. 6, 7)

Therefore, we must ask the question: How is D&I being taught in relation to the profession in the classroom? The college-to-profession D&I pipeline is an important factor in the public relations D&I narrative. However, there are only a handful of studies in public relations scholarship that focus on this aspect. This is obviously another area that needs attention from researchers.

Findings from a recent survey of practitioners and educators by the Commission on Public Relations Education (CPRE) show that when it comes to D&I knowledge, skills and abilities (KSAs), practitioners particularly note the lack of these KSAs in students graduating from public relations programs. They also seem to value D&I slightly more than educators (DiStaso, 2019; Mundy, Lewton, Hicks, & Neptune, 2018). Based on the findings of the survey, the most recent CPRE report emphasizes the urgent need for integrating D&I into the curriculum.

In order to see D&I within the public relations industry flourish, change must begin at the academic level through a more diverse student and educator base, and through changes in how D&I is taught at the educational level. This school-to-industry pipeline will result in a more diverse workforce.

(Mundy et al., 2018, p. 139)

Focusing on D&I in public relations education can help both majority and underrepresented students develop better skills for navigating diversity and cultural differences at the workplace and appreciate and work toward building inclusive organizational cultures in mindful and creative ways (Brunner, 2005). According to practitioner Kecia Carroll (n.d.), "DE&I is a crucial aspect in developing future PR practitioners. … They need to be ready to lead organizations into evolving values, culture and policies towards diversity, equity and inclusion" (para. 25)

The few extant studies that focus on this topic indicate that the state of D&I in education needs a lot of attention (Bardhan, 2003; Brown, C. White, & Waymer, 2011; Mundy et al., 2018; Pompper, 2005b; Waymer, 2012; Waymer & Brown, 2018; Waymer & Dyson, 2011). The need for D&I in public relations education exists at two levels – that of the curriculum and the people involved (i.e., educators and students) (see Carroll, n.d.). With regard to curriculum,

Pompper (2005b) found in a focus group study of African American female practitioners that the latter think the manner in which public relations is taught is "still out of step with multicultural world realities" (p. 310). In a study that focused on the role of race-related content in curriculum, Waymer and Dyson (2011) make the argument that simply teaching technical skills to undergraduate students is not enough and that the curriculum also needs to incorporate sociocultural aspects of the profession so that students are "prepared to engage in critical, reflective discussion and argument about the most pressing issues of contemporary society" (pp. 461–462). Further, they emphasize that race-related content does not get systematically included in teaching and the applied work students engage in. Faculty also reported struggling with including race-related content emphasized that what exists is "shallow and misrepresented" and expressed the need for more robust content (p. 473). McKie and Munshi (2009) have offered similar critiques of the instrumental and technical nature of current undergraduate public relations education (see also Kern-Foxworth, 1989b).

The undesirable outcomes of not including D&I content in curriculum are evident from the results of two recent studies. Place and Vanc (2016) conducted in-depth interviews with mainly White undergraduate public relations students from three mid-size universities in the United States with the goal of examining how much D&I experience students were gaining in applied aspects of the curriculum (e.g., service learning and client work). They found that students perceived diversity in negative ways, were fearful of diversity, struggled with coming to terms with their own White privilege and had a hard time connecting D&I with the professional context. The authors concluded that students' lack of preparedness to work with diverse publics (both internal and external) does not position them well for entering the profession. As mentioned earlier, this lack of D&I preparedness was also a key finding in the recent CPRE survey. In a similar study by Muturi and Zhu (2019) of mainly White mass communication (including public relations) students at a large Midwestern university, results showed that students have limited exposure to D&I issues and struggle with placing race/ethnicity in professional contexts.

In addition to curriculum, the lack of diversity among educators and students is another D&I obstacle in public relations education environments. The effort to recruit and retain more diverse students and faculty remains an ongoing challenge. In an interview-based study with undergraduate African American public relations students, Brown et al. (2011) found that while race did not seem to play a role in why the students picked public relations as a major, it did become a factor once they started in the major. Students reported not wanting to feel pigeonholed or feeling like they had to represent their entire race, said they wanted to see more faculty and mentors who looked like them, and that they initially did not feel very welcome in their Public Relations

Student Society of America (PRSSA) chapters. In another interview-based study, Waymer and Brown (2018) asked African American, Hispanic, White and Asian American practitioners with five or fewer years of professional experience how their educational experience and environment either helped or hurt them in terms of academic success and entry into the profession. The respondents of color did not report any major negative experiences but did express that they felt they had to work harder than White students to prove themselves and that being a minority was uncomfortable at times. The White respondents expressed having an understanding that students of color felt they had to work harder, and they also said that race was not an obstacle for them. However, in a more recent study of public relations undergraduate students from eight colleges and universities (66% of the respondents were White, 16% Hispanic, 9% African American, 7% of other races/ethnicities, 16% male and 84% female), Brown et al. (2019) found that race and gender play a significant role in students' experience. White female students (the majority demographic in most undergraduate public relations programs) reported having the most positive experience, both educationally and socially, and were more successful in building professional networks. Brown et al. emphasize the need to diversify the faculty and mentors available to underrepresented students who can advise them and help them network professionally.

Pompper's (2005b) study shows that according to female African-American practitioners, the curriculum cannot improve without the diversification of public relations faculty and that underrepresented student' perceptions of their prospects in the profession are directly related to role models and mentors they can relate to (and vice versa). Commenting on the current very homogenous state of faculty, they recommended all faculty keep educating and training themselves on incorporating D&I into the curriculum to avoid perpetuating an "Anglo Eurocentric" perspective (p. 310). Accreditation bodies and other scholars are also emphasizing the need to recruit more diverse adjunct faculty, bring diverse guest speakers into classrooms and expose all students to diverse experiences in professional contexts (e.g., shadowing, internships, mentoring, client work), training current faculty, and keeping D&I measurement high on the agenda of higher education leaders (Accreditation Council on Education in Journalism and Mass Communications, 2018; Brown et al., 2019; Mundy et al., 2018; Muturi & Zhu, 2019; Place & Vanc, 2016).

As we have elaborated throughout, and especially in Chapter 3, diversity and inclusion are complex phenomena and every effort should be made to address the complexities (e.g., taking an intersectional approach to diverse identities). One clear limitation of the extant research on public relations education and D&I is that studies have focused mainly on the race/ethnicity and gender dimensions of D&I in public relations education. Since race/ethnicity is a central marker of identity as well as inequity in the United States, this focus makes sense. The gender focus also makes sense given the significant gender power imbalance in public relations education and the industry. However, other aspects of diversity and difference, both primary (non-alterable) and secondary (alterable), need to be studied and intersectional approaches to D&I need to be adopted to adequately address the increasingly complex diversity landscape of the country and our world (Mundy et al., 2018). While calls are being made, actual studies of curriculum content and recruitment/retention efforts for diverse faculty and students need to be conducted.

Following the 2020 racial and social justice upheavals in the country, many professional organizations stepped up their efforts and are developing strategies, plans and content for diversifying public relations education. For example, the Institute for Public Relations (IPR) began a series of live online discussions titled "Race in the PR Classroom," jointly hosted by the IPR and the Public Relations Society of America (PRSA) Educators Academy ("Race in the PR Classroom," n.d.). This series provides valuable content and advice for educators and is also a platform for them to engage in ongoing dialogue about the challenges they face with regard to incorporating D&I in public relations pedagogy. Further, the IPR is also partnering with other organizations to offer scholarships to underrepresented students and has set up a Center for Diversity, Equity and Inclusion to step up research. It has also committed to producing a D&I teaching guide (Institute for Public Relations, 2021b). Even prior to 2020, The Plank Center for Leadership in Public Relations had started conducting D&I-focused research, uploading resources onto its website and in 2018 launched an annual D&I summit to link professionals, practitioners and students with scholarships being granted to students to attend the summit (The Plank Center, n.d.). Such action by professional associations is necessary to make the college-to-profession D&I pipeline stronger.

Views of public relations educators and student leaders

In addition to interviewing senior leaders in the profession, we also conducted in-depth interviews with ten student leaders and ten educators who are at the forefront of advocating for more inclusion of D&I in public relations education. Two questionnaires (one for students and one for educators) closely aligned with the one used to interview practitioners were developed. The interview data helped us primarily address the two following questions:

- What are the views of current public relations student leaders and educators invested in D&I about the state of D&I in education and industry?
- How do study participants view the role of industry leaders and educators in making D&I efforts successful?

We followed a purposive sampling approach and contacted students who had been previously selected for scholarships and awards for their outstanding commitment to D&I. Faculty advisers of PRSSA chapters were also contacted for recommendations of students who have demonstrated D&I leadership in their chapters. Next, educators who stand out for their D&I research and education efforts were contacted. The final student interviewee pool comprised four seniors, five juniors and one sophomore from universities/colleges in the Midwest, East Coast, Northeast and Southern parts of the United States. The educators recruited had between 8 and 39 years of teaching experience. Five had significant industry experience before entering academia (up to 35 years), four had fewer years while one had none. All interviewees were assigned pseudonyms for data reporting purposes. As in the case of the practitioner leader interviews, we asked the interviewees to describe their cultural identities in their own words (see Tables 6.2 and 6.3). (Note: All interviews were completed right before the racial upheavals of 2020.)

Open and axial coding of the two sets of interview transcripts resulted in four themes: (1) the relationship between "diversity" and "inclusion," (2) the state of D&I in the profession, (3) the responsibility of industry leadership and (4) the responsibility of educators. (Note: See Bardhan and Gower, 2020 for more details on student and educator leader responses.)

TABLE 6.2 Student leader interviewee identities

Pseudonym/year in college	Identity statement
Sharif (senior)	"I am a Muslim Arab Yemeni American."
Jasmine (senior)	"I am a Nigerian, American born."
Barb (senior)	"Upper middle class, White background. I was raised Catholic, Christian."
Mia (senior)	"I'm a multicultural individual and I have family from Brazil, Israel, France, Lebanon, Poland …a huge part of me is my nationality and my religion so I identify as a Venezuelan Jewish woman."
William (junior)	"American Colombian. I was born in Colombia and was adopted and moved to Upstate NY when I was young. I was raised in an all-White culture in a small town."
Derek (junior)	"African-American, Black, first generation college student, urban."
Dave (junior)	"African American homosexual male from the south who grew up in a predominantly White neighborhood …my cultural identity is always evolving."
Ben (junior)	"I'm American but my mother came from Jamaica… I tend to be very traditional mainly because I grew up in the Panhandle, which is like deep south."
Jane (junior)	"I'm White and from a smaller rural farm community in Minnesota."
Sheena (sophomore)	"African American woman."

TABLE 6.3 Educator leader interviewee identities

Pseudonym	Identity statements
Laura	"I'm Caucasian."
Mimi	"Eastern European and German."
John	"A White guy from a small rural Indiana town who fortunately had an amazing career that allowed him to see the larger world"
Terrence	"I identify as African American. I am biracial. My mother is White, my father is Black."
Jerry	"I am a White male, but I am a gay southerner … my dad's family is from Mexico originally. My mom's family has been in North Carolina for like 300 years."
Marie	"Female, Caucasian, heterosexual, Protestant, TAB (temporarily able bodied), mid-life aged."
Shana	"I am an African American woman. That's what I am. From the south, that's also very important."
Susan	"I really kind of think of myself as White female, lower-middle class, heterosexual, highly educated."
Gordon	"I am a father, a husband, a son, Black male, born in the southeast United States, who loves family and is concerned about how to raise a Black boy today in the southern United States, or the United States in general. Educator. Researcher. Advocate. Political Sociologist."
Valerie	"I am a Caucasian, European American. I am a lesbian. I don't know if you care about age, I'm 64-years-old. I'm middle class. So primarily your average blessed White woman …"

The relationship between "diversity" and "inclusion"

Both student and educator leaders made it clear that they understand "diversity" and "inclusion" are not the same and that recruiting diverse practitioners (or students and faculty) does not automatically lead to inclusion. They explained that diversity includes many kinds of differences in peoples' identities and inclusion means respecting all (alterable and non-alterable) differences, empowerment of all, and helping all feel like they belong. They spoke about the tendency to focus mainly on race/ethnicity and gender and believe this is not a broad enough view of diversity. Educator Marie mentioned the importance of taking an intersectional approach in how we understand and act on diversity related matters. Both groups also emphasized that equity is necessary for inclusion. Two student leaders specifically stated that representation matters when it comes to diversity. As student leader Dave put it, you "can't be what you can't see." Two educators expressed that inclusion is impossible without support from senior leadership. One emphasized a diverse organization is one that reflects the increasingly diversifying publics it works to connect with.

Both groups also emphasized that diversity and inclusion should not be lumped together but must work together or, as student leader Ben put it, they must "hold hands." Student leader Sheena shared the story of hearing a PRSSA keynote speaker say that diversity means being asked to the party and inclusion means being asked to dance. Another student Sharif and three educators also mentioned this popular analogy (attributed to D&I advocate and trainer Vernā Myers). Like Dorothy (practitioner leader), Laura (educator) was the only interviewee who explained that the term "inclusion" emerged when people began "realizing that they were getting people in the pipeline but weren't doing anything in the workplace to help them be successful."

Like the practitioner leaders in the last section, majority of the interviewees said the industry should not define D&I too tightly because diversity and how inclusion is performed are context sensitive and their meanings keep evolving with time. Overall, both groups supported the idea that a more flexible guiding vision, rather than a narrow definition, would be helpful for building a sense of what the public relations profession is working toward when it comes to D&I.

The state of D&I in the profession

Most of the student leaders and about half of the educators said while there is a higher recognition of the problem and more attention being paid to D&I, there is still a long way to go and a need for "a lot more action rather than talking" (student leader Mia). Like Mia, educator Valerie said: "It seems to me that people talk about it constantly … but there's no tangible evidence that we've really moved the needle." Jerry (educator) said recruitment is working much better than retention and Ben (student leader) emphasized steps taken "need to be intentional to help ensure that the industry is reflective of the society that's constantly changing and evolving."

Several student leaders said the industry is still too White, and some said this makes it difficult for them to feel welcome and envision their prospects for success in the future. Shana (educator) said the "White blonde sorority girl" stereotype of practitioners makes it hard for those who do not fit that image to see themselves in that role. About half of the educators used words such as "abysmal," "superficial," "terrible" and "shallow" to describe the current state of D&I in the industry. Laura (educator) added that implicit bias is a major problem and Jerry (educator) specifically emphasized the need to address gender and power disparities. Gordon (educator) said the weak college-to-profession D&I pipeline is a major obstacle in the path of moving the industry's D&I needle. A few student leaders made an important point (also made by practitioner leader Gary); they said people are often too afraid to offend and want to avoid conflict. Jasmine (student leader) and Dave (student leader) insisted that, despite such fears, it is important to find ways to have honest and respectful conversations about differences.

Several student leaders brought up the problem of the homogeneity of senior leadership who, according to William (student leader), "don't have the same perspectives as most Americans. We need new, younger and more diverse people running the PR industry to keep up with the constant changes and positive progression." Derek (student leader) added that "older leadership" has been too used to doing things the same way for too long, has been "hiring only a certain type of identity" and producing certain types of content. He acknowledged some leaders are open to change but said most are not. Sheena (student leader) noted that while there has been some progress in including more White women and LGBTQ+ individuals in leadership positions, there remains a clear lack of racial/ethnic diversity in top leadership. Beth (student leader) further pointed out it has become "normalized" to think men make better leaders, and this normalization happens not just in public relations but in larger society.

Several educators spoke about the conflict between economic and moral imperatives. John (educator) said the public relations world is "so driven by billability and the need to deliver results that people gravitate to those who look and think like they do, because it's more efficient and quicker to get the results." Marie (educator) added there is "too great a focus on the bottom line and business case arguments," and Susan (educator) said the main reason diversity is not flourishing in the industry is the "capitalistic society that is focused on profit and short-term accomplishments." Mimi (educator) added it is time to shift the conversation from "dollars and cents" to the "human element," or what is good for society, and therefore the profession. Several interviewees in both groups mentioned they perceive a lack of authenticity when it comes to D&I efforts, some cautioned diversity and inclusion are in danger of becoming just buzzwords, and that D&I is being acknowledged more now because it is a trend. Sharif (student leader) added those with privilege need to acknowledge it, internalize it and only then will authentic change take place.

The responsibility of industry leadership

Both student leaders and educators emphasized industry leaders should lead by example, although student leaders emphasized this point a little more than educators. Jane (student leader) said: "It has to start with top management because if they don't lead on it then it gets pushed down and doesn't happen." Similar to the practitioner leaders we interviewed, both groups said leaders must walk the talk and that lip service is just not enough or acceptable.

According to Ben (student leader), leaders should be "pioneers" in communicating about D&I, and according to Jasmine (student leader), they should not communicate about D&I in "stock" ways but in genuine ways that convey a real desire "to make the environment more diverse." Ben elaborated D&I language often gets put in writing (e.g., websites, mission statements) and then forgotten. He emphasized it is the leader's "responsibility to be talking about these things" and that even if D&I efforts are not going so well or are just beginning, it is important to admit faults and mistakes and encourage dialogue. William (student leader) suggested leaders need to share more positive and personal stories about how D&I engagement helped them in work and life and how they have overcome obstacles to bring about change. He added students (i.e., future leaders) should be included in these conversations.

Valerie (educator) pointed out the importance of good leadership communication:

> I think most of the people I can think of who run major organizations, corporations, they certainly do not come from a communication background, and they do not understand the value and the power of communications. They think they do, but they really don't.

Shana (educator) said that unfortunately, leaders tend to focus more on the business aspect and less on the importance of communication in building inclusive organizational cultures. Terrence (educator) said, "We need leaders to be leading conversations. … they do not have to provide the answers, but if they are asking provocative questions and getting the right people sitting around the table, that can help produce change." He explained the role of listening in communication and said listening is a lost art that must be revived. Gordon (educator) emphasized leaders need to be able to communicate to others in the organization why D&I is important for the profession itself and for building a sense of community. Susan (educator) described this as the need to communicate for "the greater good."

Both groups emphatically agreed that D&I success and authenticity are just not possible without personal engagement of top leadership. Personal engagement was linked to responsibility and accountability. Valerie (educator) said, "We need hard data and CEOs willing to look at that data and make some tough decisions and make it a priority because the demographics that they're serving in this country are changing so rapidly." She added that "we really don't see a lot of bold moves to make the field look different" and that leaders need to come together and work collectively on D&I. Laura (educator) said those heading D&I "should have a seat at the table for high level corporate strategies" and emphasized leaders need to take responsibility for outcomes. Most of the students remarked that industry leaders need to change their attitudes and perspectives regarding D&I and be more open to feedback. According to Sheena (student leader), leaders need to be "intentional" in their D&I work and in "reevaluating agency culture." Derek (student leader) observed that all leaders, and not just those who identify as belonging to marginalized groups, should talk about D&I and that "more learning and unlearning of unconscious bias" needs to happen. He said "old mentalities" can only change if more diverse leaders are in place and if current leaders can be more self-reflective, open-minded, and able to talk courageously about the biases they hold and how they are working on undoing them.

The responsibility of educators

Both groups agreed that educators are the leaders in the education setting, and just like in the case of leaders in industry, they are responsible for improving D&I in public relations education. Interviewees said D&I content should be infused organically into all the courses throughout the curriculum and should be a natural part of education. As Mia (student leader) put it, "Every single thing that has to be taught can be taught within diversity and inclusion itself. So, I think it is something that goes with educating in general." Some students said stand-alone courses that focus just on D&I would also be helpful. Others suggested including diverse authors, bringing in diverse practitioners as guest speakers in classes and organizing D&I workshops and industry tours. Diverse practitioners, according to the student leaders, could effectively mentor underrepresented students and help them feel empowered. Almost all the educators also spoke about the importance of diverse guest speakers. A few of them recommended study-abroad courses to help students understand cultural differences in embodied and fully immersed ways. According to Terrence (educator), "students need to be pushed outside of their comfort zone. For them to understand difference, they have to see difference." He also recommended using role playing activities in classes to help students embody difference. Shana (educator) said "pushing your students and giving them new experiences and new ways to think about things and new people to talk with and communicate with is very important. ... you need to challenge them."

The nature of the learning environment, along with curriculum, was also discussed by both groups as an important factor impacting D&I in educational spaces. Ben (student leader) and Sheena (student leader) said teachers should make sure they are being inclusive in the classroom and hold their students responsible when they are not. Jasmine (student leader) said educators should humanize themselves and talk more about their own experiences and struggles with D&I. She added they should "not just lecture" but help students have more "diverse conversations." Sharif (student leader) said teachers should emphasize that D&I is "important not only for the bottom line but also for humanity and for understanding privilege and disparities between people from different backgrounds and how D&I aims to make a more equal world."

Jerry (educator) said it is necessary to "embed cues into our [classroom] culture that indicate to people that they're welcome." As an example, he described how he incorporates an inclusion statement in his syllabi and said that his students seem to really appreciate this. Terrence (educator) emphasized educators must learn how to have difficult conversations about differences in classrooms and several educators offered examples of how they attempt to make their classes inclusive spaces. Mimi (educator) said that if someone is struggling or feeling isolated, she tries to find "someone who has a similar background that could be a mentor, or just someone who might understand some of the feelings that they might be feeling." John (educator) said students tend to gravitate toward their "own kind," so he mixes them up in how they sit and team up for assignments. Terrence (educator) said that as a minority identifying educator, he attempts to serve as a role model for all, but especially for underrepresented students. Shana (educator) emphasized self-reflexivity and the necessity for educators "to first examine our own biases, who we favor in our classrooms and who we favor as leaders."

Educators spoke extensively regarding the responsibility of educators to serve as leaders and advocates of D&I in public relations pedagogy. Some of them said they encourage their students to be advocates of D&I. John, Susan and Gordon (educators) noted that all educators, and not just those who identify as minorities, should use a D&I lens to teach public relations. Those educators who have held or currently hold administrative positions emphasized the need for structural changes (e.g., changes that would impact recruitment and retention of underrepresented students and faculty) that will be conducive to enhancing D&I in education. Several educators said education and industry must work together more systematically to recruit and offer opportunities (e.g., internships, scholarships) in ways that promote D&I. Susan said programs doing a good job with D&I should be upheld as models for others to learn from and emulate. Mimi (educator) observed that the current generation is much more aware about D&I issues than previous ones, and this could be a hopeful sign for the near future.

Key takeaways

The key takeaways are illuminating. There are several similar findings across the online survey and the 30 in-depth leader interviews we conducted. Some overlaps are also evident between the practitioner leader and the student leader and educator interviews:

- Across the survey and the interviews, majority of the respondents said that most public relations leaders pay lip service to D&I and that they must be personally engaged and take charge for the needle to move. The majority also said the D&I needle in the profession is moving too slowly, that the culture of Whiteness is entrenched in the industry (e.g., even though more women and LGBTQ+ professionals are being promoted, they tend to be mostly White) and that the profession needs to reflect national diversity.
- A key finding across the survey and the interviews is that inclusion (and developing organizational cultures that enhance inclusion) seems to be

the major challenge. While diversity recruitment efforts have improved some, retention of underrepresented employees (which is closely related to inclusion) remains a challenge. Underrepresented students also reported similarly and noted challenges when it comes to belonging and empowerment in the education space.

- A key finding across the survey and the practitioner interviews is that leaders seem to be shifting the responsibility for D&I to human resources.
- The perception gap that was confirmed in the survey was further confirmed by the leader practitioner interviewees.
- Majority of the interviewees in all three groups of leaders said that the meanings of diversity and inclsuionD&I are context sensitive and always evolving. A clear vision and values related to D&I and public relations are needed for industry-level collective action and change, but no definition should be fixed. All interviewees also agreed that D&I is an ongoing process and a journey.
- All interviewees in all three groups, and especially student leaders, agreed that the focus on race/ethnicity and gender is too narrow and that more differences need to be included in how diversity is conceptualized. One educator mentioned the need for an intersectional approach. While the student and practitioner leaders did not mention the term intersectionality, they spoke about diversity in ways that suggested intersectionality (that is, the need to address multiple differences simultaneously and avoid a silo approach).
- All interviewees agreed that how leaders communicate about D&I matters a lot in building inclusive organizational cultures.
- All interviewees said leaders need to be open to change and not think admitting they need to learn more about D&I is a weakness. Practitioner and student leaders also expressed concern about the homogeneity (White heterosexual male) of senior leadership.
- All interviewees agreed that unconscious and conscious biases continue to exist and hurt inclusion efforts.
- All interviewees said D&I is both a moral and business issue; however student leaders and educators emphasized the moral case more than the practitioner leaders.
- The need to better learn how to communicate in healthy ways across differences and not hesitate for fear of offending or causing conflict was mentioned by a few student and practitioner leaders.
- Equity was a term that was mentioned only by one practitioner leader. A few student leaders and educators mentioned the term but most of the interviewees focused on the term inclusion. Further, only one practitioner leader and one educator explained why the term inclusion is now becoming popular – because increasing diversity does not mean everything will work smoothly. The term inclusion suggests that there is another step,

that of relating respectfully across differences, that is necessary for the benefits of diverse organizations to materialize.

• Educators and student leaders were unanimous on the point that public relations education has a long way to go in terms of diversification (in terms of content and identities of educators and students). They emphasized that the D&I pipeline from the space of education to industry needs to be strengthened. Educators said students need to learn how to engage better with diversity and need to be shaken out of their comfort zones. Both student leaders and educators emphasized industry and academia need to work closely to enhance D&I in both realms.

Conclusion

The themes that emerged from the three sets of interviews, combined with the narratives that emerged from the online survey, indicate clearly that D&I in the public relations profession suffers from lack of leadership support and engagement. Relatedly, the space of education is also inadequately equipped to teach the students of today, who are the professionals and leaders of tomorrow, about public relations through the lens of D&I. Those employed in the profession, and the current D&I pipeline between education and industry, do not reflect the rapidly diversifying national cultural landscape. The few underrepresented professionals who do enter the industry mostly express feelings of exclusion. Inclusion seems to be a big challenge. In the words of practitioner Simon Locke (n.d.): "How will we know that we've made progress? The [PR] industry will look more like the country and less like a country club" (para. 21).

The events of 2020 led to a surge in D&I discourse in corporate America including public relations. Strategic plans were quickly developed, more D&I positions have been created and many events, summits and webinars are focusing on D&I and public relations (including public relations education). If the lessons of 2020 do not lead to improved D&I vision and practice, then the reputation and integrity of the public relations profession will be in jeopardy. Leaders need to step up, themselves diversify and take responsibility for creating organizational cultures of diversity, equity and inclusion. In the next chapter, we offer our model for envisioning and building such cultures with a clear focus on the role of leadership in this process.

7

A Leadership Model for Inclusive Diversity in Public Relations

In this chapter, we bring it all together. By this, we mean that we weave together all the previous chapters on diversity and inclusion (D&I), leadership and relevant public relations literature with our own data to do three things: (1) describe the narrative threads, or themes, that intertwine to tell the story of the current state of D&I and leadership in public relations in the United States, (2) describe the core characteristics of our leadership model for inclusive diversity in public relations and (3) present our model along with an explanation of its various components.

Tying the narrative threads together

So what's the overall story? In keeping with the story approach, we have adopted in this book, we went back to the key takeaways from each chapter and developed narrative threads (or themes) that construct the overall story of public relations leadership and D&I (see Table 7.1). The 11 themes that emerged revolve around cultural and/or structural issues pertaining to our subject matter.

Diversity and inclusion are not yet a core aspect of the US public relations professional culture

Every profession has a specific culture with core values and practices. Public relations has a long way to go when it comes to developing and incorporating D&I values and practices into its culture, especially its leadership culture. In relation to the various models and perspectives for D&I reviewed previously (see Chapter 3), the industry primarily follows the access-and-legitimacy perspective of Ely and Thomas (2001) which aligns with the business case. While the relevance

DOI: 10.4324/9781003170020-7

TABLE 7.1 Themes constituting the overall public relations, D&I and leadership narrative

1. D&I is not yet a core aspect of the US public relations professional culture
2. Public relations leadership has failed on the issue of D&I
3. A troubling perception gap exists between leaders and those not in formal leadership positions
4. Leaders lack skills for D&I-minded leadership
5. Leaders need to be better D&I communicators
6. The tendency is to understand diversity mostly in Equal Employment Opportunity (EEO) terms and language
7. The business case for D&I is prioritized over the moral case
8. Inequity-based power differentials and biases persist
9. Differences are still conceptualized in simplistic ways
10. Public relations education needs to play a pivotal role in strengthening the D&I college-to-profession pipeline
11. Scholarship on D&I and public relations leadership is almost non-existent

of diversity is recognized according to this perspective, it is incorporated more at the margins (and somewhat in the middle). Diversity is not an integrated part of the workings of the entire organization/industry and is absent especially at the core or the senior leadership level. A misperception seems to exist that there is not enough diverse talent, especially for senior leadership roles.

Our own data and previous studies suggest there is a tendency among leaders to pass the buck for diversity efforts to human resources departments. This suggests a compartmentalized approach to diversity, which hurts the goal of inclusion. While some gains have been made in recruiting for diversity, inclusion (along with equity) remains a major challenge; leaders struggle with how to describe and practice inclusion/equity, and the profession has only recently begun discussing its critical importance (Chitkara, 2018; PRSA Chapter D&I Toolkit, 2021). The problem is reportedly worse in the agency than within in-house settings (Ramaswamy, 2018). Organizational climate is also a matter of concern, and there is a sense that D&I is not practiced as an intentional and ongoing effort (i.e., as a process). No bold moves for D&I have occurred in the industry. The year 2020 did see the establishment of the Diversity Action Alliance (DAA) (see Chapter 3), which is an industry-wide effort to move the D&I needle at a faster pace. Also, the watershed turn in D&I sentiments after the killing of George Floyd spurred many industry-level promises. Actual actions, outcomes and changes are yet to be measured. However, some recent reports indicate that matters not have improved much (e.g., "Unsafe," 2022).

Public relations leadership has failed on the issue of D&I

Unfortunately, the research reviewed and conducted for this book suggests that public relations leaders, especially senior leaders, have not demonstrated commitment and accountability when it comes to D&I. They tend to pay lip service to D&I but very few are genuinely and personally engaged. Talk often does not translate into walk. The industry has been repeatedly criticized on this matter. Research clearly indicates that D&I success is not possible without authentic and genuine leadership engagement in the form of words, policies, resource support and other needed actions. Therefore, this is a case of leadership failure with regard to D&I.

Homophily has been a central feature of senior leadership in the profession for a long time. As explained in Chapter 3, the research on diversity explains that homophily leads to group-think and the tendency to stick within cultural comfort zones which ultimately drive out D&I and its advantages. This is a systemic problem that needs to be tackled with transparency and the will to change the status quo. While some recent changes have occurred in the form of promotion of more women and LGBTQ+ professionals into senior leadership positions, the attention to race/ethnicity has been poor. Whiteness remains firmly entrenched in the profession's culture, especially leadership culture (Logan, 2011, 2021; Vardeman-Winter & Place, 2017). This too is a systemic inequity issue and a major obstruction in the path of diversifying senior leadership and integrating inclusion into organizational climate. Overall, underrepresented junior employees perceive and face cultural and structural constraints (e.g., lack of mentorship and sponsorship opportunities, the history of lack of diversity in the profession) when it comes to advancing in leadership positions (Chitkara, 2018; Meng & Neill, 2021).

A troubling perception gap exists between leaders and those not in formal leadership positions

The perception gap reported in Chapter 5 and indicated in a few previous studies adds another layer to the failure of leadership on D&I. Leaders consistently report they are performing better on D&I compared to what those they lead report. Some of our senior leader interviewees explained this is probably because once leaders set a D&I vision which seems appropriate, hear the buzz every now and then around certain D&I events, and see a few individuals from underrepresented groups in the ranks, they tend to think D&I policy/vision and practice are aligned. This is a "check-the-box" D&I mentality that does not take into consideration that D&I is an ongoing process, and the work is never all done.

This perception gap begs some serious questions. Are leaders out of touch with the D&I ground realities in their organizations and the spirit of the times? Are they not concerned about increasing pressure from clients to provide more diverse teams to connect with their increasingly diverse publics? Are they not in touch with the fast-changing diversity demographics and cultural identity landscapes of the country and the world? Do they lack an understanding of the role that culture and social inequities play when it comes to communication, relationship building and inclusion/equity? Do they lack multicultural insights and competencies (including the ability to share power), which are needed for strategic thinking, alliance building and moral accountability when it comes to D&I? Finally, is it not within senior leaders' radar that millennials, who are now moving into leadership roles, along with Gen Z which is increasingly joining the workforce, are more social justice and D&I oriented than any generation before? As one of our senior leader interviewees pointed out, there are currently five generations in the workplace. It seems likely that overall, those currently in senior leadership positions have a different generational orientation to D&I than more junior level employees.

Another point that likely contributes to the perception gap is the lack of clear goal-setting and metrics for measuring D&I outcomes. One of the senior leaders we interviewed said it well: we cannot move what we cannot (or do not) measure. The DAA has recently taken up this measurement and accountability charge. This is an opportunity for leadership to step up and demonstrate genuine commitment.

Leaders lack skills for D&I-minded leadership

Research, our own and that of others, indicates that public relations leaders, especially senior leaders, lack (or need to better develop) several D&I-related skills:

- The ability to be open and eager to learn what they do not know (e.g., how to better communicate about D&I) and unlearn practices and beliefs that hurt D&I progress.
- The ability to better understand how to be personally engaged in building inclusive diversity climates. This includes helping employees feel they belong without downplaying their uniqueness.
- Humility and the ability to introspect and practice self-reflexivity.
- The ability to prioritize empowerment, relationality, two-way communication and dialogue to build trust and help inclusion thrive.
- The ability to admit mistakes and share what they have learned from them. This requires the ability to not see vulnerability and openness as weaknesses.
- Multicultural competencies, sensitivities, emotional intelligence, the ability to share power and a social justice orientation (i.e., the moral case for D&I).
- The ability to pay close attention to and help develop the D&I pipeline.
- The ability to be in touch with the D&I ground realities in their organization and in the external environment and be involved in ensuring D&I policies are being implemented. This entails developing goal measurement systems, getting regular feedback and ensuring there is no perception and policy-practice gap (e.g., see Moody, 2021).
- The ability to embrace D&I responsibility and accountability.

Leaders need to be better D&I communicators

Public relations leaders have a deep influence on the communication cultures of their organizations. This point requires significant attention, especially since public relations is a communication profession. Through a D&I lens, this means how leaders communicate about D&I matters a lot, internally and externally (Mundy, 2016).

Research shows how leaders communicate about D&I is inseparable from their role and responsibility to build inclusive relationships and cultures. Effective internal D&I leader communication entails everyday communication at all levels of the organization. Pro-diversity communication should not be reserved for just certain days and months of the year. Leaders need to talk about D&I in positive ways, be able to clearly explain the role D&I plays in the organization and how to harness its benefits, emphasize D&I is everyone's responsibility and not just of those from underrepresented groups and be upfront in communicating that policies, practices and behaviors that could be harming D&I efforts should be revised or discarded. Leaders need to humanize all by encouraging a culture of storytelling, dialogue and listening. They need to engage in building communication and dialogue across differences in respectful ways. The above internal communication skills need to be a part of external leader communication as well. Currently, these D&I-related leadership communication and intercultural skills are not being demonstrated well in the profession.

The tendency is to understand diversity in mostly EEO terms and language

Related to the above theme regarding communication is the point that the language we use to describe something shapes our perceptions, sense-making and reality (see Bardhan & Engstrom, 2021). Our online survey as well as the review of the profession's own definitions of diversity (see Chapters 2 and 5) indicate the profession's tendency to use EEO type language when describing diversity. The term "inclusion" has been used for less than a decade, and the term "equity" is even more recent in the profession's discourse. In another recent study on internal communication and D&I published just as we were wrapping up our manuscript, Wolfgruber, Stürmer and Einwiller (2021) found that formal internal/interpersonal communication within organizations can enhance or hurt perceptions and experiences of D&I. What do such studies tell us?

A lot! The language we use, or do not use, to communicate about D&I matters. Typical EEO language tends to describe diversity mainly in terms of representation, foreground equality (rather than equity) and fairness and does not touch on inclusion or indicate that D&I is a dynamic and ongoing process. It tends to have a static and generic ring to it. We do not mean to suggest that representation and fairness are not important. They are very important. But the language cannot stop there. Equal treatment assumes all are at the same starting point; this is obviously not the case when it comes to diversity, especially with regard to historical and systemic inequities. The concept of equity needs to be better understood, articulated and converted into policies and practice. Furthermore, representation becomes complicated when we look at identity through an intersectional lens. The current problem with retaining members of underrepresented groups in the profession is, in our opinion, significantly related to this point on language and primary focus on representation. Senior practitioner Hugo Balta (2017) makes the same point but in a slightly different way: "To build an inclusive workplace, companies need to look beyond representation and instead focus on integration" (para. 1). We believe representation does matter, but so do practices and the language we use; they are equally important. Unless our language and understanding of diversity flows automatically into how to practice inclusion/equity, the retention problem will remain, and recruitment efforts will be futile and a waste of resources. Diversity fatigue, or even resistance, could set in. Language adopted very recently by PRSA during the racial reckoning following the killing of George Floyd is showing some promise, although the term "equity" is still missing (PRSA Chapter D&I Toolkit, 2021).

Brunner's (2008) study found that practitioners seem to increasingly see the importance of diversity but struggle with understanding the role it plays in relationship building. The above point can explain this struggle. *There appears to be a lack of understanding of what inclusion in relation to diversity is and how it can be practiced on a daily basis.* The "D" is related to recruitment and the "I" is about retention. Both need to connect through relationship building efforts with the goal of producing and maintaining "inclusive diversity." Leaders need to be leading the way, in words and in action, in making this connection clear at micro, meso and macro levels of operation.

The business case for D&I is prioritized over the moral case

Leadership scholarship, especially more recent scholarship, emphasizes the centrality of the moral or social justice case when theorizing the relationship between D&I and leadership responsibility. The public relations professional discourse still emphasizes the business case for D&I (see Chapter 2). There has been a very recent shift toward the moral case after the 2020 racial reckoning and it remains to be seen how the narrative will evolve (Fuller, 2020).

The problem with prioritizing just the business case is that it follows the EEO sense of diversity and people tend to get commodified as being "diverse." As explained in Chapter 3 and in the previous theme, diversity is a dynamic process wherein differences (in the form of people) intersect in organizational spaces. The EEO language aligns more with the diversity management

(DM) approach, and the DM approach aligns with the business case which encourages diversity but does not focus on the work that is required to reap the creative, economic and relational benefits of diversity. Inclusive diversity requires relationship building, a focus on equity and the need to value (rather than simply "manage") diversity (Mundy, 2016). For public relations, the ideal approach would be to strike a fine balance between the business and moral case since ignoring the business case is not wise either.

Inequity-based power differentials and biases persist

Studies show that underrepresented public relations professionals continue to report feeling excluded and find themselves the targets of microaggressions which are the result of unconscious and conscious biases (see Chapter 2). Furthermore, the lack of mindfulness in the everyday communication and behaviors of dominant group professionals can alienate them and result in a lack of psychological safety and sense of empowerment. Unconscious biases also create perceptual barriers and keep in place professional and industry practices that systemically exclude underrepresented groups (e.g., hiring and promotion practices, social networking that excludes). Until 2020, the profession had not had very open discussions about power asymmetries, privilege and its entrenched culture of Whiteness. Research, however, has not been shy about these issues (e.g., Edwards, 2015; Logan, 2011; Vardeman-Winter & Place, 2017). To advance in the realm of inclusion/equity, power differentials, unearned privileges and un/conscious bias must be honestly confronted and worked through with the intent to share power. Dominant group members (White, heterosexual males and females) must be willing to join the effort as authentic allies.

Differences are still conceptualized in simplistic ways

Difference (the source of diversity) is still conceptualized mainly in singular categories in professional discourse and public relations research. Some more recent scholarship on D&I has pointed out the need for more complex and intersectional theorizing of the identities of internal and external publics/stakeholders (Ni, Wang, & Sha, 2018; Sha, 2006; Vardeman-Winter, Tindall, & Jiang, 2013). The literature on D&I and leadership reviewed in earlier chapters also underscores the importance of complex approaches to complex differences/identities and how they play out in the workplace. Further, within the more singular approach to identity in public relations trade discourse, while there is a tendency to define diversity in terms of several categories of identities and a desire to not fix the meaning of diversity since identities and societal dimensions keep evolving with time, in practice D&I gets operationalized mainly in terms of race/ethnicity and gender.

A few industry research groups are beginning to emphasize this simplistic approach needs to change to align with the increasingly fluid and complex intersectional identity map of the United States (e.g., Bililies & Ndoma-Ogar, 2021; Lucid, Insights in Color, & Think Now, n.d.). The more recent Public Relations Society of America (PRSA) and Commission for Public Relations Education (CPRE) definitions of D&I are also foregrounding this need and recognizing that the complex ways in which identity-related power works inside and outside the organization need to be brought into sharper focus. All differences are not equal, and nor are they parallel; instead, they intersect and the "new identity economy" requires a more complex approach in research and practice (Lucid et al., n.d., p. 1).

Public relations education needs to play a pivotal role in strengthening the D&I college-to-profession pipeline

The public relations students of today are the leaders of tomorrow. However, graduates currently entering the profession have a less than adequate D&I orientation. While D&I is a matter of lifelong learning, the D&I orientation students develop in their college years has a strong impact on how they perform in the workplace and how they understand and practice D&I in professional settings (Brunner, 2005; Muturi & Zhu, 2019; Place & Vanc, 2016). And as D&I practitioner and leader Kelli Newman Mason (n.d.) states, anyone interviewing for a position these days must simply expect to answer questions regarding D&I in addition to the more traditional questions about skills and background.

The most recent CPRE report (Mundy, Lewton, Hicks, & Neptune, 2018) and a handful of public relations researchers (see Chapter 6) are urging that education needs to play a more central role in developing better D&I knowledge, skills and attitudes among public relations students. Both curriculum content and learning environments need to be diversified and made more inclusive. Further, industry and education need to work together to build more D&I connections. This work is a must if the pipeline for the future is to be strengthened.

Scholarship on D&I and public relations leadership is almost non-existent

Scholarship in public relations has not specifically and systematically studied D&I and its relationship with leadership. The need to study it has been mentioned in some studies and the findings of some studies have offered some information (e.g., Men, 2014; Meng, 2014; Meng & Berger, 2018); however, this relationship has not been the central focus of study. As far as we are aware, this book is the first concerted effort to examine this relationship.

Overall, from a knowledge development point of view, there is a need for more theoretical perspectives on D&I as a process in public relations and its relationship to leadership. Several aspects of this relationship need focused examination. Some of these aspects include context (all the way from the micro to macro level of leadership operation), leaders' role in building organizational D&I culture and climate, leaders' approach to D&I, how power differentials and un/conscious biases can be addressed by leaders in diverse spaces to build inclusion/equity, leaders' role in building alliances and relationships across differences (internally as well as externally), intersectionality and leaders' approach to identity, nature of leaders' internal and external communication with regard to D&I, best practices and case studies of successful leadership on D&I, measurement of leadership performance and accountability on D&I, and models or frameworks for leadership that are conducive to supporting D&I. While our book and model address some of the above, there is still much more work to be done.

Additionally, D&I is consistently framed negatively as a problem. We cannot deny it is a problem, however, leaders must also emphasize the advantages and benefits of D&I. How this balance can be achieved is something research can grapple with. Basically, the benefits of D&I have not been the topic of much discussion. This is an obstacle in the path of envisioning the value of D&I and building a healthy attitude toward relating and communicating across differences in the public relations workplace and space.

★★★

The above 11 themes intertwine to tell the story of the weak state of leadership engagement and D&I in public relations in the United States. They clearly indicate that major cultural and structural shifts and changes are needed in how leaders approach and engage with D&I. Currently, there is no inspiring leadership "meta-narrative" for D&I in the profession (Wasserman, Gallegos, & Ferdman, 2008). We hope that our model for public relations leadership for inclusive diversity will aid leaders as they work to build this much needed meta-narrative. We now turn our attention to this model, which we developed by merging the vast span of cross-disciplinary research on leadership, D&I and public relations we have reviewed throughout the book with our own data.

A model for public relations leadership and D&I

A model for public relations leadership and D&I needs to be in tune with context, i.e., the specific state of D&I and leadership in the profession. The above 11 themes serve as this context. Collectively they suggest that inclusion and lack of leadership engagement and accountability are the core challenges. In fact, this is true at an overarching level which constitutes the larger context (or external environment) within which public relations is embedded. McKinsey & Company's ongoing study of D&I in companies in the United States and around the world recently reported that while some gains in diversity in terms of representation have been made in recent years, inclusion is the real challenge; belonging, equity and lack of leadership accountability on D&I stand out as pressing problems (Dixon-Fyle, Dolan, Hunt, & Prince, 2020). Therefore, our model is based on these core needs to build inclusive diversity climates, both internally and externally. This requires focusing on leadership's role and responsibility in building relations across cultural differences, social inequities and power differentials.

A few words about models. There are many types of models one can develop (e.g., normative models, interventionist models, process models, praxis models and so on). The choice of model should align with the task at hand and goals in mind. That is, what do we want our models to accomplish? In our case, we want our model to do at least two things: (1) We want it to serve as a theory-driven and data-informed guide for public relations leaders to practice D&I leadership successfully, knowledgeably, ethically and as a process, and (2) we would like for it to serve as a heuristic inspiration to other scholars who wish to further build on what we offer. Therefore, our model is a process and praxis model constructed through a D&I lens and embedded in the context of the public relations profession in the United States.

The process focus of our model is an attempt to foreground that D&I leadership is not a box than can be checked off but is an ongoing and dynamic process (Booysen, 2021). A process model is descriptive, prescriptive and aims toward certain desired outcomes (Bell, Raiffa, & Tversky, 1988), which in our case are inclusive diversity, leader/ship responsibility and accountability and ongoing D&I (un)learning (which requires regular feedback and goal measurement). At its heart, our model is relational and dialogic. Praxis means theory and knowledge informed practice. It involves "doing" (or action and conduct in its many forms, including communication) and, as Lather (1986) states, for praxis to be possible it needs to be guided by knowledge and theory that are "adequate to the task of changing the world" (i.e., achieve transformation), "open-ended" (not dogmatic) and "grounded in the circumstances of everyday life" (practical) (p. 262). We also draw from a praxis model for intercultural communication (which applies in the case of D&I) developed by Sorrells and Nakagawa (2008) that emphasizes critical thinking, curiosity to genuinely learn about differences and inequities, reflection and ongoing learning. The open-ended, adaptable and flexible nature of a praxis model makes it suitable for our needs since D&I and public relations leadership (the central concepts in our model) are both flexible in nature. The desired outcomes of inclusive diversity, leader/ship responsibility and accountability and ongoing D&I (un)learning can also take different forms depending on context and setting (e.g., agency, in-house, non-profit, for-profit, more diverse

TABLE 7.2 Core characteristics of leadership model for inclusive diversity in public relations

1. Primacy of a D&I lens
2. A social constructionist and interpretive approach
3. A relational and dialogic/communicative focus
4. Attention to the belonging-uniqueness dialectic
5. Beyond the transformational style of leadership

organization, more homogeneous organization, size of organization, location, domestic or global, and so on). We believe our model is broad enough so it can be adapted to specific settings. We now elaborate on five core characteristics of this model (see Table 7.2).

Primacy of a D&I lens

We state that our model is constructed through a D&I lens. What does this mean? As we described in Chapter 4, scholars have urged that leadership models for D&I should not be developed from already existing models which have been built from the experiences of privileged power elite leaders but should start from how leadership can be understood from the perspective of D&I (Chin, 2010; Ensari & Riggio, 2021). Diversity, in its most basic sense, means difference and variance from the dominant norm (Banks, 1995). Leadership D&I models should assume heterogeneity (diversity/difference) rather than homogeneity (homophily/sameness) as their starting point.

A model built through the lens of D&I, therefore, requires attention to privilege, marginalization and power inequities, professional and organizational culture and structure (which impact leadership and vice versa), how leaders can become interculturally competent and practice power sharing ("power with" and empowerment) forms of leadership rather than top-down ("power over") controlling forms, and how they must be change agents who work to dismantle oppressive cultural practices and structures (Chin & Trimble, 2015). According to Berger (2005), "any public relations theory [or model] is deficient to the extent it fails to account for power relations and structures in organizations..." (p. 23). Booysen (2021) emphasizes the importance of "mutuality and co-creation" and the reduction of leader-follower dualism in D&I-focused leadership models (p. 208). To this we add that external context/ environment and societal culture and hierarchies are especially necessary to consider since organizations do not exist in a vacuum and societal and cultural differences and inequities do not vanish in organizational life; the "internal" and "external" are not a dichotomy but a continuum (see Ferdman, 2021; Mor Barak, 2005; Mundy, 2016; Trittin & Schoeneborn, 2017).

Thus, the concepts of difference and power (or power differentials) are central to a D&I lens, and to this extent, our model falls in the critical paradigm

(Bardhan & Weaver, 2011). From a societal perspective, power is the ability of dominant groups to define reality by setting values and standards, deciding what is right and wrong and establishing policies and practices to build structures that support and maintain their power (Halualani, 2020). From an organizational perspective:

> [P]ower is the capacity or potential to get things done ... Power may come from many sources – formal authority, access to decision-makers, information, problem-solving expertise, experience, and relationships ... Power is often exercised in organizations to influence actions, agendas, decisions, and resource allocations.
>
> *(Berger & Reber, 2006, p. 4)*

Three decades ago, J. E. Grunig (1992) wrote that to practice excellent public relations and build excellent organizational cultures, public relations leaders must empower others, encourage dialogue and cooperation, build strong participative and inclusive cultures and structures and value diversity both in terms of representation and in terms of incorporating diverse values and viewpoints into the workings of the organization. The two-way symmetrical model of public relations was built on these values, and it posits that the dominant coalition (or dominant group of senior leaders) of an organization, when it includes public relations, can practice excellent public relations in a "symmetrical" manner that balances the interests of the organization and its publics (J. E. Grunig, 1992; J. E. Grunig & Hunt, 1984). Elaborating on the concept of power, J. E. Grunig and L. A. Grunig (1992) wrote: "People in power develop the culture of an organization and organizational culture influences who gains power" (p. 299). However, as Berger (2005) accurately points out, the assumption within the model is that leaders, including those who are in the dominant coalition (in-house) (or senior leadership in agencies), will do the socially responsible or "right" things. But what if they do not?

The above point on power and how public relations leaders practice their power brings us to the matter of responsibility and accountability which is a top challenge when it comes to D&I and leadership. Responsible leaders work with integrity with multiple stakeholders across micro-macro environments for the good of the organization and society (Maak & Pless, 2006a; Miska & Mendenhall, 2018). However, complaints about lack of leader responsibility, engagement and accountability abound in public relations and this is seen as a clear reason why there is not more diversity as well as inclusion/equity in current practice, especially in agencies (Ramaswamy, 2018). Therefore, this point is central to the D&I lens. Berger (2005) proposes that in such cases public relations leaders need to practice "power to" relations which is a resistive approach that advocates other leaders (whether in-house, senior leadership in agency settings, or the industry in general) take a different approach to something (e.g., practice more inclusive rather than top-down leadership; see also Berger & Reber, 2006).

According to Aldoory (2005), matters of power and diversity in public relations practice "are socially constitutive through communicative acts and should be studied as such" (p. 674). We align with this view and take a social constructionist/interpretive and relational and dialogic/communicative approach in our model.

A social constructionist and interpretive approach

In developing what he calls a "social-interpretive" approach to public relations, Banks (1995) convincingly makes the point that most scholarship and practice in public relations abide by the fundamental assumption that reality is objective and can be measured as such. Another view, which has gradually made inroads, is that reality is not objective but socially constructed (Berger & Luckmann, 1966). Building off of this approach to explain how we make sense of our world, including our professional practices and habitus, Banks explains that "social reality is the meanings assigned to it [by people]" (p. 34). According to Grint (2005):

> [W]hat counts as "true," as "objective" and as "fact" are the result of contending accounts of "reality." That implies that "reality" is constructed through language and, in turn, since language is a social phenomenon, the account of reality which prevails is often both a temporary and a collective phenomenon.
>
> *(p. 1471)*

For example, let's say a press release reports that the first Black female CEO of a public relations firm is retiring. The way this press release is written (or constructed) is one aspect of social construction of this reality (the retirement); the other element is that various stakeholders/readers of the release will not make sense of what is reported about this CEO (their accomplishments, legacy, influence and so on) in exactly the same way. Let's take another example, that of power, which is so central to our D&I lens. In a Foucauldian vein, Berger (2005) writes:

> Power is not something "out there" beyond the practice but instead constitutive of practice in shifting relations of power that both constrain and create opportunities for choices and actions. ... power ebbs and flows and moves through various venues and moments of decision making so that practice seems inevitably bound up in relations of power.
>
> *(p. 23)*

Berger's explanation of power is a social constructionist and relational one. Various other aspects of public relations communication and practice, including leadership and D&I, can be explained in similar ways. Like Berger, Bardhan and Weaver (2011) explain that a social constructionist and interpretive approach allows us to understand the world and work of public relations as "communicative and co-creational" and develop a more nuanced sense of how power works relationally and how it can create, maintain or disrupt dominance across cultural and identity-based inequities in specific contexts (p. 14).

The narrative approach and method that we have adopted in this book is also social constructionist in nature. Drawing on Fisher (1987) and like Grint (2005) above, Banks (1995) makes the point that in all public relation communication, internal and external, "the story accepted as the true story" is not the same for all individuals and publics involved (p. 40). The social constructionist approach is also suitable when it comes to studying leadership through a D&I lens. Emphasizing the need to move away from individualistic, acontextual and instrumental approaches to leadership, Alvesson (2011) writes: "Leadership is not just a leader acting and a group of followers responding in a mechanical way, but a complex social process in which the meanings and interpretations of what is said and done are crucial" (p. 152) (see also Grint, 2005). Therefore, all the concepts that are central to our concerns (leadership, public relations, D&I) are served well when studied from a social constructionist and interpretive perspective. We now turn to the relational and dialogic/communicative characteristic of our model.

A relational and dialogic/communicative focus

Relationship building with publics/stakeholders through communication is a core function of the public relations profession and relationality has been a central focus of public relations theory for decades now. Therefore, it makes good sense to take a relational and dialogic/communicative approach in our model. Second, leadership theories are increasingly moving away from more dualistic (leader-follower) and instrumental "management" foci and leaning toward relational and dialogic/communicative approaches (see Chapter 4). According to Roberson and Perry (2021), "future research should examine leader communication behaviors as a key component of inclusive leadership models" (p. 416). Third, a relational and dialogic/communicative approach makes good sense for a process where a desired outcome is the relational phenomenon of inclusive diversity. From a social constructionist perspective, the relational and the dialogic/communicative are intertwined and co-constitutive.

The relational approach to leadership draws upon constitutive (social constructionist) organizational communication scholarship (see Ashcraft, Kuhn, & Cooren, 2009). According to Uhl-Bien (2006), "The organization is actively held together not by its policies and rules and procedures, but the web of interpersonal relationships that is built through ongoing interaction," and a relational approach to leadership is "a view of leadership and organization as human social constructions that emanate from the rich connections and interdependencies of organizations and their members" (pp. 663, 654–655). This approach moves our attention from the individual to collective interdependence, helps reduce leader-follower dualism, focuses on context and helps us understand leadership as a communicative process through which meanings about organizational life are produced, maintained and/or challenged. In terms of identity, instead of the atomistic approach to self and identity, it encourages mutuality with others. According to Maak and Pless (2006c), leaders need to work with relational intelligence, which they describe as a combination of ethical and emotional intelligence:

> Most of the challenges that leaders face in an interconnected world emerge from the interaction with a multitude of stakeholders, locally, regionally and globally; both inside and outside the organization ...They require leaders to integrate people with different styles and cultural background into teams, include different voices into the dialogue, understand issues from different perspectives, solve conflicts of interests with different people, reconcile intercultural and interpersonal dilemmas.
>
> *(p. 105)*

They state that relational intelligence is necessary to build trust, which in turn aids inclusion. Thus, a culture of inclusive diversity is an everyday and ongoing relational achievement tied to how leaders, along with other organizational members, constitute organizational climate through everyday micro moments of interaction (in addition to other more formal forms of internal and external communication). Inclusion requires non-leader-centric, interdependent and relational organizational practices at micro, meso, macro (intra-organizational) and extra-organizational levels (Booysen, 2021; Wasserman, 2021). According to Ferdman (2021), such organizational relational "rhythms" are necessary for creating leadership meta-narratives of inclusive diversity. This brings us to the dialogic/communicative part. We believe any model on leadership for inclusive diversity, whether in public relations or some other profession, must include this dimension of relationality.

As Uhl-Bien (2006) explains, "relating is a constructive, ongoing process of meaning making – an actively relational process of creating (common) understandings on the basis of language" (p. 665) with a focus on "interaction, conversation, narrating, dialoguing, and multiloguing" (p. 665, 663). If relating is dialogic and communicative, then we must look closely at these terms through a social constructionist lens. According to Fairhurst (2011), communication is not a secondary phenomenon as in psychology-oriented theories of leadership (i.e., a leader communicates in a particular way to produce a particular result), rather it is at the center stage of how leadership is produced, maintained and changed; that is, "language and communication are put to use as a series of 'doings' that construct leadership in situ" (p. 495). Fairhurst and Connaughton (2014) make the case that leader communication is both transmissional (linear "sender-channel-receiver" approach) and meaning-centered (constructivist approach), i.e., "leadership actors are reflexive practitioners who shape and are shaped by realities they co-create" (p. 22). Thus, the dialogic/communicative focus, in concert with the relational focus, also foregrounds the importance of everyday (mundane) leader communication in our model. We now elaborate on the dialogic approach to communication since it is particularly important for producing inclusive and accountable leadership in diverse organizations.

In our review of the more recent research on dialogism and leadership in Chapter 4, we described that a "dialogic mindset" is a must for leaders who desire to ethically communicate and build relations with multiple publics (internal and external) and stakeholders (Bushe & Marshak, 2016). According to Cunliffe and Eriksen (2011):

> Relational leadership requires a way of engaging with the world in which the leader holds herself/himself as always in relation with, and therefore morally accountable to others; recognizes the inherently polyphonic and heteroglossic nature of life; and engages in relational dialogue.
>
> *(p. 1425)*

Such leaders take multiple voices into account and through generative dialogue (polyphony) work on carving out new narratives necessary for navigating complex organizational realities and help build behaviors and actions that serve D&I (Agger-Gupta & Harris, 2017; Gergen & Hersted, 2016). A central value of dialogic communication is moral accountability and, therefore, it is most appropriate for D&I leadership. Dialogic communication has no end point and is ongoing depending on shifting contexts and circumstances. This quality makes it particularly suitable for D&I-related relational communication. Leaders engaged in dialogic communication work on transcending their egos and building a collective sense and agency of "we" without losing the "I" (Raelin, 2016); they are at all times mindful of socially and historically generated inequities as they play out in organizational life (van Loon & van Dijk, 2015). Pless and Maak (2004) foreground reciprocal understanding and trust as core values for responsible and dialogic leadership communication. Pless, Maak and Harris (2017) write that dialogism requires treating people with dignity, which they explain is a relational term, and as subjects rather than as objects to be instrumentally utilized for organization-centric gains.

The good news for public relations scholarship (not so much practice, unfortunately) is that scholars have made strong cases for adopting dialogic approaches to communication and relationship building with internal and external stakeholders for more than three decades. Taking an ethics approach to dialogue (vs. monologue), Pearson (1989) emphasized that it is through dialogic communication that organizations should arrive at business decisions regarding right and wrong and develop attendant policies and practices (see also Botan, 1997). In the early 1990s, the model of two-way symmetrical communication emphasized dialogue for achieving balance (or "symmetry" in terms of interests) between the organization and its publics (J. E. Grunig, 1992; J. E. Grunig & Hunt, 1984). In subsequent years, Banks (1995), Kent and Taylor (1998, 2002) and Taylor and Kent (2014) further built the case for dialogic communication. Drawing from the work of philosopher Martin Buber (1970) and emphasizing the centrality of dialogic communication in both internal and external public relations communication, Banks (1995) wrote that genuine dialogue requires "turning toward the other," "active affirmation of cultural identities," communicatively creating spaces of mutuality "where genuine identities are displayed and positions on issues are negotiated," and emphasized that "genuine dialogue with relevant publics will occur only when organizational leaders personally demonstrate that they ground their own communication in solidarity and mindfulness" (pp. 75, 107, 122).

In the late 1990s, when web-based communication was on the rise, Kent and Taylor (1998) built on Pearson (1989) and applied dialogic communication as a theoretical framework for studying web-based public relations communication and relationship building. They specifically emphasized the need for a dialogic loop in all such communication so that publics can engage in meaningful dialogue with organizations. Subsequently (Kent & Taylor, 2002), and further building on Pearson, they developed a more general dialogic framework for public relations and made a case for it being more suitable for a relational approach to practice compared to the more instrumental "management" of communication approach. They emphasized that organizations must make an intentional commitment to the dialogic approach, that dialogue is not formulaic but a particular orientation to communication, and elaborated as follows:

> Dialogue as an orientation includes five features: *mutuality*, or the recognition of organization–public relationships; *propinquity*, or the temporality and spontaneity of interactions with publics; *empathy*, or the supportiveness and confirmation of public goals and interests; *risk*, or the willingness to interact with individuals and publics on their own terms; and finally *commitment*, or the extent to which an organization gives itself over to dialogue, interpretation, and understanding in its interactions with publics.
>
> *(pp. 24–25, emphasis in original)*

They noted that respecting differences, building trust and avoiding power plays are pathways to building internal and external dialogic relationships in everyday practice. They explain that dialogue is a product, an outcome of the dialogic orientation. Since dialogism is not a set of fixed rules, they suggest that public relations organizations should work on establishing what the dialogic communication process means to them specifically and how to practice it daily. Similarly, Sommerfeldt and Yang (2018) have also suggested that it is important for organizations to consider "[q]uestions such as what institutional contexts, power dynamics, and socio-cultural contexts are more conducive or constraining for dialogic communication" (p. 62).

A little over a decade later, Taylor and Kent (2014) updated their dialogic communication framework with a focus on the role of engagement in dialogism:

> Engagement represents a two-way, relational, give-and-take between organizations and stakeholders/publics with the intended goal of (a) improving understanding among interactants; (b) making decisions that benefit all parties involved, not simply the organization; and (c) fostering a fully functioning society ....
>
> *(p. 391)*

They explained that in practice, dialogic communication means that all parties must be willing to interact fairly, understand how reality is co-created, allow for self-discovery and be open to being changed. They also emphasized that it is necessary for practitioners to be trained in dialogic communication and urged scholars to explore the workings of dialogue at various levels (from micro interpersonal all the way to macro societal).

Attention to the belonging-uniqueness dialectic

We build on this previous work on relationality and dialogic communication to explain how it is specifically relevant from an inclusion perspective. There is increasing evidence in the literature on inclusion that it is necessary to maintain uniqueness and build belonging simultaneously for inclusive climates to thrive in diverse organizations. According to Sugiyama, Cavanagh, van Esch, Bilimoria and Brown (2016) (see also Shore et al., 2011): [I]nclusive leadership is carried out through the work of relating to others in a way that makes them feel valued for their unique talents and backgrounds as well as perceive that they belong and matter to the team" (p. 257). An aspiration for this tensive balance, with a full focus on power inequities, also lies at the heart of the dialogic orientation. Therefore, how we engage cultural differences and power inequities in Self-Other relational and dialogic communication becomes critical to consider. In fact, in a D&I and public relations perception study that was published as we were completing our manuscript,

Blow, Bonney, Tallapragada and Brown (2021) note that "D&I efforts need to find ways to celebrate and empower unique identities while also trying to also create a larger professional unifying identity for PR students, practitioners, and scholars" (p. 6).

Here we find it useful to bring in Russian philosopher Mikhail Bakhtin's work on dialogism. According to Bakhtin (1981), we live amidst "heteroglossia" or simultaneously unifying and diverging forces of culture, language and meanings (and identities); therefore, the Self is always in contact with Other cultural contexts and meanings. Bakhtin uses the term "polyphony" (in public relations that would be the multiple voices of different publics/stakeholders, both internal and external) from music to illustrate how it is possible for separate notes to work together (temporarily) to produce melody. Interestingly, Gary, one of our senior leader interviewees, also offered the analogy of a symphony to make this very point about simultaneously celebrating differences (uniqueness) and creating belonging among diverse identities within the organization.

In intercultural communication literature, Sobré-Denton and Bardhan (2013) also draw upon Bakhtin to explain that "the Self and cultural Other are not autonomous and sovereign. ... They may be different, but they are inevitably entangled through dialogism and could belong to each other. ... In this way, languages, cultures and identities are constantly dialogized" (p. 68). Here lies the dialectic that explains what dialogic relational communication strives for – a dual maintenance of the "I" (uniqueness) and the "we" (belonging) and a mutual connection somewhere in between. According to Baxter and Montgomery (1996), a dialectical approach to relational communication helps us get at the messiness of the communication process since it enables us to understand that when interactants communicate they engage in "simultaneous differentiation from and yet fusion with one another" (p. 24). A dialectic is an interplay between opposite seeming phenomena, it is an "and/both" perspective, and there is no perfect end state (for a more detailed explanation see Sobré-Denton & Bardhan, 2013). According to intercultural communication scholars Martin and Nakayama (1999):

> A dialectical approach recognizes the importance of similarities and differences in understanding intercultural communication. The field was founded on the assumption that there are real, important differences that exist between various cultural groups .... However, in real life there are a great many similarities in human experience and ways of communicating. ... There has been a tendency to overemphasize group differences in traditional intercultural communication research-in a way that sets up false dichotomies and rigid expectations. However, a dialectical perspective reminds us that difference and similarity can coexist in intercultural communication interactions.

(p. 16)

The dialogic communication approach is well equipped to navigate the belonging-uniqueness dialectic, which seems to be the path to building climates and relationships of inclusive diversity. How leaders relate and communicate, and how they encourage others to do so, should be in keeping with this dialectic.

Finally, a few words on how we approach identity in this attempt to find a balance between belonging and uniqueness. Some public relations scholars have already opened the conversation about the need for intersectional perspectives on the identities of publics and stakeholders in relationship building efforts (e.g., Golombisky, 2015; Pompper, 2014; Vardeman-Winter & Tindall, 2010; Vardeman-Winter et al., 2013). According to this view, people do not live, relate and experience their identities in singular categories; rather they are experienced as intersectional. And as Black feminist scholars have explained, an intersectional lens is necessary for detecting and acting to address the effects of interlocking oppressions faced by marginalized intersectional identities (Collins, 1990, 2000; Crenshaw, 1991). In Chapter 3, we discussed how some scholars in favor of an intersectional approach to D&I are arguing that predetermined categories can lead to negative effects, such as identity freezing, and hurt inclusion efforts (e.g., Risberg & Pilhofer, 2018; Tatli & Özbilgin, 2012). They are advising organizations to consider more emergent, local and intersectional approaches in their understandings of identities stating that such perspectives are capable of bringing "more dynamic views of categories, adding new intersections and linking the organizational context to the societal context" (Risberg & Pilhofer, 2018, p. 140). Such perspectives also allow for more accurate considerations of power relations between identity positionalities of publics and stakeholders in specific contexts.

Intersectionality scholar Grzanka (2019) writes that there has been an explosion in the popularity of the term intersectionality in academia and in popular/trade discourse in the last decade, but that it is used mostly in a descriptive way. The pressing praxis-related question to ask is what an intersectional approach can "do" for social justice and equity in specific contexts (see also Collins & Bilge, 2020). More specifically for our purposes, how can an intersectional approach to identity in public relations D&I leadership practice address structural and cultural power inequities in more nuanced ways in organizational life and relationship building with internal and external publics and stakeholders? For example, Vardeman-Winter et al. (2013) in their excellent article on incorporating intersectionality in public relations research and practice suggest that intersectional analyses of publics could aid more nuanced and richer understanding and segmentation of publics and help gauge public-organization/practitioner power relations in more informed ways. Internally, intersectional perspectives could prevent oversimplification of identities and help detect intersectional biases in organizational practices (e.g., more White women get promoted to leadership positions when gender is made a priority). These are just a few examples to point out how intersectional approaches can aid

D&I work in multiple ways. In sum, siloed (single category) approaches to diversity are too simplistic in today's increasingly fluid cultural landscape of identities and do not aid in building either belonging or uniqueness. How leaders communicate, and encourage others to communicate, would benefit from embracing the intersectional perspective.

Beyond the transformational style of leadership

As we saw in Chapter 4, there is a good amount of research evidence of the popularity of the transformational leadership style in public relations. In fact, Northouse (2022) states that it has been one of the most popular leadership styles in general in the last three decades. A broad style, it places a high value on leaders transforming individuals and the organization, is "concerned with emotions, values, ethics standards, and long-term goals," and with leaders empowering followers and "treating them as full human beings" (p. 185). The transformational leader needs to be charismatics, inspirational, a visionary and capable of wielding great influence that helps followers rise above normal expectations. Northouse further elaborates that such "leaders are out front in interpreting and shaping for organizations the shared meanings that exist within them" (p. 202). Transformational leaders treat each employee as an individual and can be influenced by followers as well. Moral upliftment of leaders and followers is a primary goal of this style of leadership (Díaz-Sáenz, 2011).

Within public relations, scholars have shown that the transformational approach is popular particularly from an internal communication perspective because of its focus on employee empowerment, compassion and empathy, its relational, inspirational and participatory approach, attention to intellectual stimulation, flexibility with style and emotional intelligence; from an external communication point of view, empowered and engaged employees are favorable ambassadors for the organization (e.g., Aldoory, 1998; Aldoory & Toth, 2004; Jin, 2010; Men, 2014; Men & Stacks, 2013; Werder & Holtzhausen, 2009; C. White, Vanc, & Stafford, 2010). Therefore, given this popularity, we do not want to veer too far from this approach. However, transformational leadership has its drawbacks, particularly from a D&I perspective, and we wanted to take these into consideration. The goal and spirit of "transformation" still remain central in our model since the current state of D&I in the industry needs to change for the better and leaders have the uphill task of inspiring and empowering all to change internally. However, our central problematic is a little different – it is leadership itself that needs to be inspired and "transformed" in favor of supporting and genuinely engaging with D&I. Therefore, and in keeping with the argument of Chin and Trimble (2015) that D&I leadership models should not be add-ons to already existing models, our model is D&I driven. Looking briefly at the critiques of the transformational style helps explain how our model is connected to yet significantly different from this style.

Some primary critiques of the transformational leadership style are (1) it is too leader-centric, individualistic (despite its relational focus) and more like a personality trait, (2) the focus is primarily on how the heroic, charismatic and visionary leader achieves great transformation and not enough attention is paid to how other organizational and environmental factors and actors contribute to transformation, (3) it is too broad and lacks conceptual clarity, (4) there is not much research evidence of actual and major transformations that can be attributed mainly to this style of leadership and (5) the inordinate focus on the heroic leader could lead to abuse of power (Díaz-Sáenz, 2011; Northouse, 2022). Additionally, it is not clear how this style can aid in fostering belonging and sharedness through reduction of hierarchies and inequities (Chrobot-Mason & Roberson, 2022; Ensari & Riggio, 2021). Randel et al. (2018) write that "Unlike transformational leadership, inclusive leadership helps group members feel that they belong without changing key identities and that they can contribute their uniqueness to group efforts" (p. 194). They emphasize the need for leader qualities such as pro-diversity beliefs, humility and cognitive complexity. Therefore, while the relational focus (along with attendant qualities such as compassion, empathy, and emotional intelligence) is the same, the transformational style retains leader-follower duality. And importantly, the dialogic communication and D&I lens characteristics of our model described earlier are not the central focus of the transformational style. However, as Moss (2019) rightly notes, the transformational style is a "prime candidate to act as a building block for inclusive leadership" (p. 5); she makes the case that inclusive leadership is a combination of the transformational and servant leadership styles combined with a dialogic mindset (see also Bushe & Marshak, 2016; Chrobot-Mason & Roberson, 2022).

Another particularly relevant and future-oriented critique related to the millennial generation is made by some scholars. As millennials are now increasingly in mid-level and even some senior-level leadership positions, it is necessary that leadership theories to stay in tune with this particular generation. Noting that this generation is the "Selfie" generation not likely to be easily inspired and motivated in the same intrinsic ways as previous generations and more likely to demand accountability and challenge authority, Anderson, Baur, Griffith and Buckley (2017) state: "Unfortunately, the current model of transformational leadership provides little guidance to managers who must balance helping employees reach their own goals with the achievement of group goals" (p. 248). Like Randel et al. (2018), they point out the need for a leadership style that values and works to achieve the belonging-uniqueness dialectic necessary for building inclusive diversity. Additionally, as many studies continue to show (see Chapter 2), the millennials, along with Gen Z following them, are increasingly diverse, exceptionally social justice oriented and likely to feel disengaged in and leave organizations that are not D&I focused. Therefore, models that reduce the leader-follower dualism, centralize dialogism and the belonging-uniqueness dialectic, and are D&I and social justice focused at a systemic and not just organizational level are needed. We incorporate these critiques in our leadership model for inclusive diversity in public relations.

A leadership model for inclusive diversity in public relations

We have now reached the high point of this book – our leadership model for inclusive diversity in public relations. We do not believe any such model exists and while this may be the first one of its kind, we hope it will not be the last since D&I and leadership must stay in tune with changing times and contexts. Arriving at this point has been an exciting journey of inquiry, analysis, synthesis and discovery. A great amount of work has gone into weaving together a vast span of literature in leadership theory, public relations, D&I/equity and we sincerely hope what we are offering will be of value to leaders, practitioners, scholars, educators and students of public relations and related professions. Their voices have contributed to the development of this model, and the model itself is firmly embedded in the context of the US public relations industry. We define this form of leadership as follows: *Leadership for inclusive diversity in public relations is an ongoing process with no fixed end point. It entails micro-meso-macro context sensitive leadership constituted through relationality and dialogic communication practiced through a D&I/equity lens. Such leadership aspires for the desired outcomes of climates of inclusive diversity, a culture of leadership responsibility and accountability and ongoing (un)learning at both the organizational and industry levels.* We now explain the various aspects of this model (Figure 7.1).

Context

The first aspect of our model is context. Throughout the book (and especially in Chapter 3), we have emphasized the importance of context when it comes to studying and practicing D&I oriented public relations leadership. Inclusive leadership and D&I scholars have also heavily emphasized the importance of micro-meso-macro context (e.g., Ferdman, 2021; Mor Barak, 2005; Trittin & Schoeneborn, 2017); quite simply, it is impossible to understand D&I and leadership in a systemic and process-oriented manner and account for interrelated structural and cultural power differentials and inequities without attention to context. Public relations leaders wishing to genuinely practice D&I leadership in an informed and holistic manner would first need to understand the impacts, implications and power dynamics of micro-meso-macro sociocultural, political, legal, media, ideological and economic contexts of the societies their organizations are embedded within (Botan, 1992; Sriramesh & Verčič, 2009).

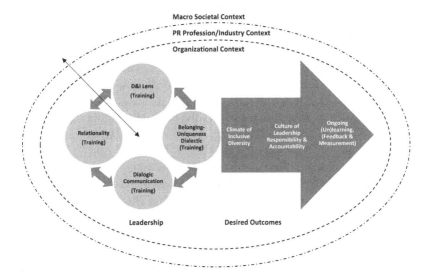

FIGURE 7.1   A leadership model for inclusive diversity in public relations

Public relations research on leadership has focused on context mainly at the organizational level. The scholarship that has focused on diversity (or lack of it) has made the important point about the need for requisite variety in the profession and referred to the macro societal context in that sense (L. A. Grunig, J. E. Grunig, & Ehling, 1992; Sha & R. Ford, 2007). International public relations research has focused heavily on societal context (e.g., Botan, 1992; Curtin & Gaither, 2012; Sriramesh & Verčič, 2009; Sriramesh & J. White, 1992), and the more critically oriented diversity scholarship has focused on macro power inequities and relations across internal and external contexts as has the scholarship on intersectionality (e.g., Edwards, 2015; Golombisky, 2015; L'Etang, McKie, Snow, & Xifra, 2016; Munshi & Edwards, 2011; Vardeman-Winter et al., 2013). Connecting internal and external contexts is necessary in any scholarship on D&I, leadership and public relations. Mundy's (2016) actionable model for D&I communication in public relations is an excellent example that accomplishes this connection. We found it to be most instructive for constructing our own model, and we quote him at length here. Explaining this model, he writes:

> [D]iversity-focused communication can be understood through one of four contexts: internal-structural; external-structural; internal-cultural; external-cultural. Internal structural communication highlights the programs, training, networking, development opportunities, and paths to advancement. External structural communication conveys the business case for diversity, while highlighting an organization's recruitment and retention efforts. Internal cultural communication focuses on how

diversity helps organizations learn and change – where diversity-centered dialogue help inform and shape organizational culture. From this perspective, organizations work to understand employees as individuals with individual stories, needs and expectations. External cultural communication, then, focuses on broader social justice issues in the communities an organization lives and serves, and how its own culture and strategic messaging reflects and addresses the diverse needs of those communities.

(Mundy, 2016, p. 18)

The Plank Center model for leadership in public relations is another model that emphasizes the importance of both internal and external contexts, particularly in terms of relationship building efforts by leaders (Berger & Meng, 2010). Additionally, Gregory and Willis (2013) have emphasized that strategic public relations leaders need to work with contextual intelligence across micro-meso-macro contexts. Several of our interviewees and the results of our online survey also indicate the importance of micro-meso-macro context in how leaders lead on D&I. Our interviewees especially emphasized the fluid nature of context in relation to D&I and that leaders need to work with this fluidity.

In our model, we consider context in three interconnected layers or nested levels: (1) the macro US societal level (which we should mention is complexly interconnected with larger world forces and flows, even though we do not focus directly on those in this book), (2) the US public relations profession/industry context which is influenced by the larger societal context and in turn influences the organizational context and (3) the organizational level context (which itself has micro and meso layers within it) which is impacted by the professional and societal contexts.

The macro societal context through a D&I lens would be the state of D&I in the workplace, education and society in general. The profession/industry context would include the historical and current struggle with D&I that public relations has experienced the details of which we have covered in this book. The organizational context is the unique context of each public relations organization or unit.

The interconnected and not necessarily linear nature of these contexts can be illustrated with a few examples. For instance, the macro societal context requires us to look carefully at the shifting and fast changing identity and cultural landscape of the United States as we assess internal and external publics/stakeholders. This context not only has implications for professional/industry culture and context, but also for organizational context. Another obvious example is how the racial reckoning after the killing of George Floyd has shifted the industry D&I discourse. Organizational context, however, is closely connected to local and regional contexts, and these may not necessarily be parallel to the macro context. For example, the diversity needs in an agency in a larger multicultural city would be different from the diversity needs of a boutique agency in a small less diverse town. Another example is the story Cheryl, one of our senior practitioner leader interviewees shared about a talented young African American man who had just been recruited into an agency. Indicating current internal-external disconnect, she described how lonely he felt when the 2017 Charlottesville incident occurred, and how he could find no one he could connect with about it at work. A third example would be the case of public relations education and the weak state of the D&I pipeline from college into the profession. This matter demonstrates the link between the macro societal (education) and professional/industry context.

Keeping such interconnections in mind, public relations leaders need to practice D&I leadership in ways that navigate and link all three contexts. They need to maintain a clear focus on complex and intersectional identity/diversity issues and power dynamics in both internal communication and inclusion/ equity building and external communication, relationship and pipeline building; they should not see the internal as being somehow separate from the external, or only being connected to the profession's context. We would like to especially underscore this latter point because we believe the disconnect across contexts (especially between the macro and the profession/industry and organizational contexts) and the D&I perception gap that we have described (see Chapter 5) are primary reasons for leadership failure when it comes to D&I in public relations.

Leadership

Across the three interrelated macro-meso-micro contexts, we conceptualize public relations leadership for inclusive diversity as being constituted through four dimensions of practice: (1) leading through a D&I lens, (2) relationality, (3) dialogic communication and (4) attention to the belonging-uniqueness dialectic. No dimension precedes any other since from a social constructionist perspective they co-constitute each other.

With regard to practicing relationality and dialogic communication through a D&I lens, it is necessary for leaders to willingly embrace professional training, coaching and education that will enhance their knowledge, attitude and skills (KAS) and prepare them to work toward the desired outcomes of climate of inclusive diversity, culture of leadership responsibility and accountability and ongoing (un)unlearning. The need for training is essential since most leaders are not experts on these practices (see Taylor & Kent, 2014; N. White, 2021). From a knowledge perspective:

- Leaders need to be able to grasp how power can work in the profession to include as well as exclude. This requires understanding that D&I is the responsibility of all identities and not just those that are marginalized or less privileged.

- The language used to define D&I matters. Using only representational EEO-type language is a static approach and does not enhance understanding of how to achieve inclusion/equity. Leaders need to understand that using dynamic language instead of cliches and flat descriptions is the path forward. Inclusion/equity will remain a challenge unless the language used to describe diversity automatically leads into how to practice inclusion across differences.
- Leaders need to appreciate the concept of standpoint plurality and the importance of considering and including different and diverse perspectives (internal and external) for organizational decision-making (Pless & Maak, 2004; Trittin & Schoeneborn, 2017)
- Organizations are communicatively and relationally constructed, maintained and changed. Leaders need to understand that the meanings and relationships jointly co-created with others impact sense-making, organizational decisions and practices, relational intelligence (which is a combination of ethical and emotional intelligence), and helps build healthy interdependence and trust (Maak & Pless, 2006c).
- Leaders need to understand and internalize that true dialogue requires the building of an interdependent sense of "we" without losing the "I." They need to understand the role of empathy in achieving this state (Raelin, 2016).
- Leaders need to understand the concept of identity and its increasingly fluid and complex cultural landscape. Relatedly, the concept of intersectionality is especially necessary to grasp.
- Leaders need to understand the concept of intercultural competence and learn how to engage in dialogic communication and relationship building across differences in ways that enhance belonging and preserve uniqueness.
- Leaders need to learn how to detect organizational and professional barriers in the path of D&I progress (e.g., homophily – especially among senior leadership, persistence of microaggressions in everyday communication, the need for more emphasis on the moral case for D&I along with the business case, inequitable hiring and promotion practices and so on).
- Leaders need to engage in building self-knowledge (Berger & Meng, 2010). This can help them assess their own D&I strengths and weaknesses and work on addressing the latter.
- Leaders need to develop a full understanding that personal engagement and genuine commitment from leaders, especially senior leaders, is necessary for D&I success. They would benefit from familiarizing themselves with research and case studies that provide evidence and information which they could then apply to develop D&I best practices for their own organizations.
- Leaders need to understand and appreciate that leadership responsibility and accountability with regard to D&I is not an option but a must.

Attitudes congruent with the knowledge component include:

- Seeing D&I as a promise rather than a problem and being passionate and eager to keep learning about D&I (Chin & Trimble, 2015).
- Humility, valuing introspection and the willingness to learn from mistakes and not see admitting mistakes as a weakness.
- The willingness to unlearn ways of thinking that obstruct D&I progress.
- Believing wholeheartedly in leadership responsibility and accountability for D&I.
- Believing in the philosophy of dialogism and creating a sense of "we" (belonging) without diminishing the "I" (uniqueness).
- The willingness to make concrete structural changes and work toward cultural changes that will assist in achieving climates of inclusive diversity.
- The willingness to "go against the grain" ("power to" approach; Berger, 2005), when necessary, to support and advocate for D&I.
- Believing wholeheartedly that the primary responsibility of a D&I oriented leader is to build climates of inclusive diversity.

The skills required to put knowledge and attitude into action (praxis) include:

- The ability to explain the relevance of D&I for the organization to all employees at all levels – both as a business and a moral case.
- The ability to communicate internally and externally with genuine passion. Build a culture of storytelling at all levels of the organization by sharing personal struggles with D&I and what was learned through the process. According to senior public relations leader R. Jeep Bryant (2016):

> People's stories are a powerful tool in advancing a common culture. Great communicators make sure those stories resonate and reverberate. ... Communicators who want to strengthen their companies' commitment to diversity and inclusion can make great strides through storytelling. The right stories, told in a memorable way, can be the most effective tools for breaking through barriers to understanding.
>
> *(pp. 30, 32)*

- The ability to jointly develop a vision for inclusive diversity (Pless & Maak, 2004).
- The ability to be personally and visibly engaged in D&I efforts, such as making structural and cultural changes necessary for building inclusive diversity and modeling D&I behavior for others (Pless & Maak, 2004).
- The ability to engage in relational and dialogic communication that helps employees feel they belong without downplaying their uniqueness.

- The ability to practice standpoint plurality, engage diverse perspectives in decision-making and mentor and guide others in how to do the same (Pless & Maak, 2004).
- The ability to bring dominant identities, i.e., White heterosexual males in this case, willingly on board the D&I effort as allies. This group holds most power in the profession and they must be engaged for change to occur. White male leadership culture has been normalized in corporate America and it remains the unquestioned norm (or just the way things are done) (Logan, 2011). This normalization must be brought into focus and made visible; White male leaders themselves need to play a big role of this effort (S. K. Johnson & Lambert, 2021; Welp & Schein, 2021). All words about power sharing will remain hollow if those holding most power remain disengaged or even alienated (Brown, 2016).
- The ability to share power and reduce leader-follower dualism and top-down hierarchies.
- The ability to engage in "power to" advocacy with senior leaders/dominant coalition/industry leadership when necessary.
- The ability to pay close attention to and help develop the D&I talent pipeline. Engage in public relations education and build stronger D&I relations (e.g., through guest lectures, internships and other relationship building efforts) between industry and colleges/universities, especially Historically Black Colleges and University (HBCUs), Hispanic Serving Institutions (HSIs), Native American University and Colleges (NAUC) and Minority Serving Institutions (MSIs) in general. Build D&I exchanges and efforts with Public Relations Student Society of America (PRSSA) chapters and other student pre-professional groups and clubs (see Bardhan & Gower, 2020; He, 2021).
- The ability to be in touch with the D&I ground realities in the organization and in the external environment and detect perception and policy-practice gaps that may exist. Measure goals/progress and get regular feedback. The latter includes engaging with resistance in a dialogic spirit (Ferdman, 2021).
- The ability to remain adaptable and flexible and work through the ambiguities and complexities of the fluid D&I landscape (Dillon & Bourke, 2016).
- The ability to embrace D&I responsibility and accountability and develop mechanisms to measure the same.

Regarding the belonging-uniqueness dialectic, leaders must understand this complex aspect of relationality and dialogism. This is not an easy note to strike. According to Ferdman (2021), inclusive leaders must have a "capacity for complexity and paradoxical thinking and behavior" (p. 18). Shore et al. (2011) and many identity scholars have explained that social identities are complex and that people do not only identify or only disidentify with social/cultural others. Interactions are usually a mix of both (i.e., identification and disidentification) with more or less of one depending on the context and identities involved. Here we draw upon Randel et al. (2018) to provide some suggestions for navigating this dialectic. They propose five categories of behavior that public relations leaders could adapt from and apply in their own organizations. The first three aim to build belonging and the latter two focus on preserving uniqueness:

> Support all organizational members.
>
> Ensure that justice and equity are part of each organizational member's experience.
>
> Provide opportunities for shared decision-making (i.e., power sharing) on relevant issues and create spaces for positive intercultural interactions.
>
> Encourage diverse contributions to the work of the organization.
>
> Help organizational members fully offer their unique talents and perspectives to enhance the work of the organization.
>
> *(p. 191)*

The intersectional perspective on identity also supports this dialectical approach to inclusion building since it helps us understand identities in complex ways; an intersectional lens can help leaders see opportunities for connections across differences in their attempts to balance belonging and uniqueness simultaneously. Additionally, the philosophy of dialogism is also well suited for this dialectic.

Desired outcomes

Our model aims for three interrelated outcomes: (1) climate of inclusive diversity, (2) culture of leadership responsibility and accountability and (3) ongoing (un)learning. We would like to emphasize that none of these are outcomes in a final sense – i.e., they are not boxes to be checked off. Achieving and maintaining a climate of inclusive diversity needs ongoing work and effort from leaders, leaders need to remain responsible and accountable at all times, and (un)learning about D&I must be on ongoing form of education that is informed by measurement of D&I achievements/failures and regular feedback from internal and external publics/stakeholders and society in general. The ongoing nature of this process and praxis is nothing extraordinary, and just like the financial health of a company requires ongoing work due to shifting internal and external contexts and changing times, so does D&I. Booysen (2014) states it well: "Once a culture of valuing inclusion is established and entrenched, it is imperative to monitor and evaluate it through a process of continuous oversight to ensure that inclusion stays institutionalized" (p. 309).

Each of the desired outcomes are self-explanatory since we have discussed them in detail throughout the book. They are interlinked and one is not possible without the others. The one point that we would like to make though is that although our model focuses on D&I leadership at the organization level, the larger goal is for these outcomes to occur at the overarching profession/industry level.

Conclusion

Public relations leaders are in position to catalyze the advancement of D&I in the profession, or they may continue to perpetuate inequities and exclusions. We certainly hope that it will be the former as we head further into this decade. If the racial and social justice reckoning of 2020 has taught us anything it is that prioritizing D&I is no longer an option but a necessity. Brumberg (2021) reports that about nine months after the death of George Floyd, US companies had pledged over $66 billion toward racial and social justice efforts: "It sure seems like we've reached a tipping point, but humans have proved incredibly adept at preserving power and the status quo – at all costs – while thwarting those in the minority" (para. 4). As we noted earlier and in Chapter 5, some recent reports are not very encouraging (e.g., "Unsafe," 2022), Pledges need to become strategic plans and concrete action which result in desired and measurable D&I outcomes.

We close this chapter on a note of tempered optimism. Operationalizing, living and communicating D&I at an everyday level is not easy and requires intentional and informed effort (Prime, Ferdman, & Riggio, 2021). As past research (e.g., Chitkara, 2018) and our own data indicate, leaders in the profession are struggling with inclusion and there is a fuzziness and lack of direction about how to build organizational cultures of inclusive diversity. And yet, as Ferdman (2021) notes:

> The ability to be inclusive and to foster and sustain an inclusive culture in groups, workplaces, and communities is a critical component of 21st century leadership. Successful and effective leadership in today's organizations and societies and in those of the future requires strong understanding of and skills for creating and catalyzing opportunities to benefit from all types of diversity and to enhance these capacities in oneself and others.
>
> *(p. 3)*

Therefore, to be up to speed on required leadership skills for today's current climate, public relations leaders need to be open to training and ongoing learning. Increasing diversity and representation is the first step and the careful cultivation of inclusion needs to occur alongside. We hope that the model we have developed will offer insights and practical guidance to leaders in their D&I journeys. And we also hope that many more studies, projects and initiatives will follow that will increase our knowledge about how to practice inclusive diversity on a daily basis in the work and world of public relations.

8

Conclusion

Looking Ahead

In this concluding chapter, we highlight the primary and unique contributions of our book. We offer some practical advice and suggestions, mostly drawn from the words of our senior leader interviewees, to guide leaders in practicing our leadership model for inclusive diversity in public relations. We conclude with suggestions for future scholarship for enhancing knowledge on diversity and inclusion (D&I) leadership in public relations as we head further into this decade and century.

Leading public relations into a diverse and inclusive future

If one is paying attention to important conversations around D&I, not just in the world of public relations but in the workplace in general and particularly with regard to leadership responsibility, it is hard to miss the central focus on inclusion in practicing equity and making diversity work. Building inclusion requires developing an inclusive mindset and behaviors which produce a certain culture and environment where all feel welcome. According to Booysen (2014):

> A culture of inclusion can be institutionalized by weaving inclusion into the everyday operation and fabric of the organization through translating the values of inclusion into its mission, vision, strategies, policies, structures, and processes as well as its leadership practices. It is thus important to put systems in place that hold everyone, especially management [leaders], accountable for achieving inclusion goals and upholding inclusion values.

(pp. 308–309)

DOI: 10.4324/9781003170020-8

In inclusive cultures, marginalized and dominant identities work together in ways that simultaneously produce feelings of interdependence (collective agency) and belonging and preserve uniqueness. The challenge seems to reside in how to achieve this complex culture.

According to Meehan (2021), one major aspect of the challenge is that it takes a lot of intentional hard work at every level backed by leadership support "to embed and cultivate equity, diversity, and inclusion competencies in the ongoing practice and culture of organizations, networks, and communities" (p. 409). As Booysen's (2014) opening quote above underscores, leadership support and deep commitment to D&I are the first steps toward gradually institutionalizing inclusion and making it a definitive part of an organization's cultural fabric. Second, leaders need to lead in tune with the times. Leaders today are leading in a world full of complexities and uncertainties, and this reality must guide their leadership on everything, including D&I. Balancing belonging and uniqueness is a complex relational challenge. As Uhl-Bien and Arena (2017) state about leadership in complex and diverse environments, "A new world requires a new way of thinking" (p. 19). Third, we need a lot more research, especially case studies, from scholars and practitioners, that illustrate how organizations with success in D&I are achieving their goals and what kinds of leadership philosophies, styles and practices are working. As Shore, Cleveland and Sanchez (2018) state:

> Never before has cooperative research been so necessary among scholars and practitioners as in the case of inclusion [and diversity] … Understanding and promoting inclusion [and diversity] will require such joint scholar/practitioner efforts involving a combination of (1) understanding of challenges associated with diversity that are facing practitioners in organizations, (2) conversations between scholars and practitioners for greater mutual insights and understanding, (3) research based on carefully designed studies, (4) organizations that provide research access for scholars to investigate inclusion, and (5) organizational leaders who are willing to proactively apply the knowledge that is gained through systematic research.
>
> *(p. 187)*

And fourth, cultures of inclusion cannot be built overnight (Crater, 2021). They arise gradually from continuing education. The hard work needed must be coupled with persistence and patience. Reinforcing this point, senior leader Aubrey Quinn of the Clyde Group recently stated: "People love to use the expression, 'This isn't a sprint, it's a marathon,' but I've accepted the fact that there is no finish line for DEI" (Schuman, 2020, para. 9).

Here we loop back to Edwards' (2011, 2015) application of sociologist Pierre Bourdieu's notion of habitus to public relations' professional culture which we described in the introductory chapter. Edwards explains that occupational cultures and practices, which reside within larger societal fields of power, are entrenched over decades, if not centuries, to form a habitus and these take time to change. The public relations habitus is no exception. What has been constructed over a long period of time will take some time to change. However, once the change begins in sincerity, we can begin entrenching the practices, dispositions, behaviors and beliefs to build a habitus of inclusive diversity, undo systemic inequities and detect and prevent new inequities from developing. And we can do so at a good pace..

Our leadership model for inclusive diversity in public relations is the primary contribution of this book, and we hope it will be a useful praxis and process tool for addressing the D&I challenge. This model is theoretically unique because of its emphasis on dialectical thinking with regard to D&I. The belonging-uniqueness dialectical focus, we believe, is a cutting-edge contribution drawn from the larger literature on D&I and leadership. While the professional discourse emphasizes belonging as the path to inclusion, our dialectical focus is based on the reasoning that belonging is not possible unless uniqueness is preserved. This form of reasoning requires us to work with two contradictory seeming ideas at the same time (Martin & Nakayama, 1999). We can attempt belonging through assimilation. In this case marginalized identities are implicitly expected to conform to dominant workplace norms in order to belong, cultural and inequity-based power differentials are not addressed in any meaningful manner, and unconscious biases remain unaddressed. On the other hand, practicing belonging through the preservation of uniqueness addresses cultural and inequity-based power differentials through power sharing and valuing uniqueness for what it can contribute.

In addition to the model and the belonging-uniqueness dialectic, we would like to highlight three points that we think are unique emphases of our research and model:

- First, and in keeping with our social constructionist and interpretive lens, we have emphasized that the language we use to describe and define diversity at the profession/industry level plays a significant role in how leaders understand and operationalize D&I/equity. The Equal Employment Opportunity (EEO) type of language that tends to be more popular aims at recruitment/representation. While recruitment/representation is extremely important, we cannot stop at that level and language. As Bernstein, Bulger, Salipante and Weisinger (2020) explain, representation sets the stage and opens up the opportunity for building inclusion/ equity, but it does not guide us much in terms of building relations across power differentials and inequities. Such complex relationships do not develop automatically once there is representation, and as past research and our own data indicate, once recruited marginalized identities need to feel heard, empowered and welcome, and not experience exclusion and inequity-based obstacles in their paths to advancement. According to Edelman's US COO Lisa Ross (2021):

> The companies that win will take hard and necessary steps both internally and externally to ensure that we move beyond representation and tokenism, into a world where voices and communities of color are authentically portrayed, elevated, and given a chance to succeed.
>
> *(para. 8)*

Furthermore, negative effects such as stereotyping and microaggressions can be the result of representation that is not carefully nurtured toward inclusion (Bernstein et al., 2020). A few years ago, Deloitte developed a four-level model for D&I that is instructive for understanding this point (Bourke, 2018). Level 1 is a compliance approach that is limited to EEO and Affirmative Action language and goals. Level 2 is a programmatic approach that uses language aimed at increasing representation of marginalized groups. Level 3 is leader-led and aims to remove cultural and systemic barriers. Level 4 is an integrated approach where D&I thinking permeates the entire organization. If organizations are to move beyond levels 1 and 2 and, as we emphasize in our model, achieve climates of inclusive diversity, then leaders and the entire organization must pay attention to the language used, internally and externally, to communicate about and construct meanings around D&I.

- Second (and a point also related to language use), because D&I has been such a challenge in public relations it tends to consistently get framed negatively in communication and professional discourse as a problem to be overcome. The focus on the positive outcomes and benefits of D&I done well (such as creativity, employee engagement, financial advantage, reputation enhancement, fulfilling social responsibility and so on) is weak. Also, there is scant mention of how successful D&I efforts can benefit organizations financially by reducing turnover costs due to low retention rates and costly discrimination lawsuits. We emphasize in our model that if we are to inspire organizational and industry culture change in favor of D&I, then leaders must effectively communicate the social/moral and financial benefits of D&I done well.
- Our model draws upon the transformational style of leadership which research suggests is the preferred model for public relations leadership (see Chapter 4). Chin and Trimble (2015) make it clear that D&I leadership models should avoid simply adding to already existing models that have been developed from the experiences of power elite leaders and start from the premise of difference/diversity rather than homogeneity. We have not simply

added on to the transformational style but borrow those of its characteristics that we believe contribute to or are a part of a D&I perspective to build a unique model. For example, we have retained certain leadership characteristics, e.g., relationality, empathy, dialogue. We have also retained the goal of transformation since D&I/equity are transformative forces (Bourke, 2018). In this way, our model incorporates what is already considered important in public relations leadership but steers it firmly in the direction of D&I.

We now turn to some suggestions and advice for leaders that we hope will be useful if they choose to put our model into action.

Advice for the future

The public relations leaders we interviewed (see Chapter 6) who stand out for their contributions to D&I in the profession provided some sound advice that synchronizes well with our model and offers practical guidance for achieving the desired outcomes. As we were coding the interviews, we made a list of the advice which we now report:

- Set clear D&I goals and measure progress regularly (just like in an ongoing campaign). Regularly check the pulse of employees on how they feel about inclusion/equity. This is necessary since D&I is an ongoing journey requiring non-stop effort.
- Create a dedicated position for D&I in senior leadership and ensure this position has teeth.
- Do not position D&I as *just* a business imperative since this commodifies and dehumanizes members of already underrepresented and marginalized groups.
- Develop programs and initiatives that help those from underrepresented backgrounds grow and advance into leadership positions (e.g., formal mentorship programs, sponsorships, training).
- If not already in place, develop employee resource groups (ERGs) as spaces where important D&I conversations can take place. Encourage interactions between ERGs to avoid silos and promote learning and interaction across different groups (workshops, lunch-and-learn sessions and so on).
- Regularly hold workshops, training and discussions about how to improve the workplace, how to embrace and affirm D&I and how to look at different points of view (i.e., develop standpoint plurality) without being reactionary, resistant or judgmental.
- Build a culture of storytelling. Share stories and promote storytelling initiatives that humanize all employees.
- Build an organizational culture where all can learn about the challenges people from different backgrounds face. Such cultures can build empathy

and help those with more privilege be mindful and self-reflexive. This, in turn, could lead to the mindset and behavioral changes needed for cultures of inclusion to grow and flourish.

- *Everyone* needs to work hard at making D&I an organic (natural) part of organizational culture. Just celebrating different groups during different months is a start but not enough.
- Hold leaders accountable and tie D&I progress to compensation. Leaders should be genuinely committed to D&I.
- Build industry-level leadership collaboration and momentum to advance D&I.

In addition to the above, we offer some suggestions of our own:

- Leaders need to participate in training, workshops and other D&I education programs along with everyone else (N. White, 2021). This would include introspecting on and examining what they need to learn as well as what pressures (internal and external) may be working against their efforts to lead on D&I (see Willis, 2019).
- Leaders must ensure that a culture of inclusion/equity permeates the entire organization. According to He (2021): "To succeed at improving DE&I within their organizations, companies need to create a cultural shift that makes everyone from front line workers to top executives invested in improving DE&I" (para. 4). This can be done by taking steps to makes sure actual D&I changes are occurring at every level, and especially ensuring middle managers understand their pivotal role in the building of this culture (Bourke, 2018).
- Make valuing (rather than resisting or fearing) difference and focusing on what we can learn and how we can grow interculturally when differences intersect a normalized way of thinking and interacting/communicating. This can assist with breaking current homophily tendencies, especially among senior leadership.
- No system/culture can change when those in dominant positions of power are not engaged or feel alienated or threatened. White, heterosexual males, who are currently this group in corporate America and in public relations, need to be intentionally brought on board the D&I effort in every organization, provided the skills needed to become more inclusive, kept accountable and made part of the solution rather than the problem (Brown, 2016; Wittenberg-Cox, 2017). This aids the argument that *everyone* needs to be part of the D&I effort.

In addition to the practical advice above, public relations scholarship also needs to do its part to assist the enhancement of D&I leadership in the profession.

Suggestions for future research

Future scholarship on D&I and leadership in public relations needs to do a few things simultaneously. Scholars need to substantially build the body of knowledge on how leaders can successfully practice D&I, what types of communication, practices and policies are effective (as well as those that may be constraining D&I efforts), and how D&I progress and leadership accountability are being measured. Therefore, on the one hand, we need applied research while on the other hand, we need to keep our critical wheels turning (i.e., remain vigilant). Critical scholarship on D&I leadership needs to keep an eye on systemic and power-related matters to ensure leaders are kept accountable and responsible. Both applied and critical research need to engage in theory-building. More specifically, we recommend the following:

- Instead of being more of a sidebar, which has been the case so far, the topic of D&I should assume a more central role in public relations leadership scholarship.
- Research/theory on D&I and public relations leadership needs to be relevant for the times (Fairhurst, 2011; Grint, 2011). According to Pless and Maak (2011), "most leadership research still assumes that leadership takes place in clearly structured, hierarchical relationships and that researchers can uncover some ultimate truth about what constitutes 'effective' leadership. The world of leadership is messier than that – more complex, diverse, and ultimately contested ..." (p. 11). Our scholarship should embrace the complexity of our times and not force fit simple lenses on complex phenomena such as D&I leadership.
- We encourage future scholarship to build on our model as well as explore its various dimensions through empirical research. For example, we believe it is particularly important to further examine the belonging-uniqueness dialectic. Additionally, there might be other dialectics, dynamics and dimensions that could enhance this model in the future.
- Our model has focused more on the organizational (internal) level of D&I process and praxis. We hope future research, following our and Mundy's (2016) model, will expand on the external level and further scrutinize how the internal and the external are linked. For example, Bourke (2018) points out that the internal and external D&I processes of organizations should match. For public relations, what are the implications of the internal D&I process and praxis we have conceptualized for external leader communication and vice versa? How can a dialectical belonging-uniqueness orientation to inclusion internally impact external leader communication and relationship building with external publics/stakeholders?
- The research on D&I and leadership tends to focus almost entirely on underrepresented and marginalized identities. White heterosexual males,

or the dominant group, are usually the presumed problem in this scenario. While the former focus is of course necessary, we also need more direct study of the dominant group to better understand how they can become part of the solution. This focus will allow for more complex understandings of power dynamics and how change can be achieved. This is particularly true for public relations since 70% of leadership positions are held by mostly White males (Logan, 2011; Place & Vardeman-Winter, 2018).

- More research is necessary on how to strike a balance between the business and the moral/social justice case for DEI in public relations. Neither case by itself is enough in current times with activism and social justice causes increasingly becoming part of operational strategy and organizational identities. Research should keep track of how leaders and companies are communicating internally and externally regarding this two-prong approach. Is there a good balance or is the scale tilting more on one side or the other?

- After the racial reckoning of 2020, there has been an uptick in the hiring of chief D&I officers in public relations and calls have been made for more transparency and sharing of D&I metrics; pledges have been made to do so and several leaders have backed their words regarding commitment to D&I with resources (Arenstein, 2020; Brumberg, 2021; Marszalek, 2020). From a critical and power relations perspective (see Berger & Reber, 2006), however, it is necessary to keep track of these hiring trends and the extent of power invested in these positions. What role are chief D&I officers expected to play? Is the work falling all on them or are other leaders stepping up? Do they report directly to the CEO and have enough resources to accomplish their goals? Are any structural and/or cultural impediments hampering their efforts? Do they feel empowered to do their work well? Why are some reports, two years into this uptick, still showing the needle may not be moving as fast as expected ("Unsafe," 2022)?

- We emphasize leadership training in our model. We believe that training tailored to the profession would be more useful and pertinent compared to more generic training. Of course, the macro societal aspects of diversity should be a part of tailored training, but the goal should be to understand D&I in terms of public relations work. Future research should explore current trainings, how effective they are and how to develop effective professions-specific D&I training for leaders and other employees. Additionally, research should explore how what veteran D&I consultant Mary-Frances Winters calls "brave spaces" can be developed within organizations. Citing Winters, Caminiti (2021) writes:

> We've spent so much time talking about creating a safe space, but that doesn't take anyone out of their comfort zone so that the really hard conversations can happen … Creating a brave space allows managers the freedom to admit that there are things they don't know about minority

employees, but that there is room to ask questions. We have to give people some slack when they don't know everything and offer some grace and forgiveness as leaders work their way through these conversations ....

(paras. 6, 7)

Since so much work in public relations occurs with external publics/stakeholders, it would also be necessary to explore how training can assist with creating external brave spaces.

- There is plenty of research that still needs to be conducted in the education space. How can we improve public relations curriculum to strengthen the college-to-profession D&I pipeline? In what ways can industry be a more engaged and effective part of this effort? How can extracurricular activities be marshalled to assist with D&I education? What cultural and structural barriers are obstructing diversifying public relations programs, and what strategies seem to be working? These, and more questions are waiting for research-backed answers.
- We live in a hyperconnected world. Future study of D&I and leadership in public relations should explore D&I in globally interconnected contexts since the profession is global in scope. While a strong body of literature in international public relations has developed over the last 30 years, D&I/equity do not quite fall into that line of scholarship. Also, diversity is related more to difference and power within societal cultures and cannot be grasped through dimensions of societal culture alone. Diversity is understood differently in different cultures and countries, and the differences that matter the most in various contexts are historically and politically shaped. For example, while race is a major category of identity and inequity in the United States and western contexts, religion, ethnicity, caste or social class may be so in some other contexts. How do different differences impact public relations leadership in globally interconnected contexts? This is a ripe area for future research.

Additionally, we encourage academic scholars and practitioners to join forces in their research endeavors. The above suggestions are not exhaustive, and we hope this much needed and highly relevant line of research will continue to grow in the near future.

Conclusion

As we wrap up our writing, we are hearing and reading mixed reports about the path forward. We began this project before the racial and social justice upheavals of 2020 and the onset of the COVID-19 pandemic. It has now been more than two years since the killing of George Floyd and the pandemic is not quite over yet. In fact, it has taken a disproportionate toll on communities of color because of systemic disparities in the healthcare system; further, women are also predicted to lose ground in leadership roles because of the pandemic's disproportionate impact on them (Brien & Fronk, 2021). These macro issues are no doubt having an impact on the public relations profession. On the other hand, the D&I conversation in public relations, and in corporate America, has taken some significant turns during our research and writing. Leaders have been vocal about their intentions to speed up D&I progress, and recent research by Fortune/Deloitte shows that CEO commitment to DEI remains strong:

> In June 2020 …, 94% of CEOs agreed that DEI was a personal strategic priority, 90% of CEOs agreed that their organization aspired to be an industry leader in DEI, and 72% of CEOs planned to disclose DEI metrics to the public. Fast forward to June 2021, and CEOs are already claiming victory on a few items. More than half of CEOs say that they have completed the following: building DEI into their strategic priorities and goals as CEO; incorporating DEI into corporate strategy, not just talent strategy; setting measurable targets for progress toward DEI goals as an executive team; and disclosing DEI metrics to their employees.
>
> *(Fan, 2021, p. 13)*

As mentioned earlier, the good news is that in the world of public relations, many agencies and companies have started hiring more chief D&I officers, committing more resources to D&I effort and programs, and reporting their D&I metrics (Arenstein, 2020; Brumberg, 2021; Marszalek, 2020). Additionally, and with regard to the D&I pipeline, current public relations students seem passionate about D&I (Sharif & Bolden, 2020; van Beuzekom & Gormley, 2020). This makes a lot of sense since Gen Z is reported to be as, if not more, committed to social justice and human rights issues compared with millennials (Dodds, 2020). If they are our future leaders, then we can certainly be hopeful and optimistic about the path forward.

While we are hopeful, we must remember the jury is still out about what has been concretely accomplished so far. Alongside our optimism, we must not forget that many agencies and companies still have not reported their D&I metrics and there are no overall metrics at an industry level (Marszalek, 2020; Shah, 2020; Sudhaman, 2020). Research supported by The Plank Center for Leadership in Public Relations, including some recent research, indicates that some drawbacks to effective leadership in public relations in the United States include internal politics, overly controlling CEOs, lack of empowerment, leaders not thinking they carry the primary responsibility for D&I and declining grades on overall leadership (Berger, Meng, Heyman, Harris, & Bain, 2014; Meng, Reber, Berger, Gower, & Zerfass, 2021; "Report Card on PR Leaders," n.d.). In such a scenario, it is hard to accurately predict how the D&I

narrative will unfold for the public relations profession. However, one thing we can say for sure: if the will to change exists then the rest will follow.

The combined impacts of the 2020 racial reckoning and the COVID-19 pandemic threw not only our country but the entire world into a crisis like we have never seen before. While we do not have a crystal ball, we believe some good change has to come out of this world-changing experience. The writing is on the wall for those who wish to read it. Ronald Roberts (2020), managing partner with Finn Partners, states powerfully that while transformation requires hard work and does not happen overnight, there is important work right now that needs to be done:

> The good news is this: What we are willing to name we can examine, and what we are willing to examine we can change. The better news is that our industry is in a position to change ourselves *and* change others. ….
>
> But before we start talking, we need to do a better job walking. We can't give expert advice on things we as agencies are not doing. Otherwise, our counsel will be rooted in empty pledges and commitments, with no understanding of how to make them real. Too many businesses and organizations have made public pronouncements and promises – then moved on. When we are a party to this, we are part of the problem.
>
> … [I]t's crucial to realize that the process of becoming truly diverse will be painful if it's done right. It will take time, energy, honesty, and self-awareness. But it is very much worth pursuing.
>
> *(paras. 2, 3, 24, emphasis in original)*

We hope what this book has to offer will be useful in this process of transformation. Like many others, we remain cautiously optimistic. In closing we quote Rosanna Durruthy (2020), LinkedIn's vice president of global diversity, inclusion and belonging: "When people from diverse backgrounds and cultures work together, we all succeed" (para. 12). Like the geese that teach us so much about leadership, we must keep pressing on with an unwavering focus on diversity, inclusion and equity. The flight ahead is a long and important one filled with opportunities.

References

Accreditation Council on Education in Journalism and Mass Communications. (2018). *Journalism and Mass Communications Accreditation 2018–2019*. http://www.acejmc. org/wp-content/uploads/2019/01/2018-19-Booklet.pdf

Acosta, K. L. (2020). Racism: A public health crisis. *City & Community, 19*(3), 506–515.

Agger-Gupta, N., & Harris, B. (2017), Dialogic change and the practice of inclusive leadership. In A. Boitano, R. Lagomarsino Dutra, & H. E. Schockman (Eds.), *Breaking the zero-sum game: Transforming societies through inclusive leadership* (pp. 305–322). Bingley: Emerald Publishing.

Ahmed, S. (2007). The language of diversity. *Ethnic and Racial Studies, 30*(2), 235–256.

Ahonen, P., Tienari, J., Meriläinen, S., & Pullen, A. (2014). Hidden contexts and invisible power relations: A Foucauldian Reading of diversity research. *Human Relations, 67*(3), 263–286.

Aldoory, L. (1998). The language of leadership for female public relations professionals. *Journal of Public Relations Research, 10*, 73–101.

Aldoory, L. (2005). A (re) conceived feminist paradigm for public relations: A case for substantial improvement. *Journal of Communication, 55*(4), 668–684.

Aldoory, L., Reber, B., Berger, B., & Toth, E. L. (2008). Provocations in public relations: A study of gendered ideologies of power-influence in practice. *Journal of Management Communication Quarterly, 85*(4), 1–28.

Aldoory, L., & Toth, E. L. (2002). Gender discrepancies in a gendered profession: A developing theory for public relations. *Journal of Public Relations Research, 14*(2), 103–126.

Aldoory, L., & Toth, E. L. (2004). Leadership and gender in public relations: Perceived effectiveness of transformational and transactional leadership styles. *Journal of Public Relations Research, 16*(2), 157–183.

Allen, B. J. (1995). "Diversity"; and organizational communication. *Journal of Applied Communication Research, 23*(2), 143–155.

Alvesson, M. (2011). Leadership and organizational culture. In A. Bryman, D. Collinson, K. Grint, B. Jackson, & M. Uhl-Bien (Eds.), *The SAGE handbook of leadership* (pp. 151–164). Thousand Oaks, CA: Sage.

Anderson, J. A., Baur, J. E., Griffith, J. A., & Buckley, M. R. (2017). What works for you may not work for (gen)me: Limitations of present leadership theories for the new generation. *The Leadership Quarterly, 28*(1), 245–260.

Appelbaum, L., & Walton, F. (2015). *An examination of factors affecting the success of underrepresented groups in the public relations profession.* The City College of New York. https://www.bic-ccny.info/2015/11/new-study-addresses-diversity-in-public.html

Arenstein, S. (2020, July 26). FleishmanHillard diversity chief: We need substantive change. *PR News.* https://www.prnewsonline.com/diversity-Graham-Fleishman Hillard

Ashcraft, K. L., Kuhn, T. R., & Cooren, F. (2009). Constitutional amendments: "Materializing" organizational communication. *Academy of Management Annals, 3*(1), 1–64.

Austin, L. (2010). Framing diversity: A qualitative content analysis of public relations industry publications. *Public Relations Review, 36*(3), 298–301.

Avolio, B. J., Walumbwa, F. O., & Weber, T. J. (2009). Leadership: Current theories, research, and future directions. *Annual Review of Psychology, 60,* 421–449.

Bakhtin, M. M. (1981). *The dialogic imagination* (M. Holquist, Ed.; C. Emerson & M. Holquist, Trans.). Austin, TX: University of Texas Press.

Balta, H. (2015, October 29). Unconscious bias: Cloning in the workplace. *Public Relations Tactics.* https://apps.prsa.org/Intelligence/Tactics/Articles/view/11283/1118/Unconscious_Bias_Cloning_in_the_Workplace#.X17aUGhKjIU

Balta, H. (2017, June 1). Diversity without inclusion is only skin-deep. *Public Relations Tactics.* https://apps.prsa.org/Intelligence/Tactics/Articles/view/11919/1143/Diversity_Without_Inclusion_Is_Only_Skin_Deep#.WVWdg-mQxPZ

Banks, S. (1995). *Multicultural public relations: A social-interpretive approach.* Thousand Oaks, CA: Sage.

Bardhan, N. (2003). Rupturing public relations metanarratives: The example of India. *Journal of Public Relations Research, 15*(3), 225–248.

Bardhan, N., & Engstrom, C. (2021). Diversity, inclusion and leadership communication in public relations: A rhetorical analysis of diverse voices. *PR Journal, 14*(2). https://prjournal.instituteforpr.org/wp-content/uploads/Bardhan_PRJ14.2-1.pdf

Bardhan, N., Engstrom, E., & Gower, G. (2018, November). *The role of leadership in diversity and inclusion in the U.S. public relations industry.* Paper presented at the National Communication Association Annual Convention, Public Relations Division, Salt Lake City, UT.

Bardhan, N., & Gower, K. (2020). Student and faculty/educator views on diversity and inclusion in public relations: The role of leaders in bringing about change. *Journal of Public Relations Education, 6*(2), 102–141.

Bardhan, N., & Patwardhan, P. (2004). Multinational corporations and public relations in a historically resistant host culture. *Journal of Communication Management, 8*(3), 246–263.

Bardhan, N., & Weaver, C. K. (2011). Introduction. In N. Bardhan & C. K. Weaver (Eds.), *Public relations in global cultural contexts: Multi-paradigmatic perspectives* (pp. 1–28). Oxfordshire: Routledge.

Bassett-Jones, N. (2005). The paradox of diversity management, creativity and innovation. *Creativity and Innovation Management, 14*(2), 169–175.

Baxter, L., & Montgomery, B. (1996). *Relating: Dialogues and dialectics.* New York, NY: The Guilford Press.

Becker, J. C. (2012). The system-stabilizing role of identity management strategies: Social creativity can undermine collective action for social change. *Journal of Personality and Social Psychology, 103*, 647–662.

Beer, J. M. (2010). Diversity management's paradoxical negation of diversity. *International Journal of Diversity in Organisations, Communities & Nations, 10*(4), 1–13.

Bell, D. E., Raiffa, H., & Tversky, A. (1988). Descriptive, normative, and prescriptive interactions in decision making. In D. E. Bell, H. Raiffa, & A. Tversky (Eds.), *Decision making: Descriptive, normative, and prescriptive interactions* (pp. 9–32). Cambridge: Cambridge University Press.

Berger, B. K. (2005). Power over, power with, and power to relations: Critical reflections on public relations, the dominant coalition, and activism. *Journal of Public Relations Research, 17*(1), 5–28.

Berger, B. K. (2007). Public relations and organizational power. In E. L. Toth (Ed.), *The future of excellence in public relations and communication management: Challenges for the next generation* (pp. 221–234). Mahwah, NJ: Lawrence Erlbaum Associates.

Berger, P., & Luckmann, T. (1966). *The social construction of reality.* New York, NY: Doubleday.

Berger, B. K., & Meng, J. (2010). Public relations practitioners and the leadership challenge. In R. L. Heath (Ed.), *The SAGE handbook of public relations* (pp. 421–434). Thousand Oaks, CA: Sage.

Berger, B. K., & Meng, J. (2014a). Preface. In B. K. Berger & J. Meng (Eds.), *Public relations leaders as sensemakers* (pp. xxiii–xv). Oxfordshire: Routledge.

Berger, B. K., & Meng, J. (2014b). Review of the leadership literature. In B. K. Berger & J. Meng (Eds.), *Public relations leaders as sensemakers* (pp. 16–37). Oxfordshire: Routledge.

Berger, B. K., & Meng, J. (2014c). Making sense of leaders and leadership. In B. K. Berger & J. Meng (Eds.), *Public relations leaders as sensemakers* (pp. 3–15). Oxfordshire: Routledge.

Berger, B. K., & Meng, J. (2014d). The global study and leadership in the future. In B. K. Berger & J. Meng (Eds.), *Public relations leaders as sensemakers* (pp. 297–313). Oxfordshire: Routledge.

Berger, B. K., Meng, J., Heyman, W., Harris, M., & Bain, M. (2014). U.S. Public relations leaders pursue talent, digital mastery, and strong cultures. In B. K. Berger & J. Meng (Eds.), *Public relations leaders as sensemakers* (pp. 3–15). Oxfordshire: Routledge.

Berger, B. K., & Reber, B. H. (2006). *Gaining influence in public relations.* Mahwah, NJ: Lawrence Erlbaum Associates.

Berger, B. K., Reber, B. H., & Heyman, W. C. (2007). You can't homogenize success in communication management: PR leaders take diverse paths to top. *International Journal of Strategic Communication, 1*(1), 53–71.

Bernstein, R. S., Bulger, M., Salipante, P., & Weisinger, J. Y. (2020). From diversity to inclusion to equity: A theory of generative interactions. *Journal of Business Ethics, 167*(3), 395–410.

Berry, J. (2016). Diversity and equity. *Cross Cultural & Strategic Management, 23*(3), 413–430.

Bililies, T., & Ndoma-Ogar, E. (2021, November 30). DEI matters more than ever in the red-hot talent war – Here's how to kick-start your journey. *Chief Executive.* https://chiefexecutive.net/dei-matters-more-than-ever-in-the-red-hot-talent-war-heres-how-to-kick-start-your-journey/

Bishop, K. (2021, December 5). Why some work environments breed toxic cultures. *BBC*. https://www.bbc.com/worklife/article/20211201-why-some-work-environments-breed-toxic-cultures

Blow, F. D., Bonney, C. F., Tallapragada, M., & Brown, D. W. (2021). PRSA's theoretical and data-driven approach to improving diversity and inclusion in public relations. *PR Journal, 14*(3).

Boekhorst, J. A. (2015). The role of authentic leadership in fostering workplace inclusion: A social information processing perspective. *Human Resource Management, 54*(2), 241–264.

Boje, D. M. (2001). *Narrative methods for organizational and communication research*. Thousand Oaks, CA: Sage.

Bolden, R. (2011). Distributed leadership in organizations: A review of theory and research. *International Journal of Management Reviews, 13*(3), 251–269.

Bommel, T. V., Shaffer, E., Travis, D. J., & Foust-Cummings, H. (2021). Inclusive leadership from the inside out. In B. M. Ferdman, J. Prime, & R. E. Riggio (Eds.), *Inclusive leadership: Transforming diverse lives, workplaces, and societies* (pp. 111–124). Thousand Oaks, CA: Sage.

Booysen, L. A. E. (2014). The development if inclusive leadership practice. In B. M. Ferdman & B. R. Dean (Eds.), *Diversity at work: The practice of inclusion* (pp. 296–329). Hoboken, NJ: John Wiley & Sons, Inc.

Booysen, L. A. E. (2021). Responsible inclusive leadership: A whole system collective process outcome. In B. M. Ferdman, J. Prime, & R. E. Riggio (Eds.), *Inclusive leadership: Transforming diverse lives, workplaces, and societies* (pp. 195–211). Thousand Oaks, CA: Sage.

Botan, C. (1992). International public relations: Critique and reformulation. *Public Relations Review, 18*(2), 149–159.

Botan, C. (1997). Ethics in strategic communication campaigns: The case for a new approach to public relations. *The Journal of Business Communication, 34*(2), 188–202.

Bourke, J. (2018, January 22). The diversity and inclusion revolution: Eight powerful truths. *Deloitte Review*. https://www2.deloitte.com/us/en/insights/deloitte-review/issue-22/diversity-and-inclusion-at-work-eight-powerful-truths.html

Bourke, J., & Titus, A. (2020, March 6). The key to inclusive leadership. *Harvard Business Review*, 2–5.

Bovet, S. F. (1994, September). Minority-owned firmed seek mainstream acceptance. *PR Journal*, 12.

Brien, D., & Fronk, R. (2021, February 24). 8 challenges for business leaders that will shape year 2 of Covid-19. *Fast Company*. https://www.fastcompany.com/90607469/8-challenges-for-business-leaders-that-will-shape-year-two-of-covid

Brewer, M. B. (1991). The social self: On being the same and different at the same time. *Personality and Social Psychology Bulletin, 17*(5), 475–48.

Brown, J. (2016). *Inclusion*. Charleston, SC: Advantage.

Brown, K., Waymer, D., & Zhou, Z. (2019). Racial and gender-based differences in the collegiate development of public relations majors: Implications for underrepresented recruitment and retention. *Journal of Public Relations Education, 5*(1), 1–30.

Brown, K., White, C., & Waymer, D. (2011). African-American students' perceptions of public relations education and practice: Implications for minority recruitment. *Public Relations Review, 37*(5), 522–529.

Brumberg, R. (2021, February 9). How communicators can facilitate DE&I breakthroughs in 2021. *PR Daily*. https://www.prdaily.com/how-communicators-can-facilitate-dei-breakthroughs-in-2021/

Brunner, B. R. (2005). Linking diversity and public relations in higher education. *Prism 3*, http://praxis.massey.ac.nz/

Brunner, B. R. (2008). Defining public relations relationships and diversity's part in the process: Practitioners' perspectives. *Journal of Promotion Management, 14*(3/4), 153–167.

Bryant, R. J. (2016, March). Creating a culture of inclusion: The power of storytelling. *Spectra, 52*(1), 30–33.

Buber, M. (1970). *I and thou* (W. Kauffman, Trans.). New York, NY: Simon & Schuster.

Burrell, Y. (2015, February 2). Respecting and valuing differences: Corporate diversity programs must be inclusive to be successful. *Public Relations Tactics*. https://apps.prsa.org/Intelligence/Tactics/Articles/view/10944/1105/Respecting_and_Valuing_Differences_Corporate_Diver

Bureau of Labor Statistics. (2020). Labor force statistics from the current population survey. United States Department of Labor. https://www.bls.gov/cps/cpsaat11.htm

Burns, J. M. (1978). *Leadership*. New York, NY: Harper & Row.

Bushe, G. R., & Marshak, R. J. (2016). The dialogic mindset: Leading emergent change in a complex world. *Organization Development Journal, 34*(1), 37–65.

Byrne, D. (1971). *The attraction paradigm*. Cambridge, MA: Academic Press.

Cameron, G. T., Cropp, F., & Reber, B. H. (2001). Getting past platitudes: Factors limiting accommodation in public relations. *Journal of Communication Management, 5*(3), 242–261.

Caminiti, S. (2021, April 19). Leaders need to create brave space, not safe space, for diversity and inclusion conversations. *CNBC Workforce Wire*. https://www.cnbc.com/2021/04/19/companies-need-brave-space-not-safe-space-for-diversity-conversation-.html

Carroll, K. (n.d.). Moving the diversity needle forward in the classroom. *PRsay*. https://prsay.prsa.org/2021/10/25/moving-the-diversity-needle-forward-in-the-classroom/?_zs=CxE8m&_zl=fTN32

Castillo-Montoya, M. (2016). Preparing for interview research: The interview protocol refinement framework. *The Qualitative Report, 21*(5), 811–831.

Chapman, M., & Choe, D. (2020, December 1). Nasdaq seeks mandatory board diversity for listed companies. *AP News*. https://apnews.com/article/business-board-of-directors-38bceb1f1579518b5b1d97df5b029569

Charmaz, K. (2006). Constructing grounded theory (1st ed.). Thousand Oaks, CA: Sage.

Chavez, C., & Weisinger, J. Y. (2008). Beyond diversity training: A social infusion for cultural inclusion. *Human Resource Management, 47*, 331–350.

Chin, J. L. (2010). Introduction to the special issue on diversity and leadership. *American Psychologist, 65*(3), 150–156.

Chin, J. L., & Trimble, J. E. (2015). *Diversity and leadership*. Thousand Oaks, CA: Sage.

Chitkara, A. (2018, April 12). PR agencies need to be more diverse and inclusive: Here's how to start. *Harvard Business Review*. https://hbr.org/2018/04/pr-agencies-need-to-be-more-diverse-and-inclusive-heres-how-to-start

Choi, J., & Choi, Y. (2009). Behavioral dimensions of public relations leadership in organizations. *Journal of Communication Management, 13*(4), 292–309.

Choi, Y., & Hon, L. (2002). The influence of gender composition in power positions on public relations practitioners' gender-related perceptions. *Journal of Public Relations Research, 14*(3), 229–263.

Chrobot-Mason, D., & Aramovich, N. P. (2013). The psychological benefits of creating an affirming climate for workplace diversity. *Group & Organization Management, 38*(6), 659–689.

Chrobot-Mason, D., & Roberson, Q. (2022). Inclusive leadership. In P. G. Northouse (Ed.), *Leadership: Theory and practice* (9th ed., pp. 322–351). Thousand Oaks, CA: Sage.

Chrobot-Mason, D., Ruderman, M. N., & Nishii, L. H. (2013). Leadership in a diverse workplace. In Q. M. Roberson (Ed.), *The Oxford handbook of diversity and work* (pp. 315–340). Oxford: Oxford University Press.

Ciszek, E. (2018). Queering PR: Directions in theory and research for public relations scholarship. *Journal of Public Relations Research, 30*(4), 134–145.

Ciszek, E. (2020). "We are people, not transactions": Trust as a precursor to dialogue with LGBTQ publics. *Public Relations Review, 46*(1), 101759.

Ciulla, J. B. (1995). Leadership ethics: Mapping the territory. *Business Ethics Quarterly, 5*(1), 5–28.

Ciulla, J. B. (Ed.). (1998). *Ethics: The heart of leadership* (2nd ed.). Santa Barbara, CA: Praeger.

Cline, C., Toth, E., Turk, J., Walters, L., Johnson, N., & Smith, H. (1986). *The velvet ghetto: The impact of the increasing percentage of women in public relations and business communication.* San Francisco, CA: IABC Foundation.

Cohen, J. (2014, October 26). Time for PR industry to 'walk the talk' on subject of diversity. *PR Week* (U.S. Edition). http://www.prweek.com/article/1318665/cohen-time-pr-industry-walk-talk-diversity

Collier, M. J. (1989). Cultural and intercultural communication competence: Current approaches and directions for future research. *International Journal of Intercultural Relations, 13*(3), 287–302.

Collins, P. H. (1990). *Black feminist thought: Knowledge, consciousness, and the politics of empowerment.* Oxfordshire: Routledge.

Collins, P. H. (2000). Gender, black feminism, and black political economy. *The Annals of the American Academy of Political and Social Science, 568*(1), 41–53.

Collins, P. H., & Bilge, S. (2020). *Intersectionality* (2nd ed.). Cambridge: Polity.

Colvin, C. (2021, August 12). Fortune 500 shows incremental progress on diversity. *HR Dive.* https://www.hrdive.com/news/fortune-500-women-diversity/604906/

Conger, J. A., & Riggio, R. E. (2007). *The practice of leadership: Developing the next generation of leaders.* Hoboken, NJ: Jossey-Bass

Connerly, M. L., & Pedersen, P. B. (2005). *Leadership in a diverse and multicultural environment.* Thousand Oaks, CA: Sage.

Cottrill, K., Lopez, P. D., & Hoffman, C. C. (2014). How authentic leadership and inclusion benefit organizations. *Equality, Diversity and Inclusion: An International Journal, 33*(3), 275–292.

Cox, T., Jr. (1991). The multicultural organization. *Academy of Management Executive, 5*, 34–47.

Cox, T., Jr. (1994). *Cultural diversity in organizations.* Oakland, CA: Berrett-Koehler.

CPRE (n.d.). *Diversity.* http://www.commissionpred.org/commission-reports/the-professional-bond/diversity/

Crater, B. (2021, September 6). Three ways to create DE&I initiatives that actually work. *MarketingDive.* https://www.marketingdive.com/news/three-ways-to-create-dei-initiatives-that-actually-work/605869/

Creary, S. J. (2021). Diversity workspaces: Pathways for cultivating inclusion in diverse organizations. In B. M. Ferdman, J. Prime, & R. E. Riggio (Eds.), *Inclusive leadership: Transforming diverse lives, workplaces, and societies* (pp. 212–220). Thousand Oaks, CA: Sage.

Creedon, P. J. (1993). Acknowledging the infrasystem: A critical feminist analysis of systems theory. *Public Relations Review, 19,* 157–166.

Crenshaw, K. (1991). Mapping the margins: Intersectionality, identity politics, and violence against women of color. *Stanford Law. Review, 43,* 1241–1299.

Cripps, K. (2015, May 30). Time for true PR leaders to seek solution to diversity issue. *PR Week* (U.S. Edition). http://www.prweek.com/article/1348754/cripps-time-true-pr-leaders-seek-solution-diversity-issue

Crouch, M., & McKenzie, H. (2006). The logic of small samples in interview-based qualitative research. *Social Science Information, 45*(4), 483–499.

Cunliffe, A. L., & Eriksen, M. (2011). Relational leadership. *Human Relations, 64*(11), 1425–1449.

Curtin, P. A., & Gaither, T. K. (2012). *Globalization and public relations in postcolonial nations.* Cambria Press.

Czarniawska, B. (1997). *Narrating the organization: Dramas of institutional identity.* Chicago, IL: University of Chicago Press.

Dass, P., & Parker, B. (1999). Strategies for managing human resource diversity: From resistance to learning. *Academy of Management Perspectives, 13*(2), 68–80.

Daymon, C., & Demetrious, K. (2016). *Gender and public relations: Critical perspectives on voice, image and identity.* Oxfordshire: Routledge.

Díaz-Sáenz, H. R. (2011). Transformational leadership. In A. Bryman, D. Collinson, K. Grint, B. Jackson, & M. Uhl-Bien (Eds.), *The SAGE handbook of leadership* (pp. 299–310). Thousand Oaks, CA: Sage.

Didion, J. (1979). *The white album.* New York, NY: Farrar, Straus and Giroux.

Diggs-Brown, B., & Zaharna, R. (1995). Ethnic diversity in the public relations industry. *The Howard Journal of Communications, 6*(1/2), 114–123.

Dillon, B., & Bourke, J. (2016). The six signature traits of inclusive leadership. *Deloitte University Press.*

Dishman, L. (2015, May 18). Millennials have a different definition of diversity and inclusion. *Fast Company.* https://www.fastcompany.com/3046358/millennials-have-a-different-definition-of-diversity-and-inclusion

DiStaso, M. (2019). Undergraduate public relations in the United States: The 2017 Commission on Public Relations Education report. *Journal of Public Relations Education, 5*(3). https://aejmc.us/jpre/2019/11/20/undergraduate-public-relations-in-the-united-states-the-2017-commission-on-public-relations-education-report/

DiTomaso, N. (2021). Inclusion in a multicultural society. In B. M. Ferdman, J. Prime, & R. E. Riggio (Eds.), *Inclusive leadership: Transforming diverse lives, workplaces, and societies* (pp. 279–288). Thousand Oaks, CA: Sage.

Diversity Action Alliance. (2021). *Race and ethnicity in public relations and communications: Benchmark report.* Diversity Action Alliance. https://static1.squarespace.com/static/5f3d4ff90cfe7a50ea56bde6/t/61114ba6723fd06b0583da00/1628558553395/DAA+Benchmark+Report+%28Jul+2021%29

Diversity Best Practices (Seramount). (2017). Bold and inclusive leadership: The time is now. https://d3oxih60gx1ls6.cloudfront.net/f0bfc15f-1e57-426a-8712-a5417952d788/1fdfb966-9d89-4384-a122-e4b6fd0f622f_insight_paper-bold_and_inclusive_leadership.compressed.pdf

Diversity fatigue. (2016, February 13). *The Economist.* https://www.economist.com/business/2016/02/11/diversity-fatigue

Dixon-Fyle, S., Dolan, K., Hunt, V., & Prince, S. (2020, May 19). Diversity wins: How inclusion matters. *McKinsey & Co.* https://www.mckinsey.com/featured-insights/diversity-and-inclusion/diversity-wins-how-inclusion-matters

Dodds, F. (2020, June 30). Gen Z considers this benefit more important than salary. *Entrepreneur.* https://www.entrepreneur.com/article/352493?utm_source=feedly&utm_medium=webfeeds

Dreachslin, J. L. (2007). The role of leadership in creating a diversity-sensitive organization. *Journal of Healthcare Management, 52*(3), 151–155.

Durruthy, R. (2020, July 16). These two factors help build racial justice and belonging in the workplace. *Fast Company.* https://www.fastcompany.com/90528350/these-the-two-factors-help-build-racial-justice-and-belonging-in-the-workplace

Dyer, R. (1997). *White: Essays on race and culture* (1st ed.). Routledge.

Eagly, A. H., & Chin, J. L. (2010). Diversity and leadership in a changing world. *American Psychologist, 65*(3), 216–224.

Edelman (2013). *2013 Edelman trust barometer.* https://www.edelman.com/trust/2013-trust-barometer

Edelman (2021). *2021 Edelman trust barometer.* https://www.edelman.com/trust/2021-trust-barometer

Edrington, C. (2021). From slacktivism to activism: Rihanna and Fenty brands "pull up". In A. Hutchins & N. T. J. Tindall (Eds.), *Public relations and online engagement: Audiences, fandom and influencers* (pp. 3–10). London: Routledge.

Edwards, L. (2009). Symbolic power and public relations practice: Locating individual practitioners in their social context. *Journal of Public Relations Research, 21*(3), 251–272.

Edwards, L. (2011). Diversity in public relations. In L. Edwards & C. M. Hodges (Eds.), *Public relations, society and culture: Theoretical and empirical explorations* (pp. 75–89). Oxfordshire: Routledge.

Edwards, L. (2015). *Power, diversity and public relations.* Oxfordshire: Routledge.

Ellis, A., & Gould, R. (2018, April 18). PR industry should move beyond discussing diversity and take action. *O'Dwyer's.* https://www.odwyerpr.com/story/public/10512/2018-04-18/pr-industry-should-move-beyond-discussing-diversity-take-action.html

Elmer, P. (2011). Public relations and storytelling. In L. Edwards & C. E. M. Hodges (Eds.), Public relations, society & culture (pp. 47–60). London: Routledge.

Ely, R. J., & Thomas, D. A. (2001). Cultural diversity at work: The effects of diversity perspectives on work group processes and outcomes. *Administrative Science Quarterly, 46*(2), 229–273.

Ensari, N., & Riggio, R. E. (2021). Exclusion of inclusion in leadership theories. In B. M. Ferdman, J. Prime, & R. E. Riggio (Eds.), *Inclusive leadership: Transforming diverse lives, workplaces, and societies* (pp. 25–38). Thousand Oaks, CA: Sage.

Erzikova, E., & Berger, B. K. (2011). Creativity vs. ethics: Russian and US public relations students' perceptions of professional leadership and leaders. *PR Journal, 5*(3). https://prjournal.instituteforpr.org/wp-content/uploads/2011ErzikovaBerger.pdf

Erzikova, E., & Berger, B. K. (2012). Leadership education in the public relations curriculum: Reality, opportunities, and benefits. *PR Journal, 6*(3). https://www.researchgate.net/profile/Elina-Erzikova/publication/273413563_Leadership_Education_in_the_Public_Relations_Curriculum_Reality_Opportunities_and_Benefits/links/55004ff10cf2d61f820d6235/Leadership-Education-in-the-Public-Relations-Curriculum-Reality-Opportunities-and-Benefits.pdf

Espinoza, O. (2007). Solving the equity–equality conceptual dilemma: A new model for analysis of the educational process. *Educational Research, 49*(4), 343–363.

Essner, D. (2017). Millennials sound off on diversity in the workplace. *Public Relations Tactics, 24*(4), 7.

Eswaran, V. (2019, April 29). The business case for diversity in the workplace is now overwhelming. *World Economic Forum.* https://www.weforum.org/agenda/2019/04/business-case-for-diversity-in-the-workplace/

Fairhurst, G. T. (2007). *Discursive leadership: In conversation with leadership psychology.* Thousand Oaks, CA: Sage.

Fairhurst, G. T. (2011). Discursive approached to leadership. In A. Bryman, D. Collinson, K. Grint, B. Jackson, & M. Uhl-Bien (Eds.), *The SAGE handbook of leadership* (pp. 495–507). Thousand Oaks, CA: Sage.

Fairhurst, G. T., & Connaughton, S. L. (2014). Leadership: A communicative perspective. *Leadership 10*(1), 7–35.

Fairhurst, G. T., & Grant, D. (2010). The social construction of leadership: A sailing guide. *Management Communication Quarterly, 24,* 171–210.

Fairhurst, G. T., & Putnam, L. L. (2004). Organizations as discursive constructions. *Communication Theory, 14,* 5–26.

Fan, D. (2021). Charting the path to equity in the workplace. *Profiles in Diversity Journal.* https://issuu.com/diversityjournal/docs/pdj-firstquarter_2021

Ferdman, B. M. (2014). The practice of inclusion in diverse organizations. In B. M. Ferdman & B. R. Dean (Eds.), *Diversity at work: The practice of inclusion* (pp. 3–54). Hoboken, NJ: John Wiley & Sons, Inc.

Ferdman, B. M. (2021). Inclusive leadership: The fulcrum of inclusion. In B. M. Ferdman, J. Prime, & R. E. Riggio (Eds.), *Inclusive leadership: Transforming diverse lives, workplaces, and societies* (pp.3–24). Thousand Oaks, CA: Sage.

Fisher, W. R. (1984). Narration as a human communication paradigm: The case of public moral argument. *Communication Monographs, 51*(1), 1–22.

Fisher, W. R. (1987). *Human communication as narration: Toward a philosophy of reason, value, and action.* Los Angeles, CA: University of South Carolina Press.

Fitch, K., James, M., & Motion, J. (2016). Talking back: Reflecting on feminism, public relations and research. *Public Relations Review, 42*(2), 279–287.

Ford, P. (2017, March 15). We all need to be diversity champions. *PR Week.* https://www.prweek.com/article/1427195/need-diversity-champions

Foucault, M. (1982). The subject and power. *Critical Inquiry, 8*(4), 777–795.

French, E. (2005). The importance of strategic change in achieving equity in diversity. *Strategic Change, 14*(1), 35–44.

Fuller, P. (2020, September 18). 3 critical steps for companies that want to move the needle on diversity. *Chief Executive.* https://chiefexecutive.net/3-critical-steps-for-companies-that-want-to-move-the-needle-on-diversity/

Gaither, T. K. (2018). Cultural diversity. In R. Heath & W. Johansen (Eds.), *The international encyclopedia of strategic communication* (pp. 472–481). Hoboken, NJ: Wiley-Blackwell.

Gallegos, P. V. (2014). The work of inclusive leadership. In B. M. Ferdman & B. R. Dean (Eds.), *Diversity at work: The practice of inclusion* (pp. 177–202). Hoboken, NJ: John Wiley & Sons, Inc.

Gallicano, T. D. (2013). Millennials' perceptions about diversity in their PR agencies. *PR Journal, 7*(2), 37–70.

Gardner, W. L., Avolio, B. J., Luthans, F., May, D. R., & Walumbwa, F. (2005). "Can you see the real me?" A self-based model of authentic leader and follower development. *The Leadership Quarterly, 16*(3), 343–372.

Gaspar, R., Pedro, C., Panagiotopoulos, P., & Seibt, B. (2016). Beyond positive or negative: Qualitative sentiment analysis of social media reactions to unexpected stressful events. *Computers in Human Behavior, 56*, 179–191.

Gelfand, M. J., Nishii, L. H., Raver, J. L., & Schneider, B. (2005). Discrimination in organizations: An organizational-level systems perspective. In R. L. Dipboye & A. Colella (Eds.), *Discrimination at work: The psychological and organizational bases* (pp. 89–116). East Sussex: Psychology Press.

Gergen, K. J., & Hersted, L. (2016). Developing leadership as dialogic practice. In J. A. Raelin (Ed.), *Leadership-as-practice* (pp. 178–197). Oxfordshire: Routledge.

Gilbert, J. A., Stead, B. A., & Ivancevich, J. M. (1999). Diversity management: A new organizational paradigm. *Journal of Business Ethics, 21*(1), 61–76.

Gill, R. (2011). *Theory and practice of leadership* (2nd ed.). Thousand Oaks, CA: Sage.

Golombisky, K. (2015). Renewing the commitments of feminist public relations theory from velvet ghetto to social justice. *Journal of Public Relations Research, 27*(5), 389–415.

Gower, K. (2001). Rediscovering women in public relations: Women in the *Public Relations Journal*, 1945–1972. *Journalism History, 27*(1), 14–21.

Gower, K. (2006). Public relations research at the crossroads. *Journal of Public Relations Research, 18*(2), 177–190.

Gregory, A., & Willis, P. (2013). *Strategic public relations leadership*. Oxfordshire: Routledge.

Grint, K. (2005). Problems, problems, problems: The social construction of 'leadership'. *Human Relations, 58*(11), 1467–1494.

Grint, K. (2011). A history of leadership. In A. Bryman, D. Collinson, K. Grint, B. Jackson, & M. Uhl-Bien (Eds.), *The SAGE handbook of leadership* (pp. 3–14). Thousand Oaks, CA: Sage.

Gronn, P. (2002). Distributed leadership as a unit of analysis. *The Leadership Quarterly, 13*(4), 423–451.

Groysberg, B., & Connolly, K. (2013, September). Great leaders who make the mix work. *Harvard Business Review.* https://hbr.org/2013/09/great-leaders-who-make-the-mix-work

Grunig, J. E. (1992). Communication, public relations, and effective organizations. In J. Grunig (Ed.), *Excellence in public relations and communication management* (pp. 1–28). Mahwah, NJ: Lawrence Erlbaum Associates.

Grunig, J. E. (1997). A situational theory of publics: Conceptual history, recent challenges and new research. In D. Moss, T. MacManus, & D. Verčič (Eds.), *Public relations research: An international perspective* (pp. 3–48). London: International Thomson Business.

Grunig, L. A. (2006). Feminist phase analysis in public relations: Where have we been? Where do we need to go? *Journal of Public Relations Research, 18*, 115–140.

Grunig, J. E., & Grunig, L. A. (1992). Models of public relations and communication. In J. Grunig (Ed.), *Excellence in public relations and communication management* (pp. 285–325). Mahwah, NJ: Lawrence Erlbaum Associates.

Grunig, L. A., Grunig, J. E., & Dozier, D. (2002). *Excellent public relations and effective organizations: A study of communication management in three countries.* Mahwah, NJ: Lawrence Erlbaum Associates.

Grunig, L. A., Grunig, J. E., & Ehling, W. P. (1992). What is an effective organization? In J. Grunig (Ed.), *Excellence in public relations and communication management* (pp. 65–90). Mahwah, NJ: Lawrence Erlbaum Associates.

Grunig, J. E., & Hunt, T. (1984). *Managing public relations.* New York, NY: Holt, Rinehart & Winston.

Grunig, L. A., & Toth, E. L. (2006). The ethics of communicating with and about difference in a changing society. In K. Fitzpatrick & C. Bronstein (Eds.), *Ethics in public relations: Responsible advocacy* (pp. 39–52). Thousand Oaks, CA: Sage.

Grunig, L. A., Toth, E., & Hon, L. (2001). *Women in public relations: How gender influences practice.* The Guilford Press.

Grzanka, P. R. (2019). *Intersectionality: Foundations and frontiers* (2nd ed.). Oxfordshire: Routledge.

Gupta, A. H. (2021, June 7). Surprise: Women and minorities are still underrepresented in corporate boardrooms. *The New York Times.* https://www.nytimes.com/2021/06/07/us/women-minorities-underrepresented-corporate-boardrooms.html?login=smartlock&auth=login-smartlock

Halualani, R. T. (2020). *Intercultural communication: A critical perspective.* San Diego, CA: Cognella Academic Publishing.

He, E. (2021, June 8). Beyond demographics: How to run a successful DE&I program. *Forbes.* https://www.forbes.com/sites/emilyhe/2021/06/08/beyond-demographics-how-to-run-a-successful-dei-program/?sh=79eb459111c0

Herring, C. (2009). Does diversity pay? Race, gender, and the business case for diversity. *American Sociological Review, 74*(2), 208–224.

Holladay, S. J., & Coombs, W. T. (1993). Communicating visions: An exploration of the role of delivery in the creation of leader charisma. *Management Communication Quarterly, 6*(4), 405–427.

Holtzhausen, D. R. (2012). *Public relations as activism: Postmodern approaches to theory & practice.* Oxfordshire: Routledge.

Homan, A. C., & Greer, L. L. (2013). Considering diversity: The positive effects of considerate leadership in diverse teams. *Group Processes & Intergroup Relations, 16*(1), 105–125.

Hon, L. C.1995). Towards a feminist theory of public relations. *Journal of Public Relations Research, 7*(1), 27–88.

Hon, L. C., & Brunner, B. (2000). Diversity issues and public relations. *Journal of Public Relations Research, 12*(4), 309–340.

Imahori, T. T., & Cupach, W. R. (2005). Identity management theory. In W. B. Gudykunst (Ed.), *Theorizing about intercultural communication* (pp. 195–210). Thousand Oaks, CA: Sage.

Institute for Public Relations (2020, April 16). *Special report: How companies are engaging employees during COVID-19.* https://instituteforpr.org/how-companies-are-engaging-employees-during-covid-19/

Institute for Public Relations (2021a, November 8). *The language of diversity.* https://instituteforpr.org/wp-content/uploads/Defining-Diversity-Equity-and-Inclusion-v14.pdf

Institute for Public Relations. (2021b, May 25). *Reflecting and reaffirming IPR's commitment to DE&I.* https://instituteforpr.org/reflecting-and-reaffirming-iprs-commitment-to-dei/

Jacques, A. (2020, July–August). Marsha R. Phillips on proactive D&I efforts. *PR Strategies & Tactics,* PRSA. https://www.prsa.org/article/marsha-r.-pitts-phillips-on-proactive-d-i-efforts?spMailingID=32360241&spUserID=MzM4NTgx-MzY5MzkS1&spJobID=1743774736&spReportId=MTc0Mzc3NDczNgS2

Jiang, H., Ford, R., Long, P. C., & Ballard, D. (2016). *Diversity & inclusion: A summary of the current status and practices of Arthur W. Page Society members*. Syracuse University, The Plank Center, PRSA Foundation, Arthur Page Society. http://plankcenter. ua.edu/wp-content/uploads/2016/07/DI-FINAL.pdf

Jin, Y. (2010). Emotional leadership as a key dimension of public relations leadership: A national survey of public relations leaders. *Journal of Public Relations Research, 22*(2), 159–181.

Johnson, C. E. (2007). Best practices in ethical leadership. In J. A. Conger & R. E. Riggio (Eds.), *The practice of leadership: Developing the next generation of leaders* (pp. 150–171). Hoboken, NJ: Jossey-Bass.

Johnson, C. E., & Hackman, M. Z. (2018). *Leadership: A communication perspective* (7th ed.). Long Grove, IL: Waveland Press, Inc.

Johnson, S. K., & Lambert, B. K. (2021). Why diversity needs inclusion and how leaders make it happen. In B. M. Ferdman, J. Prime, & R. E. Riggio (Eds.), *Inclusive leadership: Transforming diverse lives, workplaces, and societies* (pp. 60–69). Thousand Oaks, CA: Sage.

Johnston, W. B., & Packer, A. E. (1987). *Workforce 2000: Work and workers for the twenty-first century*. Washington, DC: Hudson Institute.

Jones, C. P. (2000). Levels of racism: A theoretic framework and a gardener's tale. *American Journal of Public Health, 90*(8), 1212.

Jones, J. (2014). Leadership lessons from Levinas: Revisiting responsible leadership. *Leadership and the Humanities, 2*(1), 44–63.

Jones, D., & Stablein, R. (2006). Diversity as resistance and recuperation: Critical theory, post-structuralist perspectives and workplace diversity. In A. M. Konrad, P. Prasad, & J. K. Pringle (Eds.), *Handbook of workplace diversity* (pp. 145–166). Thousand Oaks, CA: Sage.

Joshi, A., & Roh, H. (2013). Understanding how context shapes team diversity outcomes. In Q. M. Roberson (Ed.), *The Oxford handbook of diversity and work* (pp. 209–219). Oxford: Oxford University Press.

Judy, R. W., & D'Amico, C. (1997). *Workforce 2020: Work and workers in the 21ˢᵗ century*. Washington, DC: Hudson Institute.

Kanter, R. M. (1977). *Men and women of the corporation*. New York, NY: Basic Books.

Kaplan, M., & Donovan, M. (2013). *The inclusion dividend* (1st ed.). Brookline, MA: Bibliomotion, Inc.

Kelly, E., & Dobbin, F. (1998). How affirmative action became diversity management: Employer response to antidiscrimination law, 1961 to 1996. *American Behavioral Scientist, 41*(7), 960–984.

Kelly, W. S., & Smith, C. (2014, December 11). What if the road to inclusion were really an inclusion? *Deloitte Insights*. https://www2.deloitte.com/insights/us/en/ topics/talent/multidimensional-diversity.html

Kennan, W. R., & Hazleton, V. (2006). Internal public relations, social capital, and the role of effective organizational communication. In C. H. Botan & V. Hazleton (Eds.), *Public relations theory II* (pp. 311–338). Mahwah, NJ: Lawrence Erlbaum Associates.

Kent, M. L. (2015). The power of storytelling in public relations: Introducing the 20 master plots. *Public Relations Review, 41*, 480–489.

Kent, M. L., & Taylor, M. (1998). Building dialogic relationships through the World Wide Web. *Public Relations Review, 24*(3), 321–334.

Kent, M. L., & Taylor, M. (2002). Toward a dialogic theory of public relations. *Public Relations Review, 28*(1), 21–37.

Kern-Foxworth, M. (1989a). Status and roles of minority PR practitioners. *Public Relations Review, 15*, 39–47.

Kern-Foxworth, M. (1989b). Public relations books fail to show women in context. *The Journalism Educator, 44*(3), 31–36.

Kern-Foxworth, M. (1991). Black, brown, red and yellow markets equal green power. *Public Relations Quarterly, 36*(1), 27–30.

Kersten, A. (2000). Diversity management: Dialogue, dialectics and diversion. *Journal of Organizational Change Management, 13*(3), 235–248.

Ketchum Leadership Communication Monitor. (2014). *Ketchum.*

Ketchum Leadership Communication Monitor. (2016). Breaking through persistent leadership barriers. *Ketchum.*

Kirby, E. L., & Harter, L. M. (2003). Speaking the language of the bottom-line: The metaphor of "managing diversity". *The Journal of Business Communication, 40*(1), 28–49.

Kline, N., & Quiroga, M. A. (2021). Organizing for black lives and funding COVID-19 relief: Community responses to systemic racism and imagining public health 4.0. *American Journal of Public Health, 111*(S3), S201–S203.

Kochhar, S. (2016, December 6). *Millennials@Work: Perspectives on diversity and inclusion.* Institute for PR. https://instituteforpr.org/millennialswork-perspectives-diversity-inclusion/

Konrad, A. M. (2003). Defining the domain of workplace diversity scholarship. *Group & Organization Management, 28*(1), 4–17.

Kotcher, R. L. (1995). Diversity in today's workplace and marketplace. *Public Relations Quarterly, 40*(1), 6–9.

Kouzes, J. M., & Posner, B. Z. (2017). *The leadership challenge* (6th ed.). Hoboken, NJ: Jossey-Bass.

Krieger, N. (2020). Enough: COVID-19, structural racism, police brutality, plutocracy, climate change—and time for health justice, democratic governance, and an equitable, sustainable future. *American Journal of Public Health, 110*(11), 1620–1623.

Lambert, J. R., & Bell, M. P. (2013). Diverse forms of difference. In Q. M. Roberson (Ed.), *The Oxford handbook of diversity and work* (pp. 13–31). Oxford: Oxford University Press.

Laskin, A., & Kresic, K. (2021). Inclusion as a component of CSR and a brand connection strategy. In D. Pompper (Ed.), *Public relations for social responsibility: Affirming DEI commitment with action* (pp. 149–163). Bingley: Emerald Publishing.

Lather, P. (1986). Research as praxis. *Harvard Educational Review, 56*(3), 257–278.

Leading diversity: How firms can walk the talk. (2021, January 20). *Knowledge@ Wharton.* https://knowledge.wharton.upenn.edu/article/leading-diversity-firms-can-walk-talk/

Lee, A. J. (2005). Unconscious bias theory in employment discrimination litigation. *Harvard Civil Rights – Civil Liberties Law Review, 40*, 481–503.

Lee, S. T., & Cheng, I. H. (2010). Characteristics and dimensions of ethical leadership in public relations. *Journal of Public Relations Research, 23*(1), 46–74.

Len-Ríos, M. (1998). Minority public relations practitioner perceptions. *Public Relations Review, 24*(4), 535–555.

Leong, N. (2021). *Identity capitalists: The powerful insiders who exploit diversity to maintain inequality.* Redwood City, CA: Stanford University Press.

Leroy, H., Buengeler, C., Veestraeten, M., Shemla, M., & J. Hoever, I. (2021). Fostering team creativity through team-focused inclusion: The role of leader harvesting the benefits of diversity and cultivating value-in-diversity beliefs. *Group & Organization Management*. Advance online publication. doi:10.1177/10596011211009683

L'Etang, J., McKie, D., Snow, N., & Xifra, J. (Eds.). (2016). *The Routledge handbook of critical public relations*. Oxfordshire: Routledge.

Limaye, M. R. (1994). Responding to work-force diversity: Conceptualization and search for paradigms. *Journal of Business and Technical Communication*, 8(3), 353–372.

Lindlof, T., & Taylor, B. (2011). *Qualitative communication research methods* (3rd ed.). Thousand Oaks, CA: Sage.

Linnehan, F., & Konrad, A. M. (1999). Diluting diversity: Implications for intergroup inequality in organizations. *Journal of Management Inquiry*, 8(4), 399–414.

Littlejohn, S., Foss, K. A., & Oetzel, J. G. (2016). *Theories of human communication* (11th ed.). Long Grove, IL: Waveland Press.

Lo Wang, H. (2018). Generation Z is the most ethnically and racially diverse yet. *National Public Radio*. https://www.npr.org/2018/11/15/668106376/generation-z-is-the-most-racially-and-ethnically-diverse-yet

Locke, S. E. (n.d.). Diversity and PR communications: The role of implicit bias. *CommPro*. https://www.commpro.biz/diversity-in-pr-communications-the-role-of-implicit-bias/

Logan, N. (2011). The white leader prototype: A critical analysis of race in public relations. *Journal of Public Relations Research*, 23(4), 442–457.

Logan, N. (2021). Breaking down barriers of the past and moving toward authentic DEI adoption. In D. Pompper (Ed.), *Public relations for social responsibility: Affirming DEI commitment with action* (pp. 3–17). Bingley: Emerald Publishing.

Lorbiecki, A., & Jack, G. (2000). Critical turns in the evolution of diversity management. *British Journal of Management*, 11, S17–S31.

Lorenzo, R., Voigt, N., Tsusaka, M., Krentz, M., & Abouzahr, K. (2018, January 23). How diverse leadership teams boost innovation. *Boston Consulting Group*. https://www.bcg.com/en-us/publications/2018/how-diverse-leadership-teams-boost-innovation

Lucid, Insights in Color, & Think Now. (n.d.). *Redefining identity in research* [PowerPoint slides]. SlideShare. https://static1.squarespace.com/static/5eef98897ee5706373248c60/t/60ba5a345c36bc4c7e0affef/1622825539477/REDEFINING+IDENTITY+IN+RESEARCH_.pdf

Luque, F. (n.d.). Why DE&I shouldn't be an afterthought. *Prsay*. https://prsay.prsa.org/2021/10/29/why-dei-shouldnt-be-an-afterthought/?_zs=CxE8m&_zl=tod32

Maak, T., & Pless, N. M. (2006a). Responsible leadership: A relational approach. In T. Maak & N. M. Pless (Eds.), *Responsible leadership* (pp. 33–53). Oxfordshire: Routledge.

Maak, T., & Pless, N. M. (2006b). Introduction. In T. Maak & N. M. Pless (Eds.), *Responsible leadership* (pp. 1–13). Oxfordshire: Routledge.

Maak, T., & Pless, N. M. (2006c). Responsible leadership in a stakeholder society—A relational perspective. *Journal of Business Ethics*, 66(1), 99–115.

MacAfee, B. (2017, October 2). The case for driving diversity for clients. *Provoke Media*. https://www.provokemedia.com/agency-playbook/sponsored/article/the-case-for-driving-diversity-for-clients

Mannix, E., & Neale, M. A. (2005). What differences make a difference? The promise and reality of diverse teams in organizations. *Psychological Science in the Public Interest*, 6(2), 31–55.

Maritz, R., Pretorius, M., & Plant, K. (2011). Exploring the interface between strategy-making and responsible leadership. *Journal of Business Ethics, 98*(1), 101–113.

Marketinsite (2020, December 4). How companies can tap into diversity and add value. *Nasdaq.* https://www.nasdaq.com/articles/how-companies-can-tap-into-diversity-and-add-value-2020-12-04

Marszalek, D. (2020, July 28). Weber Shandwick reveals diversity data as calls for change outpace industry. *Provoke Media.* https://www.provokemedia.com/latest/article/weber-shandwick-reveals-diversity-data-as-calls-for-change-outpace-industry?utm_source=dlvr.it&utm_medium=twitter&utm_campaign=provoke_news

Martin, J., & Nakayama, T. (1999). Thinking dialectically about culture and communication. *Communication Theory, 9*(1), 1–25.

Mason, K. M. (n.d.). 8 Interview questions about diversity and inclusion every job seeker should be able to answer. *The Muse.* https://www.themuse.com/advice/diversity-inclusion-interview-questions-answers-examples

Mazzei, A., & Ravazzani, S. (2012). Leveraging variety for creativity, dialogue and competition. *Journal of Communication Management, 16*(1), 59–76.

McIntosh, P. (1989, July/August). White privilege: Unpacking the invisible knapsack. *Peace and Freedom.* https://psychology.umbc.edu/files/2016/10/White-Privilege_McIntosh-1989.pdf

McKie, D., & Munshi, D. (2007). *Reconfiguring public relations: Ecology, equity, and enterprise.* Routledge.

McKie, D., & Munshi, D. (2009). Theoretical holes: A partial A to Z of missing critical thought in public relations. In R. L. Heath, E. L. Toth, & D. Waymer (Eds.), *Rhetorical and critical approaches to public relations II* (pp. 61–75). Oxfordshire: Routledge.

Mease, J. J. (2012). Reconsidering consultants' strategic use of the business case for diversity. *Journal of Applied Communication Research, 40*(4), 384–402.

Mease, J. J., & Collins, B. L. (2018). Asset, liability, possibility: Metaphors of human difference and the business case for diversity. *Equality, Diversity and Inclusion, 37*(7), 664–682.

Meehan, D. (2021). How to develop and support leadership that contributes to a more equitable, diverse, and inclusive society. In B. M. Ferdman, J. Prime, & R. E. Riggio (Eds.), *Inclusive leadership: Transforming diverse lives, workplaces, and societies* (pp. 407–418). Thousand Oaks, CA: Sage.

Men, L. R. (2014). Why leadership matters to internal communication: Linking transformational leadership, symmetrical communication, and employee outcomes. *Journal of Public Relations Research, 26*(3), 256–279.

Men, L. R., & Jiang, H. (2016). Cultivating quality employee-organization relationships: The interplay among organizational leadership, culture, and communication. *International Journal of Strategic Communication, 10*(5), 462–479.

Men, L. R., & Stacks, D. W. (2013). Measuring the impact of leadership style and employee empowerment on perceived organizational reputation. *Journal of Communication Management, 17*, 171–192.

Meng, J. (2014). Unpacking the relationship between organizational culture and excellent leadership in public relations: An empirical investigation. *Journal of Communication Management, 18*(4), 363–385.

Meng, J., & Berger, B. K. (2013). An integrated model of excellent leadership in public relations: Dimensions, measurement, and validation. *Journal of Public Relations Research, 25*(2), 141–167.

Meng, J., & Berger, B. K. (2017). Millennial communication professionals in the workplace. *The Plank Center for Public Relations.* http://plankcenter.ua.edu/resources/research/millennial-communication-professionals-inthe-workplace/

Meng, J., & Berger, B. K. (2018). Maximizing the potential of millennial communication professionals in the workplace: A talent management approach in the field of strategic communication. *International Journal of Strategic Communication, 12*(5), 507–525.

Meng, J., Berger, B. K., Gower, K. K., & Heyman, W. C. (2012). A test of excellent leadership in public relations: Key qualities, valuable sources, and distinctive leadership perceptions. *Journal of Public Relations Research, 24*(1), 18–36.

Meng, J., Berger, B. K., Heyman, W., & Reber, B. H. (2019). *Public relations leaders earn a "C+" in The Plank Center's report card 2019.* The Plank Center for Leadership in Public Relations. http://plankcenter.ua.edu/wp-content/uploads/2019/09/Report-Card-Full-Report.pdf

Meng, J., & Neill, M. S. (2021). *PR women with influence. Breaking through the ethical and leadership challenges.* Bern: Peter Lang.

Meng, J., Reber, B. H., Berger, B. K., Gower, K. K., & Zerfass, A. (2021). North American Communication Monitor 2020-2021. *The Plank Center for Leadership in Public Relations.* http://plankcenter.ua.edu/wp-content/uploads/2021/06/NACM-Report-2020-21-1.pdf

Meyer, J. W., & Rowan, B. (1977). Institutionalized organizations: Formal structure as myth and ceremony. *The American Journal of Sociology, 83*, 340–363.

Meyerson, D. E. (2001). *Tempered radicals: How people use difference to inspire change at work.* Boston, MA: Harvard Business School Press.

Miller, F. A. (1998). Strategic culture change: The door to achieving high performance and inclusion. *Public Personnel Management, 27*(2), 151–160.

Miller, F. A., & Katz, J. (2002). *The inclusion breakthrough: Unleashing the real power of diversity.* Oakland, CA: Berrett-Koehler.

Milliken, F. J., & Martins, L. L. (1996). Searching for common threads: Understanding the multiple effects of diversity in organizational groups. *Academy of Management Review, 21*(2), 402–433.

Miska, C., Hilbe, C., & Mayer, S. (2014). Reconciling different views on responsible leadership: A rationality–based approach. *Journal of Business Ethics, 125*(2), 349–360.

Miska, C., & Mendenhall, M. E. (2018). Responsible leadership: A mapping of extant research and future directions. *Journal of Business Ethics, 148*(1), 117–134.

Moody, K. (2021, November 11). Study: Talent leaders miss 'the simple things' to increase DEI. *HRDive.* https://www.hrdive.com/news/study-talent-leaders-miss-the-simple-things-to-increase-dei/609889/

Mor Barak, M. E. (2005). *Managing diversity: Toward a globally inclusive workplace* (1st ed.). Thousand Oaks, CA: Sage.

Mor Barak, M. E. (2017). *Managing diversity: Toward a globally inclusive workplace* (4th ed.). Thousand Oaks, CA: Sage.

Mor Barak, M. E., Lizano, E. L., Kim, A., Duan, L., Rhee, M. K., Hsiao, H. Y., & Brimhall, K. C. (2016). The promise of diversity management for climate of inclusion: A state-of-the-art review and meta-analysis. *Human Service Organizations: Management, Leadership & Governance, 40*(4), 305–333.

Mor Barak, M. E., Luria, G., & Brimhall, K. C. (2021). What leaders say versus what they do: Inclusive leadership, policy-practice decoupling, and the anomaly of climate for inclusion. *Group & Organization Management.* Advance online publication. doi:10.1177/10596011211005916

Moss, G. (2019). *Inclusive leadership* (1st ed.). Oxfordshire: Routledge.

Moule, J. (2009, January). Understanding unconscious bias and unintentional racism. *Phi Delta Kappan.*

Mundy, D. E. (2015). From principle to policy to practice? Diversity as a driver of multicultural, stakeholder engagement in public relations. *PR Journal, 9*(1). https://prjournal.instituteforpr.org/wp-content/uploads/2015v09n01Mundy.pdf

Mundy, D. E. (2016). Bridging the divide: A multidisciplinary analysis of diversity research and the implications for public relations. *PR Journal, 3*(1). https://prjournal.instituteforpr.org/wp-content/uploads/Dean-Mundy-1-1.pdf

Mundy, D. (2019). Diversity. In B. Brunner (Ed.), *Public relations theory: Application and understanding* (pp. 49–62). Hoboken, NJ: Wiley Blackwell.

Mundy, D., Lewton, K., Hicks, A., & Neptune, T. (2018). Diversity. In *Fast forward: Foundations + future state. Educators + practitioners: The Commission on Public Relations Education 2017 Report on undergraduate education* (pp. 139–148). Commission on Public Relations Education. http://www.commissionpred.org/wp-content/uploads/2018/04/report6-full.pdf

Munshi, D., & Edwards, L. (2011). Understanding 'Race' in/and public relations: Where do we start and where should we go? *Journal of Public Relations Research, 23*(4), 349–367.

Munshi, D., & Kurian, P. (2005). Imperializing spin cycles: A postcolonial look at public relations, greenwashing, and the separation of publics. *Public Relations Review, 31*(4), 513–520.

Muturi, N., & Zhu, G. (2019). Students' perceptions of diversity issues in public relations practice. *Journal of Public Relations Education, 5*(2), 75–104.

Nagda, B. R. A. (2006). Breaking barriers, crossing borders, building bridges: Communication processes in intergroup dialogues. *Journal of Social Issues, 62*(3), 553–576.

Nakayama, T. K., & Krizek, R. L. (1995). Whiteness: A strategic rhetoric. *Quarterly Journal of Speech, 81*(3), 291–309.

Newcomb, T. M. (1961). *The acquaintance process.* New York, NY: Holt, Rinehart, and Winston.

Ni, L. (2007). Redefined understanding of perspectives on employee-organization relationships: Themes and variations. *Journal of Communication Management, 11*(1), 53–70.

Ni, L., Wang, Q., & Sha, B.-L. (2018). *Intercultural public relations.* Oxfordshire: Routledge.

Nishii, L. H., & Leroy, H. L. (2020). Inclusive leadership: Leaders as architects of inclusive workgroup climates. In B. M. Ferdman, J. Prime, & R. E. Riggio (Eds.), *Inclusive leadership: Transforming diverse lives, workplaces, and societies* (pp. 162–178). Thousand Oaks, CA: Sage

Nkomo, S. M. (2014). Inclusion: Old wine in new bottles? In B. M. Ferdman & B. R. Dean (Eds.), *Diversity at work: The practice of inclusion* (pp. 580–592). Hoboken, NJ: John Wiley & Sons, Inc.

Nkomo, S., & Cox, T. (1996). Diverse identities in organizations. In S. Clegg, C. Hardy, & W. Nord (Eds.), *Handbook of organization studies* (pp. 338–356). Thousand Oaks, CA: Sage Publications.

Northouse, P. G. (2022). *Leadership: Theory and practice* (9th ed.). Thousand Oaks, CA: Sage.

Offermann, L. R., & Matos, K. (2007). Best practices in leading diverse organizations. In J. A. Conger & R. E. Riggio (Eds.), *The practice of leadership: Developing the next generation of leaders* (pp. 277–299). Hoboken, NJ: Jossey-Bass.

Oswick, C., & Noon, M. (2014). Discourses of diversity, equality and inclusion: Trenchant formulations or transient fashions? *British Journal of Management, 25*(1), 23–39.

Özbilgin, M., & Tatli, A. (2011). Mapping out the field of equality and diversity: Rise of individualism and voluntarism. *Human Relations, 64*(9), 1229–1253.

Page, S. E. (2007). Making the difference: Applying a logic of diversity. *Academy of Management Perspectives, 21*(4), 6–20.

Pandey, V. K., Shanahan, K. J., & Hansen, S. W. (2005). The relationship between shareholder wealth effects, diversity, and publicity as a marketing strategy. *Journal of the Academy of Marketing Science, 33*(4), 423–432.

Pearson, R. (1989). Business ethics as communication ethics: Public relations practice and the idea of dialogue. In C. H. Botan & V. Hazleton, Jr. (Eds.), *Public relations theory* (pp. 111–131). Mahwah, NJ: Lawrence Erlbaum Associates.

Pelled, L. H. (1996). Demographic diversity, conflict, and work group outcomes: An intervening process theory. *Organization Science, 7*, 615–631.

Pham, T. (2021, July 27). Diversity and inclusion best practices for your workforce. *Entrepreneur.* https://www.entrepreneur.com/article/376424

Phillips, K. W., Liljenquist, K. A., & Neale, M. A. (2010). *Better decisions through diversity.* Kellogg School of Management at Northwestern University. https:// insight.kellogg.northwestern.edu/article/better_decisions_through_diversity

Pieczka, M. (2002). Public relations expertise deconstructed. *Media, Culture & Society, 24*(3), 301–323.

Place, K. (2012). Power-control or empowerment? How women public relations practitioners make meaning of power. *Journal of Public Relations Research, 24*(5), 435–450.

Place, K. (2015). Binaries, continuums, and intersections: Women public relations professionals' understanding of gender. *Public Relations Inquiry, 4*(1), 61–78.

Place, K., & Vanc, A. (2016). Exploring diversity and client work in public relations education. *Journal of Public Relations Education, 2*(2), 83–100.

Place, K., & Vardeman-Winter, J. (2018). Where are the women? An examination of research on women and leadership in public relations. *Public Relations Review, 44*(1), 165–173.

Plank, B. (1991). Remarks. PRSA Conference. Plank Papers, The Plank Center for Leadership in Public Relations, University of Alabama.

Pless, N. M., & Maak, T. (2004). Building an inclusive diversity culture: Principles, processes and practice. *Journal of Business Ethics, 54*(2), 129–147.

Pless, N. M., & Maak, T. (2011). Responsible leadership: Pathways to the future. *Journal of Business Ethics, 98*(1), 3–13.

Pless, N. M., Maak, T., & Harris, H. (2017). Art, ethics and the promotion of human dignity. *Journal of Business Ethics, 144*(2), 223–232.

Pompper, D. (2004). Linking ethnic diversity and two-way symmetry: Modeling female African American practitioners' roles. *Journal of Public Relations Research, 16*(3), 269–299.

Pompper, D. (2005a). "Difference" in public relations research: A case for introducing Critical Race Theory. *Journal of Public Relations Research, 17*, 139–169.

Pompper, D. (2005b). Multiculturalism in the public relations curriculum: Female African American practitioners' perceptions of effects. *The Howard Journal of Communications, 16*, 295–316.

Pompper, D. (2007). The gender-ethnicity construct in public relations organizations: Using feminist standpoint theory to discover Latinas' realities. *The Howard Journal of Communications, 18*(4), 291–311.

Pompper, D. (2012). On social capital and diversity in a feminized industry: Further developing a theory of internal public relations. *Journal of Public Relations Research, 24*(1), 86–103.

Pompper, D. (2014). *Practical and theoretical implications of successfully doing difference in organizations.* Bingley: Emerald Publishing.

Pompper, D. (2015). *Corporate social responsibility, sustainability and public relations: Negotiating multiple complex challenges.* Oxfordshire: Routledge.

Pompper, D. (2020). Public relations' role as diversity advocate: Avoiding micro-aggressions and nurturing microaffirmations in organizations. *PR Journal, 13*(2). https://prjournal.instituteforpr.org/wp-content/uploads/Pompper-_Diversity_ Advocate_EDITED2.12.pdf

Pompper, D., & Jung, T. (2013). "Outnumbered yet still on top, but for how long?" Theorizing about men working in the feminized field of public relations. *Public Relations Review, 39*, 497–506.

Powell, G., Jayasinghe, L., & Taksa, L. (2015). Intersectionality, social identity theory, and explorations of hybridity: A critical review of diverse approaches to diversity. In R. Bendl, I. Bleijenbergh, E. Henttonen, & A. J. Mills (Eds.), *The Oxford handbook of diversity in organizations* (pp. 518–535). Oxford: Oxford University Press.

PR Coalition (2005). *Focus on diversity: Lowering the barriers, raising the bar.* PR Coalition. https://instituteforpr.org/wp-content/uploads/Focus_Diversity_2005.pdf

PR Council (2016). *Diversity perception study shows it is time for actionable change in PR agencies.* https://prcouncil.net/news/diversity-perception-study-highlights-it-is-time-for-actionable-change-in-pr-agencies/

PR Council (n.d.) *PR Council diversity and inclusion pledge.* https://prcouncil.net/ pr-council-diversity-inclusion-pledge/

Prasad, P. (1997). The Protestant ethic and the myth of the frontier: Cultural imprints, organizational structuring, and workplace diversity. In P. Prasad, A. J. Mills, M. Elmes, & A. Prasad (Eds.), *Managing the organizational melting pot: Dilemmas of workplace diversity* (pp. 129–147). Thousand Oaks, CA: Sage.

Prasad, A., & Elmes, M. (1997). Issues in the management of workplace diversity. In P. Prasad, A. J. Mills, M. Elmes, & A. Prasad (Eds.), *Managing the organizational melting pot: Dilemmas of workplace diversity* (pp. 367–375). Thousand Oaks, CA: Sage.

Prasad, P., & Mills, A. J. (1997). From showcase to shadow: Understanding the dilemmas of managing workplace diversity. In P. Prasad, A. J. Mills, M. Elmes, & A. Prasad (Eds.), *Managing the organizational melting pot: Dilemmas of workplace diversity* (pp. 3–27). Thousand Oaks, CA: Sage.

Prince, C. J. (2021, February 19). How eight CEOs are making diversity happen (really). *Chief Executive.* https://chiefexecutive.net/how-eight-ceos-are-making-diversity-happen-really/

Pringle, J. K., & Ryan, I. (2015). Understanding context in diversity management: A multi-level analysis. *Equality, Diversity and Inclusion, 34*(6), 470–482.

Prime, J., Ferdman, B. M., & Riggio, R. E. (2021). Inclusive leadership: Insights and implications. In B. M. Ferdman, J. Prime, & R. E. Riggio (Eds.), *Inclusive leadership: Transforming diverse lives, workplaces, and societies* (pp. 421–429). Thousand Oaks, CA: Sage.

PRSA (n.d.). *Diversity and inclusion.* https://www.prsa.org/about/diversity-inclusion

PRSA (2016). *Diversity and inclusion toolkit.* https://www.prsa.org/docs/defaultsource/about/diversity/prsa-diversity-and-inclusion-tool-kit-2016

PRSA Chapter D&I Toolkit. (2021). Public Relations Society of America. https://www.prsa.org/docs/default-source/about/diversity/prsa-2021-toolkit—6-3-21.pdf?sfvrsn=26ff3dfd_0

Pusch, M. D. (2004). Intercultural training in historical perspective. In D. Landis, J. M. Bennett, & M. J. Bennett (Eds.), *Handbook of intercultural training* (3rd ed., pp. 13–36). Thousand Oaks, CA: Sage.

Qin, J., Muenjohn, N., & Chhetri, P. (2014). A review of diversity conceptualizations: Variety, trends, and a framework. *Human Resource Development Review, 13*(2), 133–157.

Race in the PR classroom (n.d.). Institute for Public Relations. https://instituteforpr.org/race-in-the-pr-classroom/

Raelin, J. A. (2016). Imagine there are no leaders: Reframing leadership as collaborative agency. *Leadership, 12*(2), 131–158.

Ramaswamy, S. (2018, September 27). Diversity and inclusion in the PR profession: A case for change. *PR Week.* https://www.prweek.com/article/1494228/diversity-inclusion-pr-profession-case-change

Randel, A. E., Galvin, B. M., Shore, L. M., Ehrhart, K. H., Chung, B. G., Dean, M. A., & Kedharnath, U. (2018). Inclusive leadership: Realizing positive outcomes through belongingness and being valued for uniqueness. *Human Resource Management Review, 28*(2), 190–203.

Reagans, R. (2013). Demographic diversity as network connections: Homophily and the diversity-performance debate. In Q. M. Roberson (Ed.), *The Oxford handbook of diversity and work* (pp. 192–206). Oxford: Oxford University Press.

Report card on PR leaders (n.d.). *The Plank Center for Public Relations.* http://plank-center.ua.edu/resources/research/report-card/

Risberg, A., & Pilhofer, K. (2018). Diversity and difference research: A reflection on categories and categorization. *Ephemera, 18*(1), 131–148.

Roberson, Q. A. (2006). Disentangling the meanings of diversity and inclusion in organizations. *Group & Organization Management, 31,* 212–236.

Roberson, Q., & Perry, J. L. (2021). Inclusive leadership in thought and action: A thematic analysis. *Group & Organization Management.* Advance online publication. doi:10.1177/10596011211013161

Roberts, R. (2020, October 28). How PR agencies can initiate a culture of DE&I change. *PR Daily.* https://www.prdaily.com/how-pr-agencies-can-initiate-a-culture-of-dei-change/

Roberts, L. M., & Creary, S. J. (2013). Navigating the self in diverse work contexts: In Q. M. Roberson (Ed.), *The Oxford handbook of diversity and work* (pp. 73–97). Oxford: Oxford University Press.

Rosenbaum, M. E. (1986). The repulsion hypothesis: On the nondevelopment of relationship. *Journal of Personality and Social Psychology, 51,* 1156–1166.

Ross, L. O. (2021, May 6). Business and systemic racism: The next step in a long journey. *Edelman Insights.* https://www.edelman.com/trust/2021-trust-barometer/insights/business-and-systemic-racism-next-step-long-journey

Ruck, K., & Welch, M. (2012). Valuing internal communication; management and employee perspectives. *Public Relations Review, 38*(2), 294–302.

Sabharwal, M. (2014). Is diversity management sufficient? Organizational inclusion to further performance. *Public Personnel Management, 43*(2), 197–217.

Sarup, M. (1996). *Identity, culture and the postmodern world*. Edinburgh: Edinburgh University Press.

Schuman, N. (2020, November 12). Checking in on DEI: The work is just beginning. *PR News*. https://www.prnewsonline.com/DEI-progress#:~:text=DEI%20In%20 the%20Workplace&text=Aubrey%20Quinn%2C%20Clyde%20Group's%20 managing,and%20creating%20an%20inclusive%20culture

Scott, M. (2020, August 27). A diversity lesson from HP CEO Enrique Lores. *ChiefExecutive*. https://chiefexecutive.net/a-diversity-lesson-from-hp-ceo-enrique-lores/

SEC approves Nasdaq's proposed rule changes to increase corporate board diversity. (2021, August 11). *The National Law Review*. https://www.natlawreview.com/article/ sec-approves-nasdaq-s-proposed-rule-changes-to-increase-corporate-board-diversity

Sha, B. L. (2006). Cultural identity in the segmentation of publics: An emerging theory of intercultural public relations. *Journal of Public Relations Research*, *18*(1), 45–65.

Sha, B.-L., & Ford, R. (2007). Redefining "requisite variety": The challenge of multiple diversities for the future of public relations excellence. In E. L. Toth (Ed.), *The future of excellence in public relations and communication management: Challenges for the next generation* (pp. 381–398). Mahwah, NJ: Lawrence Erlbaum Associates.

Shah, A. (2020, July 27). Analysis: Do D&I leaders make a difference? *PRovoke media*. https://www.provokemedia.com/long-reads/article/analysis-do-d-i-leaders- make-a-difference?utm_source=dlvr.it&utm_medium=twitter&utm_cam- paign=provoke_news

Sharif, H. N., & Bolden, A. (2020, July 7). What future PR pros want brands to know about DE&I. *PR Daily*. https://www.prdaily.com/what-future-pr-pros-want-brands- to-know-about-dei/

Sherbin, L., & Rashid, R. (2017, February 1). Diversity doesn't stick without inclu- sion. *Harvard Business Review*. https://hbr.org/2017/02/diversity-doesnt-stick- without-inclusion

Shore, L. M., & Chung, B. G. (2021). Inclusive leadership: How leaders sustain or dis- courage work group inclusion. *Group & Organization Management*. Advance online publication. doi:10.1177/1059601121999580

Shore, L. M., Cleveland, J. N., & Sanchez, D. (2018). Inclusive workplaces: A review and model. *Human Resource Management Review*, *28*, 176–189.

Shore, L. M., Randel, A. E., Chung, B. G., Dean, M. A., Ehrhart, K. H., & Singh, G. (2011). Inclusion and diversity in work groups: A review and model for future research. *Journal of Management*, *37*, 1262–1289.

Simons, T., Leroy, H., Collewaert, V., & Masschelein, S. (2015). How leader align- ment of words and deeds affects followers: A meta-analysis of behavioral integrity research. *Journal of Business Ethics*, *132*(4), 831–844.

Sison, M. D. (2017). Communicating across, within and between, cultures: Toward inclusion and social change. *Public Relations Review*, *43*(1), 130–132.

Smith, D. G. (2021). Leadership excellence in a pluralistic society: The role of iden- tity and inclusive leadership. In B. M. Ferdman, J. Prime, & R. E. Riggio (Eds.), *Inclusive leadership: Transforming diverse lives, workplaces, and societies* (pp. 289–301). Oxfordshire: Routledge

Smith, C., Turner, S., & Levit, A. (2018). The radical transformation of diversity and inclusion: The millennial influence. *Deloitte*. https://www2.deloitte.com/ content/dam/Deloitte/us/Documents/about-deloitte/us-the-radical-transforma- tion-of-diversity-and-inclusion-the-millennial-influence.pdf

Sobré-Denton, M., & Bardhan, N. (2013). *Cultivating cosmopolitanism for intercultural communication: Communicating as global citizens.* Oxfordshire: Routledge.

Sommerfeldt, E. J., & Yang, A. (2018). Notes on a dialogue: Twenty years of digital dialogic communication research in public relations. *Journal of Public Relations Research, 30*(3), 59–64.

Sorrells, K., & Nakagawa, G. (2008). Intercultural communication praxis and the struggle for social responsibility and social justice. In O. Swartz (Ed.), *Transformative communication studies: Culture, hierarchy, and the human condition* (pp. 17–43). Kibworth Harcourt: Troubador Publishing Ltd.

Sriramesh, K. (2007). The relationship between culture and public relations. In E. Toth (Ed.), *The future of excellence in public relations and communication management* (pp. 507–526). Mahwah, NJ: Lawrence Erlbaum Associates.

Sriramesh, K. (2009). Introduction. In K. Sriramesh & D. Verčič (Eds.), *The global public relations handbook* (expanded and revised ed.; pp. xxxiii–xl). Oxfordshire: Routledge.

Sriramesh, K., & Verčič, D. (2009). A theoretical framework for global public relations research and practice. In K. Sriramesh & D. Verčič (Eds.), *The global public relations handbook* (expanded and revised ed., pp. 3–21). Oxfordshire: Routledge.

Sriramesh, K., & White, J. (1992). Societal culture and public relations. In J. Grunig (Ed.), *Excellence in public relations and communication management* (pp. 597–614). Mahwah, NJ: Lawrence Erlbaum Associates.

Strauss, A., & Corbin, J. (1990). Grounded theory research: Procedures, canons, and evaluative criteria. *Qualitative Sociology, 13*(1), 4–21.

Strenski, J. (1993). Stress diversity in employee communications. *PR Journal, 50*(7), 33.

Sudhaman, A. (July 28, 2017). "If you don't have inclusion, people run away": PR CEOs face up to diversity challenge. *The Holmes Report.* https://www.holmesreport.com/latest/article/'if-you-don-t-have-inclusion-people-run-away'-pr-ceos-face-up-to-diversity-challenge

Sudhaman, A. (June 23, 2020). Amber Micala Arnold: 'Accountability is one of the industry's biggest problems.' *PRovokeMedia.* https://www.provokemedia.com/latest/article/amber-micala-arnold-'you-have-to-put-bold-goals-and-quotas-in-place

Sugiyama, K., Cavanagh, K. V., van Esch, C., Bilimoria, D., & Brown, C. (2016). Inclusive leadership development: Drawing from pedagogies of women's and general leadership development programs. *Journal of Management Education, 40*(3), 253–292.

Tajfel, H. (Ed.). (1978). *Differentiation between social groups: Studies in the psychology of intergroup relations.* Cambridge, MA: Academic Press.

Tajfel, H. (1981). *Human groups and social categories.* Cambridge: Cambridge University Press.

Tajfel, H., & Turner, J. C. (1979). An integrative theory of inter-group conflict. In W. G. Austin & S. Worchel (Eds.), *The social psychology of inter-group relations* (pp. 33–47). Pacific Grove, CA: Brooks/Cole.

Tatli, A., & Özbilgin, M. F. (2012). An emic approach to intersectional study of diversity at work: A Bourdieuan framing. *International Journal of Management Reviews, 14*(2), 180–200.

Taylor, M., & Kent, M. L. (2014). Dialogic engagement: Clarifying foundational concepts. *Journal of Public Relations Research, 26*(5), 384–398.

Ternynck, J. (2021, October 5). Why executive sponsorship is critical for achieving D&I goals. *Smart Brief*. https://www.smartbrief.com/original/2021/10/why-executive-sponsorship-critical-achieving-di-goals

Thaxter, C. (1886). *The cruise of the mystery and other poems.* Boston, MA: Houshton, Mifflin and Company.

The Alliance (n.d.). Diversity Action Alliance. https://www.diversityactionalliance. org/

The Museum of Public Relations (2021, November 2). *Silence is not an option.* YouTube. https://www.youtube.com/watch?v=5rlNTtdhw0g

The Plank Center. (n.d.). The Plank Center for Leadership in Public Relations. http://plankcenter.ua.edu/?s=student+scholarships

The Plank Center Mission. (n.d.). *Mission.* The Plank Center for Leadership in Public Relations. http://plankcenter.ua.edu/mission/

Thomas, E. F., Zubielevitch, E., Sibley, C. G., & Osborne, D. (2019). Testing the social identity model of collective action longitudinally and across structurally disadvantaged and advantaged groups. *Personality and Social Psychology Bulletin, 46*(6), 823–838.

Thompson, H., & Matkin, G. (2020). The evolution of inclusive leadership studies: A literature review. *Journal of Leadership Education, 19*(3), 15–31.

Tindall, N. T. J. (2009). The double bind of race and gender: Understanding the roles and perceptions of black female public relations faculty. *Southwestern Mass Communication Journal, 25*(1), 1–26.

Tindall, N. T. J. (2016, March 29). *Get in where you fit in: The challenge of diversity and fit in the PR industry.* Institute for Public Relations. http://www.instituteforpr.org/get-in-where-you-fit-in-the-challenge-of-diversity-and-fit-in-the-pr-industry/

Tindall, N. T. J., & Waters, R. (2012). Coming out to tell our stories: Using queer theory to understand the career experiences of gay men in public relations. *Journal of Public Relations Research, 24*(5), 451–475.

Tindall, N. T. J., & Waters, R. (Eds.). (2013). *Coming out of the closet: Exploring LGBT issues in strategic communication with theory and research.* Bern: Peter Lang.

Tomlinson, J. (1999). *Globalization and culture.* Chicago, IL: University of Chicago Press.

Tomlinson, F., & Schwabenland, C. (2010). Reconciling competing discourses of diversity? The UK non-profit sector between social justice and the business case. *Organization, 17*(1), 101–121.

Toth, E. L. (1988). Making peace with gender issues in public relations. *Public Relations Review, 14,* 36–47.

Toth, E. L. (1989). Whose freedom and equity in public relations? The gender balance argument. *Mass Communication Review, 16,* 70–76.

Triandis, H. C. (1959). Cognitive similarity and interpersonal communication in industry. *Journal of Applied Psychology, 43*(5), 321.

Trittin, H., & Schoeneborn, D. (2017). Diversity as polyphony: Reconceptualizing diversity management from a communication-centered perspective. *Journal of Business Ethics, 144*(2), 305–322.

Turnbull, H., Greenwood, R. A., Tworoger, L., & Golden, C. (2010). Skill deficiencies in diversity and inclusion in organizations: Developing an inclusion skills measurement. *Academy of Strategic Management Journal, 9*(1), 1–14.

Turner, J. C. (1985). Social categorization and the self-concept: A social cognitive theory of group behaviour. In E. J. Lawler (Ed.), *Advances in group processes: Theory and research* (pp. 77–121). Stamford, CT: JAI.

United Minds study reveals gap between company DE&I efforts and employee experiences. (2021, May 14). *Weber Shandwick.* https://www.webershandwick.com/news/united-minds-study-reveals-gap-between-company-dei-efforts-employee-experiences/?utm_source=social&utm_medium=linkedin&utm_campaign=codeifypost4

Uhl-Bien, M. (2006). Relational leadership theory: Exploring the social processes of leadership and organizing. *The Leadership Quarterly, 17*(6), 654–676.

Uhl-Bien, M., & Arena, M. (2017). Complexity leadership: Enabling people and organizations for adaptability. *Organizational Dynamics, 46*, 9–20.

Uhl-Bien, M., Marion, R., & McKelvey, B. (2007). Complexity leadership theory: Shifting leadership from the industrial age to the knowledge era. *The Leadership Quarterly, 18*(4), 298–318.

Unsafe, unheard, unvalued: A state of inequity (2022). Hue and The Harris Poll. https://www.stateofinequity.wearehue.org/

Uysal, N. (2013). Shifting the paradigm: Diversity communication on corporate web sites. *PR Journal, 7*(2), 8–36.

van Beuzekom, R., & Gormley, A. (2020, November 5). How future communicators are embracing DE&I in PRSSA chapters. *PR Daily.* https://www.prdaily.com/how-future-communicators-are-embracing-dei-in-prssa-chapters/

Van Camp, S. (2012, September 10). Diversity and communication must be communicated from the inside-out. *PR News.* http://www.prnewsonline.com/diversity-and-inclusion-must-be-communicated-from-the-inside-out/

Van Dijk, H., van Engen, M., & Paauwe, J. (2012). Reframing the business case for diversity: A values and virtues perspective. *Journal of Business Ethics, 111*(1), 73–84.

van Knippenberg, D., & van Ginkel, W. P. (2021). A diversity mindset perspective on inclusive leadership. *Group & Organization Management.* Advance online publication. doi:10.1177/1059601121997229

van Knippenberg, D., van Ginkel, W. P., & Homan, A. C. (2013). Diversity mindsets and the performance of diverse teams. *Organizational Behavior and Human Decision Processes, 121*, 183–193.

van Loon, R., & van Dijk, G. (2015). Dialogical leadership: Dialogue as condition zero. *Journal of Leadership, Accountability and Ethics, 12*(3), 62–75.

Vardeman-Winter, J., & Place, K. (2017). Still a lily-white field of women: The state of workforce diversity in public relations practice and research. *Public Relations Review, 43*, 326–336.

Vardeman-Winter, J., & Tindall, N. T. (2010). Toward an intersectionality theory of public relations. In R. Heath (Ed.), *The SAGE handbook of public relations* (pp. 223–235). Thousand Oaks, CA: Sage.

Vardeman-Winter, J., Tindall, N. T. J., & Jiang, H. (2013). Intersectionality and publics: How exploring publics' multiple identities questions basic public relations concepts. *Public Relations Inquiry, 2*(3), 279–304.

Vasquez, G. M. (1993). A homo narrans paradigm for public relations: Combining Bormann's symbolic convergence theory and Grunig's situational theory of publics. *Journal of Public Relations Research, 5*(3), 201–216.

Voegtlin, C. (2011). Development of a scale measuring discursive responsible leadership. *Journal of Business Ethics, 98*(1), 57–73.

Voegtlin, C., Patzer, M., & Scherer, A. G. (2012). Responsible leadership in global business: A new approach to leadership and its multi–level outcomes. *Journal of Business Ethics, 105*(1), 1–16.

Walden, J., Jung, E. H., & Westerman, C. Y. (2017). Employee communication, job engagement, and organizational commitment: A study of members of the millennial generation. *Journal of Public Relations Research, 29*(2–3), 73–89.

Waldman, D. A. (2011). Moving forward with the concept of responsible leadership: Three caveats to guide theory and research. *Journal of Business Ethics, 98*(1), 75–83.

Wasserman, I. C. (2021). Inclusive leadership in complex times: Leading with vulnerability and integrity. In B. M. Ferdman, J. Prime, & R. E. Riggio (Eds.), *Inclusive leadership: Transforming diverse lives, workplaces, and societies* (pp. 83–98). Thousand Oaks, CA: Sage.

Wasserman, I. C., Gallegos, P. V., & Ferdman, B. M. (2008). Dancing with resistance: Leadership challenges in fostering a culture of inclusion. In K. M. Thomas (Ed.), *Diversity resistance in organizations* (pp. 175–200). Mahwah, NJ: Lawrence Erlbaum Associates.

Waymer, D. (Ed.). (2012). *Culture, social class, and race in public relations.* Lanham, MD: Lexington Books.

Waymer, D., & Brown, K. (2018). Significance of race in the U.S. undergraduate public relations educational landscape: Reflections of former public relations students. *Journal for Multicultural Education, 12*(4), 353–370.

Waymer, D., & Dyson, O. (2011). The journey into an unfamiliar and uncomfortable territory: Exploring the role and approaches of race in PR education. *Journal of Public Relations Research, 23*(4), 458–477.

Welp, M., & Schein, E. H. (2021). The role of white male culture in engaging white men to be inclusive leaders. In B. M. Ferdman, J. Prime, & R. E. Riggio (Eds.), *Inclusive leadership: Transforming diverse lives, workplaces, and societies* (pp. 263–278). Thousand Oaks, CA: Sage.

Werder, K. P., & Holtzhausen, D. (2009). An analysis of the influence of public relations department leadership style on public relations strategy use and effectiveness. *Journal of Public Relations Research, 21*(4), 404–427.

White, C., Vanc, A., & Stafford, G. (2010). Internal communication, information satisfaction, and sense of community: The effect of personal influence. *Journal of Public Relations Research, 22*(1), 65–84.

White, N. (2021, January 25). 10 Reasons why a DEI coach is good for business. *Entrepreneur.* https://www.entrepreneur.com/article/363684

Wills, C. M. (2020). Diversity in public relations: The implications of a broad definition for PR practice. *PR Journal, 13*(3). https://prjournal.instituteforpr.org/wp-content/uploads/Wills_final_formatted_June2020.pdf

Willis, P. (2019). From knowing to doing: Reflexivity, leadership and public relations. *Public Relations Review, 45*(3), 101780. https://doi.org/10.1016/j.pubrev.2019.05.001

Winters, M.-F. (2014). From diversity to inclusion: An inclusion equation. In B. M. Ferdman & B. R. Dean (Eds.), *Diversity at work: The practice of inclusion* (pp. 205–228). Hoboken, NJ: John Wiley & Sons, Inc.

Winters, M.-F. (2021). Engaging in bold, inclusive conversations. In B. M. Ferdman, J. Prime, & R. E. Riggio (Eds.), *Inclusive leadership: Transforming diverse lives, workplaces, and societies* (pp. 221–235). Routledge.

Wittenberg-Cox, A. (2017, August 3). Deloitte's radical attempt to reframe diversity. *Harvard Business Review.* https://hbr.org/2017/08/deloittes-radical-attempt-to-reframe-diversity

Wolfgruber, D., Stürmer, L., & Einwiller, S. (2021). Talking inclusion into being: Communication as a facilitator and obstructor of an inclusive work environment. *Personnel Review*. Advance online publication. https://doi.org/10.1108/PR-01-2021-0013

Wooten, L. P. (2008). Guest editor's note: Breaking barriers in organizations for the purpose of inclusiveness. *Human Resource Management, 47*(2), 191–197.

Zanoni, P., Janssens, M., Benschop, Y., & Nkomo, S. (2010). Unpacking diversity, grasping inequality: Rethinking difference through critical perspectives. *Organization, 17*(1), 9–29.

Zerbinos, E., & Clanton, G. A. (1993). Minority practitioners: Career influences, job satisfaction, and discrimination. *Public Relations Review, 19*(1), 75–91.

Index

Italicized pages refer to figures and **bold** pages refer to tables

access-and-legitimacy perspective on diversity 49
accountability 40, 73, 82, 137
advertising 4
affirmative action (AA) 45–46, 51
African Americans: leadership positions in companies 25; in public relations 14–15
allyship/alliance building/allies 17, 56, 64–65, 71, 119–120, 159, 162, 184
antenarratives 111–112, 120, 122
Arthur W. Page Society 33
Asian Americans 15, 25
assimilation 14
authentic leader 79, 82

Bakhtin, Mikhail 81–82
Bauman, Zygmunt 54
belonging 55, 173–176, 184
belonging-uniqueness dialectic 184–185, 189–190
bias 162; conscious 134–135, 162; unconscious 62–64, 73, 134–135, 162
Black, Indigenous and people of color (BIPOC) *see* people of color
Black Public Relations Society 14
Bourdieu, Pierre 5, 58, 188
brave spaces 93

Burns, James McGregor 79
business case for D&I 50–52, 69–70, 161–162

Charlottesville incident, 2017 181
Civil Rights movement 13
code of ethics 6
collective agency 84
Commission for Public Relations Education (CPRE) 66, 72, 143, 163
communication culture 37
complexity 79; leadership 85–86
connectional intelligence 96
conscious bias 134–135, 162
context 89, 178–181; definition 53–54; of diversity 67; leadership phenomena and 79; macro 5, 52–53, 70–71, 178–181, 194; macro-historical 70–71; normative 54; power differentials and 70–72; relational 54; social/racial justice movements 70; structural 54; in theorizing and practicing D&I 54–55, 115–116
COVID-19 pandemic 2
critical empathy 64
critical public relations scholarship 3
critical race theory 29–30
cultures 18, 20, 33, 62, 68, 86, 96, 103–104, 110, 142, 151–152, 164, 166, 174; cultural difference in public

relations 6–7; cultural diversity 7; cultural identities 14, 28, 49, 89, 112–114, 127–128, 147, 158, 172; cultural inequities 88; cultural power inequities 175; cultural sandbox 6; dominant 14, 29, 31, 54, 69; exclusive 62; of inclusion/inclusivity 20, 37, 54, 56, 58–60, 69, 76–77, 91, 118, 133, 167, 172, 187–188; intercultural/ multicultural communication 21; multiculturalism 13, 28, 34, 135–136, 144; occupational 5; shifts 14; of US public relations industry 23, 38–40, 46, 71–72, 123, 156–157; US public relations' professional 6; of Whiteness 27, 31, 153, 162; *see also* organizational culture

dialogic communication 169–173
dialogic mindset 83
dialogic relational leadership 81–84
dialogue 64–65, 70, 82–83; across power differentials 64; intergroup 64
Didion, Joan 107
discrimination 69
discrimination-and-fairness perspective on diversity 49
diversity 13, 36, 40, 42–43, 57, 66–67, 70; across disciplines 54; for building good relationships 27; categories 68; conceptualization of differences 162–163; context, definition 53–54; as core company value 32; debates and arguments 50–54; definition 17–22; friendly policies 31; generative interactions 59; idea of 'counting' 32; impact on team/group performance 47; inclusion of 30; intersectional approach to 48; management (DM) 45–46, 52, 69; mandate and programs 33; millennials value diversity 33; mindset 88; models 49–50, 72; moral/social justice *vs* business case 50–52; movement in the United St 14; power inequities between groups 52–54; in public relations 23–24; race and ethnicity as dimensions of 14; representational 59; requisite variety approach 32; as social responsibility 26; theories 46–48; in United States 13–17; workforce composition 37–38, 49

Diversity Action Alliance (DAA) 12, 66–68
diversity and inclusion (D&I) leadership 2–3, 5, 11; actionable model of 34; in agency setting 39–40; code of ethics 6; envisioning 66–69; history of 10; interdisciplinary research 10; in internal communication 35–36; narrative perspective 8–9; perception gap 108–110, 116–118; problem/ challenge 3–6, 9–10; role of 22–23; support for 34; vision 109–110
dominant groups

educators and student leaders 146–153; interviewee identities **147–148**; responsibility of 152–153; *see also* public relations education
emplotment 111
empowerment 37, 55, 79
equal employment opportunity (EEO) 45–46, 51, 160–161
equity/equality 2–3, 6–8, 30, 55–57, 70, 73; difference between "equality" and 35; professional cultures of 58
equity in profession 14
ethical selfhood 81–82
Excellence in Public Relations and Communication Management project 23–24
exclusion 55, 59

failures of public relations leaders 157–158; lack of D&I-related skills 159; lack of mentorship and sponsorship opportunities 158; perception gap 158–159; tendency to understand diversity in EEO terms 160–161
feminism 28
feminist scholarship in public relations 24
fields 58
Fisher, Walter 107
fit 5
full participation 55
functional leadership 78

gay pride movements 13
gender disparities 24–25; gender-related power differentials 72; in public relations 5; in relation to D&I 118–119

gender research 24–25; as cultural and social construction 28; gendered performance of power and leadership 28
generative diversity interactions 59
Gen Z 32–33, 96, 159, 177
George Floyd killing 2, 13
glass ceiling constraints 14
Global Alliance for PR 6
Greenleaf, Robert 78

habitus 5, 188–189
hegemonic systemic practices 3
heterogeneity 62
Hispanic Public Relations Association 14
Hispanics 15, 40; leadership positions in companies 25
Hispanic Serving Institutions (HSIs) 67, 184
Historically Black Colleges and Universities (HBCUs) 67, 184
homogeneity 62, 149; of leadership 62, 74, 77, 93, 149, 154, 166, 190
homophily 26, 42, 47, 49, 52, 58, 62, 71–74, 77, 109–110, 158, 166, 182, 192
human dignity model for inclusion 60
human resources (HR), role in D&I efforts and resources 120–121

identity 112–114; cultural identities 14, 28, 49, 89, 112–114, 127–128, 147, 158, 172; dominant and non-dominant identity practitioners 33; privileged identity groups 52, 64, 135; self-professed 63; social identity theory (SIT) 47–48, 71
identity freezing 48
immigration 13
incentives and rewards programs 40
inclusion 131–133; inclusive organizational environments 132–133; path of creating inclusive cultures 132–133; relational culture and 62; role for diversity 131–132
inclusion/inclusiveness 3, 7–8, 27, 30, 36–38, 41, 43, 54–56, 66–67, 70; cultures of 56; definition 55–56; of 'diversity' 30; human dignity model for 60; inclusive climates, building 61; inclusive diversity in public relations 2; inclusive leadership 7–8; link between diversity and 54–55;

micro relational level of 59; multilevel model 59–60; organizational climate and 60–62; of power relations 52; practices 56; professional cultures of 58; in public relations 23–24; skills 56; as social responsibility 26; theories and models 58–60; in United States 13–17; *see also* inclusive leadership
inclusive leadership 82, 88–94, 177; creation of climates 89, 92; inclusive leaders as role models 91; role of balancing belonging and uniqueness 90; traits 92; work 92–93; *see also* inclusion/inclusiveness
in-group/out-group divisions 47, 50
Institute for Public Relations (IPR) 35, 146
integration-and-learning perspective on diversity 49
intercultural communication interactions 174
intergroup dialogue 64
internal communication 35–36
International Association of Business Communicators (IABC) 6, 23
International Public Relations Association 6
intersectionality 29, 32, 48, 55, 95
introspection 104

job-relatedness of D&I 54
Johnson's (President) 1965 Executive Order 11246 44

Kennedy's (President) 1961 Executive Order 10925 44
kernel 111
knowledge, attitude and skills (KAS) 143, 181–184

lavender ceiling 31
leadership 1, 120, 188; authentic leader 79, 82; communication-based definition of 80; complexity 85–86; core characteristics of **166**; definitions of 78; dialogic relational leadership 81–84; engagement and accountability 137; formal role 137–139; functional 78; gender differences 4, 96–97; good communication skill 151; at IBM and HP 11; implications of digital revolution and globalization 102; inclusive 82, 88–94, 177;

interpersonal focus 78; intersectional lens 95; leader communication skill 140–142; leader's primary responsibility 139–140; link between D&I and 38–41; non-leader-centric and intersubjective 83–84; non-profit 78; position difference 93; in public relations 2–3; racial discrimination and 25–26; racial/ethnic diversity 4; responsibility of industry leaders 150–152, 187; responsible 84–86; role in achieving D&I goals 39, 72–73, 75–77; scholarship 79–81; situational 78; stakeholder theory and 84–85; task focus 78; transactional 79, 86; transformational 79, 81, 86, 94, 98–99, 103–104, 176–177, 190–191; true dialogical leaders 83; White (male) dominance in 31
leadership engagement 13
leadership model for inclusive diversity in public relations **166**, 178–186, *179*, 189; attitudes 183; belonging-uniqueness dialectic 184–185; context 178–181; interrelated outcomes 185–186; knowledge perspective 181–182; practical guidance for desired outcomes 191–192; skills 183–184
leadership theory 77–104; being in a leadership position 87; communication style 97–99; from ethics and responsibility perspective 87; intersection of D&I and leadership 86–96; leader-follower relationship 78; leader-member exchange theory 78; modern 86; North American bias 86; optimal distinctiveness theory 89; Plank Center's role 99–103; for public relations 96–99; relationship between diverse teams and leadership 87; social constructionist and discursive approach 80–81, 83; theorizing process 93–96
Leveraging Variety Model of diversity 49
LGBTQ+ 71, 150, 158; identities 31–32

marginalized groups 66; AA/EEO focus on 51; power inequities and 56
marginalized identities 42, 65, 189, 193
marketing 4
mentorship opportunities 25

microaggressions 15, 33, 52, 61, 63, 124, 162, 182, 190
micro/meso/macro continuum 88
millennials 96, 177; perceptions of D&I in agencies 109; in public relations 32–33
minority practitioners: leadership positions in companies 25; mentorship opportunities for 25
Minority Serving Institutions (MSIs) 184
model for public relations leadership and D&I 164–165; belonging-uniqueness dialectic 173–176; praxis model 165; primacy 166–168; process model 165; relational and dialogic/communicative approach 169–173; social constructionist and interpretive approach 168–169; types 165
moral case 50–52, 161–162
moral/social justice: approach to diversity 57; *vs* business case 50–52, 70

narrative analysis/lens/paradigm 8–9, 104–105, 123; antenarratives 111–112, 120, 122; bias and racism 134–135; broad and flexible approach 129–130; communication and story-centered approach 110–111; conflict between economic and moral imperatives 150; context 115–116; diversity identity categories 112–114; emplotment 111; Equal Employment Opportunity (EEO) responses 116; formal leadership roles 137–139; inclusion 131–133; leaders' views on D&I 110–113, **113**; lip service theme 108; masterplots 111; narrative plots 116–121; narrators' cultural identities 112; organizational culture 130–131; pace of change 119–120, 135–137; perception gap 108–110, 117, *117*, 123, 125, 128, 139, 145, 154, 158–159; practitioner leaders 126–129, **127**; public relations industry 133–134; respondent demographic data **113**; sentiment analysis 112–121; themes **157**; views of educators and student leaders 146–153, **147–148**
Native Americans 15
Native American Universities and Colleges (NAUC) 184
normative context 54

occupational culture 5
organizational climate 7, 37, 42, 60–62, 68, 88, 91, 102, 134–135, 157–158, 170; inclusive workplace climates 89, 92
organizational culture 37, 54, 56, 68, 74, 80; and climate 60–62; and diversity and inclusion 65, 76, 90–91, 120–121, 130–131, 153–155, 180; and leadership 101–103, 142–143, 151, 166–167, 186, 191–192; and storytelling 111; responsibility for 124, 137; and retention of minorities 134–135
organizational reward systems 91

participatory environment 7
pay discrepancy 25
pay equity 14
people of color 3, 38, 65; bias towards 135; discrimination and microaggressions against BIPOC 124; leadership positions 25–26, 138
perception gap 108–110, 117, *117*, 123, 125, 128, 139, 145, 154, 158–159
The Plank Center for Leadership in Public Relations 2, 99–104, 180; traits of public relations leaders 100–101
polyphony 81
power: differentials 66, 70–72, 162; inequities 3, 56, 71; relations 28–29, 51–54
PR Coalition 26–27, 39
PR Council 20, 66, 72
primacy 166–168
privileges: racial 5: dominant groups 14, 33, 51–53, 58, 90, 135, 166; awareness of 21, 150, 152, 162, 181; and power 29–30, 32, 56, 77; and unconscious bias 62–65, 69–71, 192; and leadership 87, 89, 92, 94, 109; White privilege 30, 144
profitability 69
public relations communication 8
public relations D&I scholarship 23; antenarratives 111–112, 120, 122; communication and story-centered approach 110–111; concept of intersectionality 29; connection between relationship building and diversity 27; critiques 28–32; dominant and non-dominant identity

practitioners 33; Excellence project 23–24; experiences of women of color 29; gendered performance of power and leadership 28; gender research 24–25; HR's role in D&I efforts and resources 120–121; inclusion 36–38; leaders' views on D&I 110–113, **113**; LGBTQ+ identities 31–32; limitations 29; mentorship opportunities for minority practitioners 25; millennials' views 32–33; narrators' sentiments 113–114, 116–121; need for diverse workforce and inclusion 27; online survey approach 111–112; organizational commitments 115–116; pace of change 119–120, 135–137; perception gap 108–110; priority practice 27; race/ethnicity research 25–26, 28–29; relationship between leadership, communication and D&I 116–121; research in new millennium 26–28; sentiment toward D&I efforts 114–115; in United Kingdom 28–29; White leadership 30–31
public relations education 163; curriculum 143–145; diversity at classroom level 142–143; educational experience and environment 144–145; limitations 145–146; professional organizations and 146; responsibility of educators 152–153; views of educators and student leaders 146–153, **147–148**; *see also* educators and student leaders
public relations leadership 2, 41, 105–107; categories of behavior 185; challenges related 2; as corporate social responsibility (CSR) 34; definition 101; multicultural and social responsibility approach 34; organizational D&I realities 35; senior 108–109; social constructionist perspective 110; *see also* failures of public relations leaders
Public Relations Society of America (PRSA) 6, 13–14, 24, 66–67, 72, 99–100, 106, 115, 146
Public Relations Student Society of America (PRSSA) 67, 149, 184

race/ethnicity research 25–26, 66
racial discrimination 25–26
racial leadership landscape 31

racial/social justice 2, 14, 32, 34–36, 66, 70, 111, 122
reciprocal understanding 60
relational context 54
representational diversity 59
requisite variety 23–24, 31–32, 53, 179
resistance perspective on diversity 50
Ricoeur, Paul 81

scholarship in public relations 163–164, 193–195; *see also* public relations D&I scholarship
self-categorization theory 47, 71
self-identification 47
"Selfie" generation 177
self-professed identity 63
senior leadership in public relations 108–109, 118–119, 159
sentiment analysis 112–121
sexual harassment 14
similarity-attraction theory 47, 71
situational leadership 78
social capital 36, 88
social constructionist and interpretive approach 168–169
social identity theory (SIT) 47–48, 71
social responsibility approach of D&I 34, 38
Society for Human Resource Management (SHRM) 67
sociopsychological theories 71
Sodexo 75–76
Statement of Equality of Opportunity for Women 24
stereotyping 25, 59, 91, 190

storytelling 9
structural context 54
symphony analogy 131

Title VII of the 1964 Civil Rights Act 44
tokenism 25, 30
transactional leadership 79
transformational leadership 79, 81, 94, 98–99, 103–104, 176–177, 190–191; critiques of 177
trust 60, 103

unconscious bias 62–64, 73, 134–135, 162
uniqueness 55, 173–176, 184–185
US culture of individualism 46
US diversity narrative 44–46; AA/EEO policies 45; Civil Rights era 44–45; in education and workplace 70; moral/social justice *vs* business case 50–52; subjugation and segregation of minority groups 44–45; *see also* diversity; inclusion/inclusiveness
US public relations industry 66, 73; assessing 65–73; history 44–46
"Us *vs* Them" dynamics 46–47

White heterosexual males 52, 64–65
Whiteness 27, 31, 72, 149, 153, 162; power in US public relations 42
White norms of leadership 30–31
women 150; in leadership 98, 118–119; liberation movement 13–14; research in public relations 25
Workforce 2000 45
Workforce 2020 26
workforce diversity 37–38, 49, 51

Printed in the United States
by Baker & Taylor Publisher Services